Justification Defenses and Just Convictions

This major study advances an interpretation of criminal justification defenses that views them as an integral component of the structure of the criminal law defined as the institutional representation of the underlying principles of political morality in a liberal society.

Criminal offense definitions prohibit certain types of conduct and prescribe criminal punishment for those engaging in that conduct. Yet people sometimes violate those prohibitions in circumstances that render their conduct acceptable. Justification defenses provide legal devices that allow courts to exonerate those who violate criminal offense definitions in such circumstances. Such controversial cases as the use of force by battered women or the violation of trespass laws by those engaged in civil disobedience raise important questions about the proper scope and limits of justification defenses. The purpose of the book is to explain the function and limits of these defenses in a way that will enable the reader to apply them to difficult cases.

The book extends the traditional scope of the legal and philosophical discussion of justification defenses. It integrates philosophical analysis with a consideration of contemporary applications, it shows how these defenses are key components of criminal law, and it explores the relationship between legal and moral justification.

Cambridge Studies in Philosophy and Law

Other books in the series:

Justification Defenses and Just Convictions

ROBERT F. SCHOPP

University of Nebraska College of Law

CAMBRIDGE
UNIVERSITY PRESS

PUBLISHED BY THE PRESS SYNDICATE OF THE UNIVERSITY OF CAMBRIDGE
The Pitt Building, Trumpington Street, Cambridge CB2 1RP, United Kingdom

CAMBRIDGE UNIVERSITY PRESS
The Edinburgh Building, Cambridge CB2 2RU, United Kingdom
40 West 20th Street, New York, NY 10011-4211, USA
10 Stamford Road, Oakleigh, Melbourne 3166, Australia

First published 1998

Printed in the United States of America

Typeset in Times Roman

Library of Congress Cataloging-in-Publication Data
Schopp, Robert F.
Justification defenses and just convictions / Robert F. Schopp.
p.   cm. – (Cambridge studies in philosophy and law)
Includes index.
ISBN 0-521-62211-5 (hardback)
1. Justification (Law) – United States.   2. Self-defense (Law) –
United States.   3. Judgments, Criminal – United States – Moral and
ethical aspects.   I. Title.   II. Series.
KF9246.S36   1998   97-26889
345.73'04 – dc21   CIP

*A catalog record for this book is available from
the British Library.*

ISBN   0 521 62211 5 hardback

Contents

Preface   *page* ix
Frequently Cited Sources   xi

1   Justification Defenses: The Issues   1
    1.1 The Theoretical Debate about the General Category of
         Justification Defenses   2
         1.1.1   The Context   2
         1.1.2   Justified Conduct as Right or as Permissible   4
         1.1.3   Unknowingly Justified Defendants   5
         1.1.4   Putative Justification   6
         1.1.5   The Social Matrix and the Incompatibility Thesis   7
         1.1.6   Duress as a Problematic Classification   10
         1.1.7   Summary   10
    1.2 Self-defense as a Problematic Specific Justification Defense   11
         1.2.1   General Self-defense   11
         1.2.2   Battered Women and Self-defense   12
    1.3 Necessity, Nullification, and Crimes of Conscience   13
    1.4 Summary and Plan   14

2   Justification Defenses and the Conventional Public Morality   16
    2.1 Right or Permissible   16
    2.2 Knowledge and Justification   21
    2.3 Moral Condemnation and Criminal Punishment   22
         2.3.1   Five Types of Condemnation in Criminal Punishment   22
         2.3.2   Hard Cases for Moral Condemnation   25
         2.3.3   Moral Condemnation and Justification Defenses   26
    2.4 Knowledge and Justification Revisited   29
         2.4.1   Moral Condemnation, Prohibitory Norms, and
                 Unknowingly Justified Defendants   29
         2.4.2   Justification Defenses with Subjective Elements   31
         2.4.3   Hard Cases and the Knowledge Requirement   37

2.5   The Social Matrix and the Incompatibility Thesis   40
      2.5.1   Assisting Justified Acts   40
      2.5.2   The Duty Not to Interfere and the Incompatibility Thesis   42
      2.5.3   Hard Cases and the Revised Matrix of Social
              Responsibility   47
2.6   Conclusion   52

3   Self-defense   55
3.1   Contemporary Theories   56
      3.1.1   Self-defense and the Social Order   56
      3.1.2   Self-defense and Distributive Justice   60
3.2   Legal Defenses and Individual Interests   62
3.3   The Normative Structure   64
      3.3.1   Political Liberalism   65
      3.3.2   The Criminal Justice System in the Liberal Society 71
      3.3.3   Justification Defenses   73
3.4   Self-defense as Justified Conduct in a Liberal Society   75
3.5   Self-defense as Morally Justifiable Law   83
3.6   Conclusion   87

4   Self-defense and Battered Women   89
4.1   Self-defense Doctrine   90
4.2   The Battered Woman Syndrome and Self-defense   92
      4.2.1   The Battered Woman Syndrome   92
      4.2.2   The Putative Relevance of the Battered Woman
              Syndrome to Self-defense   93
4.3   Battered Woman Syndrome Research   94
4.4   The Battered Woman Syndrome and Conventional
      Self-defense Law   98
      4.4.1   Imminence or Immediacy   98
      4.4.2   Imminent or Immediately Necessary: The
              Justificatory Foundation   99
      4.4.3   Learned Helplessness as Disordered Thought and
              Special Capacity   102
      4.4.4   Necessary Force: Battered Woman Syndrome or the
              Pattern of Battering   104
      4.4.5   Reasonable Belief in the Necessity of Deadly Force 106
      4.4.6   Retreat as a Legal Alternative to Defensive Force   108
      4.4.7   Institutional Legal Alternatives   109
      4.4.8   The Pattern of Battering as Support for
              Reasonable Belief   111
      4.4.9   Credibility and the Failure to Leave Previously   111
4.5   Self-defense by Battered Women as Justification and Excuse 114
      4.5.1   Reasonable Belief   114

	4.5.2	Battered Woman Syndrome and Mental Illness	116
	4.5.3	Reasonable Belief: Justification and Excuse	120
	4.5.4	Culpability and Battered Women as Justified or Excused	126
4.6	Conclusion		134

5	Duress and Systemically Complete Mitigation		136
	5.1	The Theoretical Interpretation	138
	5.2	Systemically Complete Mitigation	142
	5.3	Two Potential Criticisms	146
	5.4	Conclusion	151

6	The Limits of Justification: Necessity and Nullification		153
	6.1	Crimes of Conscience	154
	6.2	Jury Nullification	156
		6.2.1 The Central Explicit Debate	156
		6.2.2 The Arguments	157
		6.2.3 Deception and the Moral Force of the Criminal Law	163
	6.3	Necessity and Nullification in a Liberal Society	167
		6.3.1 Deception and the Integrity of a Liberal Criminal Justice System	167
		6.3.2 Necessity and Nullification: The Conceptual Puzzle	168
		6.3.3 Necessity	170
		6.3.4 Nullification as Necessity: Intrasystemic Appeals to Justice	177
		6.3.5 Nullification beyond Necessity: Intrasystemic Appeals to Mercy	180
		6.3.6 Nullification beyond Necessity: Extrasystemic Nullification	183
		6.3.7 Summary	185
	6.4	The Responsibilities of Persons in a Liberal Society	187
		6.4.1 The Zenger Trial and Jurors as Persons	187
		6.4.2 Judicial Nullification	193
		6.4.3 Conflicting Obligations: Tension Rather than Contradiction	197
	6.5	Conclusion	198

| 7 | Conclusions | | 199 |

| Index | | | 205 |

Preface

The contemporary debate regarding justification defenses in the criminal law tends to emphasize the logical relationships among offense elements, justification defenses, and excuses in the context of the traditional justifications for criminal punishment. These are important concerns, and this book joins that debate. This book seeks a broader foundation, however, in the principles of political morality represented by the criminal law. The theory advanced here demonstrates the importance of the expressive function of criminal conviction and punishment in a system of criminal law that serves as an official representation of liberal principles of political morality. It also contends that appreciation of the abstract foundations and functions of the criminal law can inform the search for the most defensible resolution of difficult contemporary applications, such as those involving claims of justification by defendants who kill their batterers or engage in crimes of conscience.

As with any extended intellectual project, this book builds upon the contributions of many individuals. I am particularly grateful to Barbara Sturgis and Megan Sullivan, who served as my coauthors in writing one of the articles in which we initially presented some of the arguments developed in this book. Many of my colleagues at the University of Nebraska participated in an extended (some of them might say interminable) series of discussions and faculty colloquia regarding many of the issues and arguments presented here. Robert Audi, Marty Gardner, Steve Kalish, Jo Potuto, and John Snowden read and commented upon various manuscripts that contributed to the analysis in this book. I am also grateful to the faculty of the University of Utah College of Law for providing resources, stimulation, and hospitality during a sabbatical semester in which I worked on this project. In light of the dedication, I should also mention Ed, who listened to parts of this in a truck, Ralph, who listened to it in New Jersey, and Josiah S. Carberry. I have searched my memory for some contribution for which I would be able to thank Professor Carberry. Alas, I can think of none.

Many of the arguments developed in this book were initially presented in prior articles. I am grateful for permission to draw on these in developing the analysis defended here. These include: *Justification Defenses and Just Convictions,* 24 Pacific Law Journal 1233 (1993) (copyright held by the University of the Pacific, McGeorge School of Law); *Self-defense,* in In Harm's Way 255 (Jules L. Coleman and Allen Buchanan, eds.; Cambridge University Press, 1994); *Battered Woman Syndrome, Expert Testimony, and the Distinction between Justification and Excuse,* 1994 University of Illinois Law Review 45 (coauthored with Barbara J. Sturgis and Megan Sullivan; the copyright to the University of Illinois Law Review is held by the Board of Trustees of the University of Illinois); and *Verdicts of Conscience: Nullification and Necessity as Jury Responses to Crimes of Conscience,* 69 Southern California Law Review 2039 (1996) (copyright held by the University of Southern California).

Frequently Cited Sources

This book employs abbreviated citation forms for the following frequently cited sources. The abbreviated form follows the full citation below in square brackets.

American Law Institute, *Model Penal Code* (Official Draft and Revised Comments 1985) [MPC].

Joshua Dressler, *Understanding Criminal Law* (New York: Mathew Bender, 2d ed. 1995) [Understanding].

George P. Fletcher, *Rethinking Criminal Law* (Boston: Little, Brown and Co., 1978) [Rethinking].

Wayne R. LaFave and Austin W. Scott Jr., *Criminal Law* (St. Paul, Minn.: West Publishing Co., 2d ed. 1986) [Criminal Law].

Oxford English Dictionary (Oxford: Oxford University Press, compact ed. 1971 with 1987 supplement) [Oxford English Dictionary].

Paul H. Robinson, *Criminal Law Defenses* (St. Paul, Minn.: West Publishing Co., 1984) [Defenses].

For the teachers, students, and friends
with whom we seek to understand,
especially JOEL FEINBERG

1

Justification Defenses

The Issues

The fully competent, culpable, and malevolent Spike attacks Mother Beneficence with a tire iron in order to steal the alms she has collected for the poor.
Mother Beneficence defends herself by kicking Spike in the shins, and Dudley
Doright rushes to her rescue, smiting Spike sharply, knocking him to the ground,
and holding him until the police arrive. Dudley acts solely for the purposes of
preventing harm to Mother Beneficence and bringing Spike to Justice.

Both Mother Beneficence and Dudley fulfill the offense elements for assault
in that they purposely cause bodily injury to another human being.[1] Most
readers, jurors, and theorists would probably agree, however, that their actions
are justified. The Model Penal Code (MPC) provides justification defenses of
self-defense for Mother Beneficence and defense-of-others for Dudley.[2] These
defenses would not only exempt Mother Beneficence and Dudley from punishment, but also ratify their defensive force as acceptable under the circumstances.[3]

Most theorists accept the general characterization of justification defenses
as affirmative criminal defenses that ratify the defendant's conduct as acceptable under the circumstances, despite fulfilling all offense elements for some
criminal offense. This formulation distinguishes justification defenses from
excuses that exempt the defendant from punishment due to some disability, but
do not mark the defendant's conduct as acceptable under the circumstances.[4]

Despite the broad acceptance of this basic distinction, important questions
remain regarding both the general class of justification defenses and specific
defenses that fall within this category. Difficult issues regarding the general category of justification defenses involve the conceptual and moral foundations of
this class of defense, the significance of the defendant's knowledge regarding
justificatory circumstances, the effects of these defenses on the rights and
duties of third parties, and the boundaries that differentiate justification
defenses from related defenses and mitigation.

---

1 MPC at § 211.1.
2 *Id.* at §§ 3.04, 3.05.
3 Defenses at § 24(a); Rethinking at 759.
4 Defenses at §§ 24, 25; Rethinking at 759.

These theoretical concerns contribute to at least two types of practical problems. First, the manner in which legislatures and courts formulate, interpret, and apply legal provisions representing these defenses can depend on their understanding of the answers to some of these theoretical questions. Should a statute privileging the exercise of force in self-defense, for example, require that the defensive force is necessary, believed necessary, or reasonably believed necessary to prevent the use of unlawful force against the defendant? Does the presence of a psychological syndrome, such as the battered woman syndrome, contribute to or undermine a claim of self-defense? Second, many jurisdictions recognize a residual justification defense, known as the necessity, lesser-evils, or choice-of-evils defense. This defense serves as a residual corrective device intended to address conduct that violates an offense definition in circumstances that render it more acceptable than the available alternatives but do not qualify for any specific justification defense. The manner in which courts define the parameters of this defense can depend partially on their understanding of some of the theoretical issues.

This book advances an integrated theory of justification defenses. It interprets the role and parameters of justification defenses by appealing to the expressive function of the criminal law as an official representation of a conventional public morality. Roughly, justification defenses apply to conduct that violates some criminal offense definition in circumstances that preclude the expression of condemnation inherent in criminal conviction and punishment. The parameters of such defenses in a liberal democracy must reflect underlying principles of liberal political morality.

1.1   The Theoretical Debate about the General Category of Justification Defenses

1.1.1   The Context

In order to establish the guilt of a defendant for a criminal offense in contemporary American criminal law, the state must prove that the defendant fulfilled the material elements of the offense as defined in the relevant criminal code.[5] The MPC defines offenses in a manner that includes both objective offense elements stated in the form of conduct, circumstances, or results and culpability elements. One commits assault, for example, by purposely, knowingly, or recklessly causing bodily injury to another human being.[6] "Causing bodily injury to another human being" represents the objective offense elements for assault,[7]

---

5 MPC at § 1.12(1).
6 *Id.* at § 211.1(1).
7 *Id.* at § 1.13(9) (material elements); *see* Defenses at § 11(a).

and "purposely, knowingly, or recklessly" represents the culpability element.[8] In addition, the conduct constituting the offense must include a voluntary act as defined in the MPC.[9]

Defendants may offer several types of defenses in response to the state's case-in-chief. Defendants advance failure-of-proof defenses when they attempt to show that the state has failed to carry its burden of proving one or more offense elements.[10] Defendants can escape liability despite fulfilling all offense elements by establishing general defenses. For the purposes of this book, justifications and excuses are the two categories of general defenses of primary interest. Those who raise justification defenses contend that although they have engaged in conduct that fulfills the material elements of a criminal offense, circumstances render that conduct socially acceptable and perhaps even desirable and, thus, immune from punishment. Excuses, in contrast, address the accountability of the defendant rather than the acceptability of the conduct. Those who raise excuses admit that they engaged in criminal conduct that was wrongful in the circumstances, but they contend that they are not appropriately held accountable for that behavior due to some disability-based excusing condition.[11]

In short, justifications exonerate defendants who perform ordinarily criminal conduct in special circumstances that render their behavior socially acceptable. These defenses would apply to any other actor who performed the same conduct in the same circumstances. Excuses, in contrast, are specific to defendants because they exculpate these individuals for their criminal conduct due to disabilities, such as infancy or psychological disorder, that undermine the attribution of culpability for this conduct to these defendants.

Although this general distinction between justification and excuse is relatively well settled, a series of difficult cases and theoretical issues regarding the parameters of the justification defenses remains. The central theoretical questions include the following: (1) Do justification defenses render conduct right or merely tolerable or permissible? (2) Must defendants act with awareness of justificatory circumstances in order to qualify for justification defenses? (3) Should defendants who commit criminal conduct with the reasonable but mistaken belief that justificatory circumstances prevail qualify for excuse, justification, or neither? (4) Do justification defenses create a matrix of social responsibility such that other persons may assist and may not resist or interfere with justified conduct? (5) Does this social matrix generate a corollary incompatibility thesis such that no more than one party in violent confrontation can be justified? The following subsections examine each of these contentious issues in order to clarify the parameters of the contemporary debate.

---

8 MPC at § 2.02 (culpability elements).
9 *Id.* at § 2.01.
10 Defenses at §§ 21, 22.
11 *Id.* at §§ 24, 25; Rethinking at 759.

1.1.2 Justified Conduct as Right or as Permissible

According to George Fletcher's theory, offense definitions proscribe conduct forbidden by prohibitory norms that constitute morally coherent imperatives for the society to which the law applies. Justification defenses provide a license or permission to violate a general prohibitory norm when certain relatively well-defined conditions indicate that doing so will promote a superior right or social interest.[12] Justification defenses enhance the criminal justice system's ability to fulfill some of its important functions.

The criminal law provides both a guide for voluntary self-regulation by individual citizens and criteria for evaluation of each person's conduct by other citizens and by courts. In order to fulfill these functions, justifications should identify right, rather than merely permissible, behavior, because doing so guides individual decision making toward correct conduct under the circumstances.[13] The criminal law seeks to prevent violent confrontation and, in order to promote this purpose, it avoids rules giving rise to inconsistent claims. Justifications that render conduct objectively right, establishing the justified actor's right to perform that conduct, prevent conflicts among legally sanctioned acts. If the actor has a right to engage in that conduct, then others have no right to interfere. Thus, justifications that establish objectively right conduct, as opposed to merely permissible behavior, avoid situations in which two parties in conflict might both be justified.[14]

Joshua Dressler and Kent Greenawalt reject the claim that justifications always identify right conduct that the actor has a right to perform, contending that some justified behavior is merely permissible or tolerable. Law sometimes allows conduct that is morally less preferable than available alternatives.[15] The offense definitions for most serious crimes forbid conduct that harms others. Justifications sometimes exempt certain behavior from punishment because it does not cause the proscribed type of harm. Such conduct might qualify for exception because it is not harmful, although it is not beneficial, morally ideal, or conduct that the actor has a positive right to perform.[16]

The criminal law does not attempt to promote morally ideal behavior; rather, it establishes minimal standards of social morality, leaving considerable lati-

---

12 Fletcher presents his theory in several sources: Rethinking at 553–77; *The Right and the Reasonable*, 98 Harv. L. Rev. 949 (1985); *The Right to Life*, 13 Geo. L. Rev. 1371 (1979); *Should Intolerable Prison Conditions Generate a Justification or an Excuse for Escape?* 26 U.C.L.A. L. Rev. 1355 (1979).

13 *The Right and the Reasonable, id.* at 976–7.

14 *Prison Conditions, supra* note 12, at 1358–65.

15 Joshua Dressler, *New Thoughts about the Concept of Justification in the Criminal Law: A Critique of Fletcher's Thinking and Rethinking*, 32 U.C.L.A. L. Rev. 61 (1984); Kent Greenawalt, *Distinguishing Justifications from Excuses*, 49 Law & Contemp. Probs. 89 (1986); Kent Greenawalt, *On the Perplexing Borders of Justification and Excuse*, 84 Colum. L. Rev. 1897 (1984).

16 Dressler, *id.* at 83.

tude within which individuals can prefer their own interests over those of others. People can defend themselves with deadly force in their own homes without retreat, for example, and in many jurisdictions, they can also do so in public places. Arguably, this rule provides legal permission for conduct that is only morally tolerable in that retreat to avoid killing would be the morally superior option.[17] Perhaps the rule allowing the use of deadly force in self-defense against innocent aggressors provides more compelling support for the contention that some justified conduct is merely tolerable rather than superior conduct. At the least, the critics contend, the law ought to be able to provide the justification while leaving open the question regarding whether such conduct is superior or merely tolerable.[18]

1.1.3 Unknowingly Justified Defendants

Fletcher contends that justifications apply only to those who act with awareness of the justificatory circumstances because justifications exonerate defendants for violations of general prohibitory norms, and only those who act with such knowledge merit exoneration. In some passages he seems to demand also that they act for the right reasons in that they must be motivated by the justifying conditions.[19] Paul Robinson contends that current American law reveals no consensus on the knowledge requirement. According to Robinson, case law is rare and approximately equally divided regarding this issue, and some jurisdictions justify on the basis of defendants' beliefs regarding justifying conditions while others do not. Finally, he interprets the MPC provisions that justify defendants on the basis of their beliefs in the justifying conditions as intended to include putatively justified defendants rather than to exclude unknowingly justified ones.[20]

In addition to disputing Fletcher's position as a descriptive account of current law, the critics argue that justifications ought to apply to unknowingly justified actors. Justification defenses provide exceptions to prohibitory norms for classes of behavior that do not cause the harm the norms are intended to prevent, yet the knowledge requirement would deny the defense to those who do not perform socially harmful conduct as well as to some who actively prevent the relevant harm.[21]

Furthermore, the knowledge requirement fails to satisfy Fletcher's purpose of limiting justifications to those who deserve them because it would extend the defense to defendants who are aware of the justifying circumstances but act

---

17 *Perplexing Borders, supra* note 15, at 1904–7.
18 Dressler, *supra* note 15, at 84–6.
19 *Compare* Rethinking at 562–5; *The Right to Life, supra* note 12, at 82–3 *with* Rethinking at 557, 559; *The Right to Life, supra* note 12, at 1384–5.
20 Defenses at § 122(e).
21 *Id.* at § 122(c); Dressler, *supra* note 15, at 79.

from vicious motive. Suppose, for example, that X learns of justifying conditions that would provide a defense for force exerted against Y. Although X cares not at all about these justifying circumstances, he takes advantage of them in order to exercise his long-standing hatred for Y by shooting Y. The critics deny that X deserves the defense merely because X knows of the justificatory circumstances if that knowledge does not motivate the conduct that violates the offense definition.[22]

Greenawalt interprets this problem regarding the unknowingly justified actor as demonstrating that no clear parameters can be drawn for justification defenses because moral evaluation involves behavior, consequences, and knowledge, blurring the distinction between justification and excuse. He offers the hypothetical Ann who attacks Ben out of hate while she is unknowingly justified because Ben was in the process of setting a bomb in a crowded place. Ann provides no grounds for excuse, so her act is either justified or wrongful. Greenawalt contends that Ann's act seems justified if we concentrate on the consequences but unjustified if we focus on her behavior and reason for acting. He concludes that Ann's action was warranted, although she was wrong to attack Ben.[23] Finally, Robinson argues that extending justifications to unknowingly justified actors who act for evil purposes will not result in gross injustice or social approval of evil actions because these actors remain liable for criminal attempts.[24]

1.1.4   *Putative Justification*

Putative justification arises when the actor reasonably but mistakenly believes that the act is justified. Fletcher argues that putatively justified actors should be excused but not justified because including these defendants within the scope of justification would frustrate the violence-preventing function of the criminal law by justifying both parties in violent confrontation under certain conditions.[25] Suppose, for example, that X reasonably but mistakenly believes that Y is attacking her. If putative justification justifies, then X is justified in responding with force against Y, and Y, who is unaware of X's mistaken belief, reasonably but mistakenly believes that X is unjustifiably attacking her. Thus, Y is justified by putative justification in responding in kind. As a result, both parties are justified in engaging in armed combat. Should the police intervene in this altercation, they would interfere in mutually justified behavior.

The justificatory approach to putative justification also results in cases in which the actor is not justified in acting in a manner that seems intuitively to be clearly justified. Suppose, for example, that B attacks C because B reasonably

---

22 Defenses at § 122(e); Dressler, *supra* note 15, at 80.
23 *Distinguishing, supra* note 15, at 95.
24 Defenses at § 122(d).
25 Rethinking at 762–9.

but mistakenly believes that C is attacking her. If putative justification justifies, then B is justified, and if C is aware of B's mistake, then C is aware that B's violence against her is justified and, hence, not unlawful. C, therefore, may not justifiably exert any force in protecting herself from this unprovoked attack.

For these reasons, Fletcher argues that putative justification should be interpreted as a mistake-based excuse that exculpates the defendant for the putatively justified conduct but does not render it lawful. With this approach, C can legally defend herself from B's excused but unlawful conduct. B's conduct does not actually serve any superior social interest or right that would ground an exception to the general prohibitory norm and support the matrix of interlocking social relationships created by a true justification.[26]

Greenawalt resists the attempt to consistently categorize putatively justified defendants, arguing that some are most appropriately justified rather than excused. He cites the example of a forest ranger who reasonably but erroneously concludes that he must burn a section of forest in order to create a fire break and protect a town and its inhabitants from a forest fire. Greenawalt contends that the ranger should be justified rather than excused because his choice and action were justified under the circumstances although the consequences fortuitously were not.[27] Any choice that is the best that could be expected under the circumstances should be justified.[28]

Greenawalt advances cases intended to demonstrate the significance of defendants' mental states for justification. Recall Ann who strikes Ben out of hatred while she is unknowingly justified, and compare her to Anna who strikes Bill because she reasonably but mistakenly believes that he is about to attack her. If justification is purely a matter of the external circumstances without regard to perception, then Ann is justified while Anna is not, yet it seems clear that Ann is blameworthy while Anna is not. Greenawalt contends that Anna's blameless perception should be sufficient for justification and that the fact that Ann would be subject to attempt liability demonstrates that her act was not fully justified. He concludes that actors who act on a faultless appraisal of the facts should be justified.[29]

1.1.5   The Social Matrix and the Incompatibility Thesis

Fletcher's classification of putative justification as excuse rather than as justification reflects his claim that justifications identify conduct that is right despite violating the prohibitory norm. Any actor would be right to perform such conduct in order to promote the superior right or social interest that justifies it. Excuses, in contrast, are specific to the individual because they arise from the

---

26 *Id.; Prison Conditions, supra* note 12, at 1361–5.
27 *Perplexing Borders, supra* note 15, at 1907–11.
28 *Id.; Dressler, supra* note 15, at 93.
29 *Distinguishing, supra* note 15, at 101–3.

individual's disability rather than from the superior right or interest that gives rise to the justification.[30] This foundation in superior rights or social interest supports a matrix of complimentary legal rights and duties for third parties. If person X is justified in doing act A because doing A serves the superior right or social interest, then any other person Y has a right to assist and a duty not to resist or interfere with X in doing A because assisting X will promote the justificatory right or social interest and resisting or interfering will frustrate that right or interest.[31] That is, the related legal rights and duties in the social matrix cohere with one another because they share a common foundation in the superior social interests, abstract rights, and norms that provide the normative foundation for all specific legal rights and duties in the set.

Fletcher's interpretations of justified conduct as right behavior, of putative justification as excuse, and of the social matrix arguably promote the violence-preventing function of law by supporting the incompatibility thesis, which holds that no more than one party to a violent confrontation can be justified.[32] That is, if a common foundation of justificatory rights or abstract social interests provides the underlying normative foundation for a set of related legal rights and duties, that set should generally cohere in such a way as to preclude situations in which two or more participants in violent confrontation with each other have access to legal justification. If justification defenses apply only to cases in which justificatory circumstances actually occur, and if third parties have a duty not to resist justified acts, then situations should not ordinarily arise in which two justified parties engage in violent behavior. If X and Y engage in violent conflict, then each resists or interferes with the other. If both were justified, then both would be justified in resisting or interfering with justified actors, in direct contradiction of the claim that one may not resist or interfere with justified actions.

The claim that the social matrix provides a coherent set of interlocking duties and responsibilities encounters tension with Fletcher's knowledge requirement. Suppose that X is unknowingly justified in killing Y and that Z assists X in performing that act with knowledge of the justifying circumstances. Due to the knowledge requirement, X has no justification defense, but Z is justified in assisting X.[33] It seems that it is true both that Z is justified and that he

---

30 Rethinking at 759–62.
31 *Id.* at 761–3; *The Right to Life, supra* note 12, at 77; *Prison Conditions, supra* note 12, at 1357–65. Fletcher refers to a matrix of social relationships. One could use this phrase to refer to an interlocking set of specific legal rights and duties or to the complex set of conventional moral principles that support the legal rights and duties related to justification defenses. In the former sense, the matrix would be the set of related legal rights and duties. In the latter sense, the matrix would be the relevant part of the conventional public morality that provides the normative foundation for that set of legal rights and duties. For the sake of clarity, I refer to the set of interlocking rights, privileges, and duties as the social matrix, and I refer to the underlying normative foundation as the conventional public morality.
32 *Prison Conditions, supra* note 12, at 1357–65.
33 Dressler, *supra* note 15, at 95–6.

is not; Z is justified in that he acts in furtherance of the superior social interest with knowledge of the justifying circumstances, but Z is not justified in that he promotes X's unjustified action.

Critics advance difficult cases calling both the social matrix and the incompatibility thesis into question. Dressler advances the example in which X is an undercover police officer who believes mistakenly but with probable cause that Y is a mass murderer. X draws her gun and approaches Y in order to arrest her. Before X has an opportunity to identify herself as a police officer, Y sees X draw her gun and reasonably but mistakenly concludes that X is about to attack her. Dressler contends that it is at least arguable that under these circumstances Y is justified in defending herself from the apparent deadly attack, and X is justified in defending herself from Y's exercise of force. This example suggests that, contrary to the incompatibility thesis, both parties in a violent conflict might be justified when both act on mistaken perceptions.[34]

Dressler advances other cases that raise doubts about the incompatibility thesis, and he contends that the resolution of these cases may vary with the underlying moral theory. Suppose, for example, that X and Y are both swimming from their sinking ship toward the only available plank that is floating in the water. It is sufficient to keep either of them afloat, but not both. Dressler contends that it is at least arguable that each party is justified in fighting for her life by preventing the other from gaining the plank.[35] He advances another example, which he interprets as a conflict between irreducible values. Suppose X can save a thousand innocent children only by killing the innocent Y. Dressler contends that one could plausibly conclude that X would be justified in killing Y and that Y would be justified in exerting deadly force against X in self-defense. Thus, both sides in the violent conflict would be acting rightly.[36]

Greenawalt advances actual (as opposed to hypothetical) cases in which he claims both sides in violent conflict might be justified. In *People v. Young*, the defendant Young intervened in an apparent mugging that was actually a legal arrest in progress.[37] Young was arguably justified in that he should be praised rather than blamed for his decision and in that society should encourage people to make similar decisions when confronted with similar information. Yet, the police who violently resisted Young's intervention were also justified in doing so, and society should generally encourage police to resist those who interfere in legal arrests by police officers. Greenawalt presents a similar analysis of prison escape cases in which prisoners might be justified in escaping in order to avoid some imminent violence and prison guards might also be justi-

---

34 *Perplexing Borders, supra* note 15, at 94.
35 Dressler, *supra* note 15, at 88–9.
36 *Id.* at 89–91.
37 People v. Young, 11 N.Y.2d 274, 183 N.E.2d 319, 229 N.Y.S.2d 1 (1962), *rev'g* 12 A.D.2d 262, 210 N.Y.S.2d 358 (1961).

fied in fulfilling their responsibilities by preventing those prisoners from escaping.[38] While Dressler interprets his incompatible justification cases as reflecting tensions among underlying moral theories, principles, and values, Greenawalt explains them as manifestations of the complex process of justifying decisions and acts in light of the information available.[39]

1.1.6 Duress as a Problematic Classification

The defense of duress constitutes a problematic category for any attempt to systematically classify justifications and excuses because it contains elements that are ordinarily attributed to each. Duress is frequently classified as an excuse, but it often includes an objective component such as the MPC's "person of reasonable firmness."[40] Cases, codes, and commentators vary, addressing duress as an excuse, a justification, or some hybrid combination.[41] Under the MPC some cases could fall under both the choice-of-evils justification and the duress excuse.[42]

1.1.7 Summary

The debate among Dressler, Fletcher, Greenawalt, and Robinson emphasizes the following theoretical issues with accompanying difficult cases.[43]

(1) Right or Permissible: Do justifications render conduct right, or do they include merely permissible or tolerable behavior?

  1.1 X exercises deadly force in self-defense against Y in X's house without retreating.

  1.2 X exercises deadly force in self-defense against Y who is an innocent aggressor.

(2) The Knowledge Requirement: Must defendants be aware of the justifying circumstances in order to be eligible for the defense, or are justifications purely objective in the sense that they are determined by the presence of the justifying circumstances independent of the actor's awareness?

  2.1 The unknowingly justified X attacks Y out of hate. (Greenawalt's Ann)

---

38 *Perplexing Borders, supra* note 15, at 1919–21.
39 *Compare* Dressler, *supra* note 15, at 87–91 *with id.*
40 MPC at § 2.09.
41 Joshua Dressler, *Exegesis of the Law of Duress: Justifying the Excuse and Searching for Its Proper Limits,* 62 S. Calif. L. Rev. 1331, 1349–67 (1989).
42 MPC at §§ 3.02 (choice of evils), 2.09 (duress).
43 In later sections of this book, I refer to cases identified in this summary by number. "Case 2.1," for example, refers to the case of the unknowingly justified Ann who attacks out of hate.

(3) Putative Justification: Does putative justification establish a justification, an excuse, or either one depending on other conditions?

    3.1 X attacks Y out of the reasonable but mistaken belief that Y is attacking X. (Greenawalt's Anna)

    3.2 X burns a section of forest in the reasonable but mistaken belief that doing so is necessary to save a town and its inhabitants from a forest fire.

    3.3 X and Y attack one another out of the mutually mistaken but reasonable beliefs that doing so is necessary to defend their lives.

(4) The Social Matrix: Do justifications consistently accompany third-party rights and duties such that others may assist justified actors but may not resist or interfere with them?

    4.1 Unknowingly justified X kills Y with Z's knowingly justified assistance: X is not justified; Z is both justified and unjustified.

(5) Incompatibility Thesis: Can two or more parties in violent confrontation be justified in exercising force?

    5.1 New York *Young* case.

    5.2 Prison escape cases.

    5.3 X and Y contest possession of the plank.

    5.4 X attempts to kill the innocent Y to save a thousand innocents, and Y attempts to kill X in self-defense.

(6) Duress: Can duress be consistently categorized as either a justification or an excuse?

1.2 Self-defense as a Problematic Specific Justification Defense

1.2.1 General Self-defense

Mother Beneficence and Dudley justify their exercise of force against Spike as falling within the scope of the specific justification defenses of self-defense and defense of others, respectively. These defendants in these circumstances present easy cases in that the statutory provisions clearly apply, and most readers would probably find that this outcome seems intuitively correct. These easy cases represent a standard form in that a fully competent aggressor purposely attacks an innocent victim for profit, and the defendants exercise proportionate force in order to save the innocent victim in circumstances in which they can do so only through the exercise of force.

Although intuitions tend to converge regarding standard cases, theoretical accounts of self-defense encounter at least three types of difficulty. First, cases that vary from the standard form elicit ambivalent intuitive responses and raise substantial doubts regarding justification. Consider, for example, cases involving innocent aggressors who endanger the lives of innocent victims. Perhaps the innocent aggressor is a child who does not realize that the gun in his hand will harm the victim or a severely impaired person who attacks the victim out of delusional terror. Other intuitively problematic cases involve culpable aggressors who initiate attacks in circumstances that prevent their victims from taking preventive action without endangering innocent parties. Suppose the victim can stop the aggressor only by ramming the car in which the aggressor and an innocent bystander are sitting or that the aggressor shoots at the victim while holding a hostage in front of him as an innocent shield such that the victim can protect herself only by shooting the innocent shield as well as the aggressor.

Second, several controversial questions arise regarding the appropriate parameters of the use of force in self-defense. Must victims retreat from places they legitimately occupy in order to avoid inflicting injury on aggressors? Must they wait until the harm that justifies force is imminent, or can they injure aggressors in "preemptive strikes"? Can victims protect themselves by inflicting injuries substantially more severe than those with which they are threatened, or must they observe a rule of proportionality requiring that they accept less serious injury rather than inflicting severe harm? Suppose, for example, that a weaker victim can escape blackened eyes only by fatally stabbing a stronger aggressor.

Finally, the theoretical foundations of self-defense remain unsettled. Some writers have traced self-defense to historical roots in a public duty to prevent crimes, while others have justified the use of self-protective force through appeal to a lesser-evils rationale. Some theorists treat aggressors as central, arguing that they forfeit the right to life by engaging in aggression, while others emphasize the victim's perspective by appealing to a right to protect some interest such as personal autonomy. Each of the proffered rationales accommodates certain cases, but none provides a completely satisfactory theoretical foundation for all aspects of self-defense.

1.2.2   *Battered Women and Self-defense*

A series of controversial criminal cases address claims of self-defense by battered women who have exercised deadly force against their mates with whom they had engaged in extended relationships involving patterns of repetitive physical abuse of the women by the mates. These cases raise a series of perplexing questions about the parameters of the general category of justification defenses and specifically about the law of self-defense. In some of these cases the defendants exercised force during an episode of physical abuse by the batterers. In others the defendants exerted deadly force against their mates in the absence of any occurrent abuse but in anticipation of renewed attacks. Some of the latter cases have occurred in circumstances in which the mates presented no overt evidence of immediate threat because they were reclining in another room or sleeping.[44] Commentators ordinarily refer to these two contrasting factual patterns, respectively, as confrontation and nonconfrontation cases. Although they dispute the relative frequency of each type of case, commentators agree that both occur and that the latter present more difficult circumstances for defendants who claim self-defense under traditional legal doctrine.[45]

These cases call particular attention to the significance of the defendants' mental states for the distinction between justification and excuse. This distinction characterizes justification as directed toward conduct and excuse as directed toward the defendant's accountability. Yet, many justification provisions require reasonable belief regarding the justificatory conditions rather than their actual occurrence, and these battered women's cases often emphasize the reasonableness of the defendants' beliefs and the relevance of the battered woman syndrome. By virtue of this emphasis on a syndrome involving the defendants' psychological processes, these cases present circumstances that deviate from the standard form of self-defense in a manner that requires clarification of the parameters of, and the justification for, self-defense provisions specifically and the category of justification defenses more generally.

1.3   Necessity, Nullification, and Crimes of Conscience

The necessity defense provides a residual justification defense that serves as a corrective device within the criminal law when people violate offense definitions in circumstances that render their conduct socially acceptable but do not fulfill the requirements of any specific justification defense. Defendants who have violated offense definitions as acts of conscience sometimes advance perplexing claims under the necessity defense. Consider three types of atypical criminal defendants. The first trespasses at a nuclear weapons plant (or a segregated bus station or women's health clinic) in order to publicly protest some law or public policy represented by that facility or by the activity that occurs there. The second operates an underground railroad in violation of the Fugitive Slave Act (or smuggles South American residents into the United States or breaks into a women's health clinic in order to disable equipment and prevent scheduled abortions). The third causes the death of a loved one by disconnecting that person from life-sustaining medical machinery in order to fulfill a promise to that person or to spare that person the pain or indignity of such an existence.

All three types of defendants violate valid law from a sense of conscience. All understand the nature and consequences of their acts, and none suffers

---

44 State v. Norman, 378 S.E.2d 8, 9 (N.C. 1989); State v. Allery, 682 P.2d 312, 313–14 (Wash. 1984); Holly Maguigan, *Battered Women and Self-Defense: Myths and Misconceptions in Current Reform Proposals,* 140 U. Pa. L. Rev. 379, 391–7 (1991).
45 *Compare* Charles P. Ewing, Battered Women Who Kill 34, 99–142 (Lexington, Mass.: Lexington Books, 1987), *with* Maguigan, *id.* at 388–401.

any disability that might ground a legal excuse. No ordinary defense clearly applies, yet punishment raises intuitive discomfort. Many readers might ask, "Are these the types of people and conduct we had in mind when we built the prisons?" Such defendants sometimes seek judicial instructions regarding either the necessity defense or jury nullification.[46] Appellate courts almost universally reject these requests, although trial courts occasionally instruct regarding the necessity defense, and these instructions sometimes generate acquittals.[47] Commentators debate each separately without clear resolution or clarification of the relationship between the necessity defense and jury nullification or of the relationships between each and crimes of conscience.[48] These debates demonstrate both the lack of a clear conception of the necessity defense as a defense that defines the boundaries of the general category of justification defenses and the importance of developing such an understanding.

1.4 Summary and Plan

Although the basic distinction between justification and excuse is well established, difficult issues remain regarding the boundaries of the distinction, the parameters of the general category of justification defenses and of specific defenses, and hard cases for the general category as well as for specific defenses within that category. Some of the problematic cases reflect complex or perplexing factual circumstances or difficult moral choices. Some, however, reveal the absence of a clear understanding of the parameters of and justifications for the specific defense in question or the more general category of justification defenses.

This book advances and defends an integrated theory of justification defenses intended to enhance our understanding of the role of justification defenses in the criminal law and our ability to apply these defenses to hard cases. Pursuing both analytic and normative goals, it addresses the analytic project insofar as it explicates the broad principles of justification embodied in contemporary criminal law, but it does not attempt to defend every aspect of

---

46 Matthew Lippman, *The Necessity Defense and Political Protest,* 26 Crim. L. Bull. 317 (1990); Alan Scheflin & Jon Van Dyke, *Jury Nullification: The Contours of a Controversy,* 43 Law & Contemp. Probs. 51 (1980).

47 Arlene D. Boxerman, Comment, *The Use of the Necessity Defense by Abortion Clinic Protesters,* 81 J. Crim. L. & Criminology 677, 690n90 (1990); Lippman, *id.* at 38–43; Scheflin & Van Dyke, *id.* at 63–8; Laura J. Schulkind, Note, *Applying the Necessity Defense to Civil Disobedience Cases,* 64 N.Y.U. L. Rev. 79, 81n13 (1989).

48 Regarding the necessity defense, *see* Steven M. Bauer & Peter J. Eckerstrom, Note, *The State Made Me Do It: The Applicability of the Necessity Defense to Civil Disobedience,* 39 Stan. L. Rev. 1173 (1987); Boxerman, *id.;* Lippman, *supra* note 46; Schulkind, *id.* Regarding nullification, *see* Scheflin & Van Dyke, *supra* note 46; Alan W. Scheflin & Jon M. Van Dyke, *Merciful Juries: The Resilience of Jury Nullification,* 48 Wash. & Lee L. Rev. 165 (1991); Gary J. Simson, *Jury Nullification in the American System: A Skeptical View,* 54 Tex. L. Rev. 488 (1976).

current doctrine. The book pursues the normative project in that it advances and defends an integrated theory of justification defenses, including some provisions that would alter current doctrine. This theory appeals to the expressive function of the criminal law and to the principles of political morality underlying the broader criminal justice system in order to articulate the role of justification defenses in institutions of criminal law representing liberal principles of political morality.

Chapter 2 examines the difficult theoretical issues raised in Section 1.1 and the expressive function of criminal conviction and punishment in order to clarify the parameters of the conceptual framework for justification defenses as a general category. Chapter 3 advances a theory of self-defense as a justification defense in a liberal society, and Chapter 4 examines the issues raised by claims of self-defense in a series of perplexing cases involving battered women. Chapter 5 demarcates some of the boundaries of the category of justification defenses by differentiating duress from justification in a manner that accommodates some troubling cases left unaddressed by earlier chapters. Chapter 6 clarifies the parameters of the necessity defense as a residual justification defense and differentiates it from jury nullification in the context of crimes of conscience. Chapter 7 summarizes and concludes the project.

2

Justification Defenses and the Conventional Public Morality

This chapter examines the central theoretical issues and difficult cases raised in Section 1.1 regarding the general category of justification defenses. It advances a theoretical framework that accommodates these difficult cases and clarifies the parameters of this category of defense, and it provides a foundation for this class of defenses in the broader structure of criminal offenses and defenses and in the moral condemnation inherent in criminal punishment. As part of the process of articulating a theory of justification defenses, this chapter begins to explore the boundaries that separate justifications from related legal categories, including excuse and mitigation. It does not attempt to develop a comprehensive theory of criminal defenses, however, as it addresses these related issues only insofar as doing so advances the primary purpose of articulating the contours of justification defenses.

2.1 Right or Permissible

Several arguments support the contention that justified conduct is right rather than merely permissible. Justified cannot mean merely not liable to punishment because excused conduct is not punishable, yet it is not justified. As an ideal guide for individual conduct, the law should provide a right answer for each situation. If justified conduct is objectively right, the actor has a right to do it, and, thus, others have a duty not to interfere. This formulation promotes the purpose of law by avoiding mutually justified violent conflicts. If justified conduct were merely permissible, however, two or more permissible alternatives might conflict, leading to incompatible justifications.[1] Although Fletcher explicitly contends that justified conduct is right rather than merely permissible or tolerable, he does not specify a precise interpretation of "right." In one sense, the right act might be understood as the morally best or ideal act. Some teleological moral theories identify the right act as that act that is such that no available alterna-

---

1 *See supra* § 1.1.2.

tive is superior.[2] Justification defenses that identified the right act in this sense would provide the ideal guidance Fletcher seeks in that they would direct the individual toward the best action in the circumstances.

As others have argued, however, the criminal law generally proscribes harmful acts rather than prescribing ideal conduct. As a set of specific behavioral directives, the criminal law provides minimal standards rather than ideals of aspiration. If justification defenses identified the morally best conduct, then it would be impossible to surpass the standard set by those defenses by forgoing the justified behavior. Yet, under some circumstances those who refrain from acting on available justifications behave in an heroic rather than substandard manner. Suppose, for example, police officer X enters a house to investigate reported gunfire; X encounters a six-year-old Y who has found a loaded gun and killed his sister, apparently unaware that they are not playing a game. When X enters the room, Y laughs, points the gun at X, and begins to pull the trigger. X may justifiably shoot Y in self-defense, but if X refrains from shooting, choosing instead to risk lethal injury to himself rather than harming the dangerous but innocent Y, most observers would praise X for heroically rising above the standard set by the law. It seems, therefore, that one can sometimes exceed the standard set by justification defenses, precluding the interpretation of "right" as the morally ideal or best.

Alternately, one might interpret "right" as morally obligatory. On this interpretation, right conduct is not only that which one not may do but also that which one has a duty to do.[3] This interpretation differs from that which was just discussed because morally obligatory conduct does not necessarily coincide with the best conduct. According to some views, the morally best conduct may be superogatory rather than obligatory. Only a relatively less demanding level of conduct is required. Individuals are not, however, obliged to take advantage of justifications. The police officer described previously altruistically forgoes an available justification, and other actors may refuse to exercise available justifications for reasons of self-interest rather than of morally or socially superior interest. Suppose X observes Y snatching Z's purse. X is in a position to tackle Y in order to prevent the theft and would be justified in doing so.[4] X steps aside rather than risk injury in the confrontation. X refrains from exercising the justification, yet X does not violate an obligation, barring some independent duty to come to Z's aid.

One might interpret right action as including all action that is not wrongful by the appropriate standard. Legally right action, according to this interpretation, includes all action that is not illegal. Although Fletcher apparently would

---

2 William K. Frankena, Ethics 14 (Englewood Cliffs, N.J.: Prentice Hall, 2d ed., 1973); Dagobert Runes, Dictionary of Philosophy 272 (Totowa, N.J.: Littlefield, Adams, 1962).
3 II Oxford English Dictionary 2547.
4 MPC at § 3.06(1).

prefer a more stringent formulation of "right," this interpretation meets his demand that "right" mean more than merely not liable to punishment.[5] Excuses and nonexculpatory policy defenses, such as diplomatic immunity, preclude punishment of the defendants who establish them, but they do not render the offensive conduct permissible. The law expressly condemns the conduct performed by defendants exculpated under these types of defenses and attempts to prevent repetition through provisions designed to remove these defendants from society or to control their behavior. Insanity defense statutes, for example, provide for postacquittal commitment, and defendants who establish diplomatic immunity are subject to restraint, expulsion, trial, and punishment in their own country, or punishment in the host country if the represented country waives immunity.[6] Thus, actors who establish these types of defenses are not liable to punishment, but their conduct that gives rise to these defenses remains illegal rather than permissible.

Fletcher's theory contains the seed from which one can explicate the formulation of justified conduct as permissible. He interprets justifications as modifying prohibitory norms by creating exceptions.[7] Excuses and nonexculpatory policy defenses merely exempt certain defendants from punishment without modifying the prohibitory norms. Prohibitory norms direct those subject to the norms to refrain from engaging in certain types of conduct. These directives take the form "You may not perform acts of type *A*," where the type of act is defined in terms of the conduct or consequences prohibited by the offense definition. Justification defenses create exceptions to these norms by specifying certain circumstances under which the directives do not apply. They take the form "except when circumstances *C* occur." Thus, the modified norm reads, "You may not perform acts of type *A*, except under circumstances *C*," allowing otherwise prohibited acts under specified conditions.

The assault provision of the MPC embodies the following prohibitory norm: "You may not cause bodily injury to another."[8] The self-defense provision modifies that prohibition by adding the exception "except under circumstances such that causing bodily injury to another person is immediately necessary for the purpose of protecting yourself against the use of unlawful force by that other person on the present occasion."[9] By specifying an exception to the prohibitory norm under certain circumstances, a justification defense informs the individual that the norm does not apply under those circumstances. The norm

---

5 George P. Fletcher, *Should Intolerable Prison Conditions Generate a Justification or an Excuse for Escape?* 26 U.C.L.A. L. Rev. 1355, 1359 (1979).

6 MPC at § 4.08; Defenses at § 203(c).

7 *See supra* § 1.1.2.

8 MPC at § 211.1(a).

9 *Id.* at § 3.04(1). I have omitted "believes" from the MPC provision in order to reserve the issue of justificatory knowledge for the section that addresses that issue. *See infra* §§ 2.2, 2.4.

and justification together effectively state, "You may not perform acts of type *A,* except that it is not the case that you may not perform acts of type *A* when circumstances *C* obtain." The phrase "it is not the case that you may not" is the equivalent of "you may." It is not the equivalent of "you should," "you must," "it would be best if you did," or "it would be morally ideal if you did." In short, an exception to a prohibitory norm *allows* individuals to engage in conduct of the ordinarily proscribed type, but it does not instruct them to do so or mark conduct of that type as superior or obligatory.

Justifications grant permission or establish privileges by specifying exceptions to prohibitory norms. The relationship among prohibitory norms, offense definitions, and justifications as exceptions or privileges requires some clarification. If one thinks that offense definitions constitute prohibitory norms and that justifications create exceptions to prohibitory norms, then it seems that justifications create exceptions to offense definitions. Understood in this manner, all offense definitions seem to contain an indefinite number of implicit negative offense elements referring to all possible justificatory circumstances. Justifications then collapse into failure-of-proof defenses because defendants who assert justification defenses contend that they did not commit the offenses with which they have been charged because they did not fulfill one of these negative offense elements.

The precise interpretation of these concepts intended by the theorists discussed here remains unclear. This book integrates them in the following manner. A prohibitory norm is a broad statement of principle, providing a broadly applicable moral imperative in the conventional public morality represented by the legal system. Offense definitions are more specific legal applications of the prohibitory norm, drafted with consideration for other important social principles and policies to give notice, guide citizens and officials, and articulate the relative severity of various offenses.

A complete set of offense definitions and applicable justification defenses would address the entire universe of behavior relevant to the more abstract moral principles represented by the criminal law. A fully articulated conventional public morality would contain a complete set of conventional moral principles, including those embodied in the prohibitory norms underlying the various offense definitions, and it would clarify the relationships among the various principles. Justification defenses would apply to conduct that violates an offense definition in circumstances such that some other principle of the conventional public morality takes priority over the principle represented by the prohibitory norm represented by the offense definition. Thus, the overriding principle justifies an exception to the prohibitory norm.[10]

---

10 *See infra* § 3.3 for discussion of the criminal law as embodying a conventional public morality.

According to this interpretation, justifications do not create implicit exceptions to offense definitions, rendering them failure-of-proof defenses regarding negative elements. Rather, they specify exceptions to the broad prohibitory norm, granting permission to violate offense definitions. Understood in this manner, defendants who fulfill all offense elements for a particular offense under conditions providing a justification defense commit the offense, but they are not liable to conviction, punishment, or condemnation because they have not violated the comprehensive set of norms underlying the offense definition.

As exceptions to the general prohibitory norms, justification defenses take the form of privileges rather than rights. If X has a right to perform act A, then any Y against whom X holds this right has a duty not to interfere with X performing A. If X has a privilege to do A, however, then Y has no legal right that X not do A, but Y has no legal duty to avoid interfering with X's doing A.[11] That is, if X has a privilege to do A, X violates no legal right of Y's by doing A, but Y may legally prevent X from doing A. Privileges allow parties to compete against each other, for example, in ordinary business or athletic competition in which each party pursues some lawful goal while attempting to prevent the other from achieving it. Thus, the privileges created by justification defenses render conduct permissible by establishing exceptions to prohibitory norms, but they do not entail correlative legal duties to refrain from interfering. Fletcher is correct, therefore, in stating that if justification defenses render conduct permissible rather than right, they do not prelude the possibility of conflicting privileges.[12]

Although the mere fact that X has a privilege to engage in conduct of type A does not create a duty for Y to refrain from interfering in X's behavior, it does not follow that Y may legally interfere. Y may have a duty to refrain that arises from other legal sources. Suppose police officer X causes bodily injury to Z because Z's resistance to a lawful arrest renders that injury necessary to the completion of the arrest. X's conduct is justified by the MPC provision privileging the use of force in law enforcement.[13] Although this privilege does not entail a duty for Y to refrain from interfering, Y retains the duty to refrain established by other provisions. Y's duty to refrain arises from the provisions proscribing assault if Y would interfere in a manner causing bodily injury or from other offense definitions addressing various methods of obstructing official functions.[14]

Those who act on legal privileges, understood as the lack of any duty to refrain from so acting, may encounter situations in which they are privileged to act but others are similarly privileged to resist or interfere with their actions.

---

11 Wesley Newcomb Hohfeld, Fundamental Legal Conceptions 38–50 (Walter Wheeler Cook ed., Westport, Conn.: Greenwood Press, 1964) (1919).
12 *See supra* § 1.1.2.
13 MPC at § 3.07.
14 *Id.* at §§ 211.1, 242.1, 242.2, 242.3, *respectively.*

Perhaps the most obvious cases arise in legally sanctioned boxing matches in which both participants are privileged to exercise force against one another and to interfere with one another's exercise of the privilege.[15] Similarly, those who engage in legal competitive business practices perform conduct from which they have no duty to refrain but with which others have no duty to refrain from interfering. Yet, the methods of all parties in these instances of mutually privileged competition are limited by all relevant law. Thus, business enterprises may compete with their competitors, but they may not do so through violence. The boxers may exercise mutually privileged violence, but they may not employ weapons. In short, a statute providing a privilege does not preclude the possibility of lawful conflict with other legal behavior, but it does not follow that all privileged conduct may be interfered with or that those who may interfere may do so in any manner they choose.

In summary, justification defenses specify exceptions to prohibitory norms, rendering the justified conduct permissible. Interpretations of justified conduct as morally ideal, superior, or obligatory comport neither with the general logical form of prohibitory norms and justifications nor with the circumstances in which they sometimes apply. This formulation of justifications as creating privileges leaves open the logical possibility of conflicts between mutually justified actors because the mere fact that conduct is privileged does not preclude legal interference. In order to determine whether this formulation generates instances of mutually justified violent conflict in practice, one must examine the difficult cases in the context of the larger legal structure.

2.2 Knowledge and Justification

Fletcher limits justification defenses to those who perform the proscribed action with awareness of the justificatory circumstances, and he interprets putative justification as an excuse. Thus, the defendant's belief in the existence of the justificatory circumstances is necessary but not sufficient for justification. Others dispute Fletcher's explanation for the knowledge requirement and advance difficult cases. Problematic cases include those involving unknowingly justified defendants and putative justification.

The argument for the knowledge requirement from the premise that only those who act with such knowledge merit the special exception provided by the defense arguably supports a requirement of justificatory motive as well as knowledge. The knowledge condition would make the defense available to actors who were aware of the justificatory conditions but acted from vicious motives. Greenawalt raises pivotal cases described earlier as case 2.1 involving

---

15 *Id.* at § 2.11(2)(b).

the vicious but unknowingly justified Ann and 3.1 involving the putatively justified Anna.[16] Greenawalt interprets these cases as demonstrating that no clear line separating justifications and excuses can be drawn because moral evaluation addresses behavior, consequences, and knowledge.[17] Consider also the case of Alice who is both knowingly justified and vicious. Alice accurately perceives that Bert is about to attack Carol. Alice cares not a whit about Carol, but she takes advantage of this opportunity to attack Bert out of hate.

Arguably, common intuitions would hold the putatively justified Anna justified in her action but not the unknowingly justified Ann or the justified but vicious Alice. The knowledge requirement would deprive Ann and Anna of the justification, but it would provide Anna with an excuse, while it would justify Alice. Penal codes that base justifications on the defendants' beliefs or reasonable beliefs about justificatory conditions would justify Anna and Alice but not Ann. Finally, codes that recognized actual necessity or beliefs about necessity as alternative grounds for justification would justify all three defendants, vesting no significance in the important moral differences among them. These cases and the perplexing issues of putative justification and unknowingly justified actors require consideration of the moral condemnation inherent in criminal punishment.

2.3   Moral Condemnation and Criminal Punishment

2.3.1   *Five Types of Condemnation in Criminal Punishment*

Recall the initial clear case of justification involving Spike, Mother Beneficence, and Dudley. Assume that Spike and Dudley are both charged with assault. Both fulfill all material elements of the assault offense in that each purposely causes bodily injury to another. Neither suffers any disability that would ground an excuse. Each is either justified or guilty. Clearly, Spike is a guilty assailant who deserves punishment, while Dudley merits a justification defense. In what relevant ways do they differ?

Intuitively, Dudley merits praise for his actions while Spike deserves condemnation. Joel Feinberg argues that moral condemnation inheres in the concept of punishment, but the precise nature and focus of the condemnation expressed by criminal punishment remains difficult to specify.[18] Social institutions of punishment, including the criminal justice system, consist of rules, practices, and roles regarding the nature, justification, and distribution of punishment. Specific applications of the institution of punishment to a particular

---

16 *See supra* § 1.1.7.
17 *See supra* § 1.1.3.
18 Joel Feinberg, Doing and Deserving 95–118 (Princeton: Princeton Univ. Press, 1970).

person at a particular time constitute punishment as events. One can address questions regarding the concept, efficacy, or justification of punishment both at the level of the institution and at the level of the specific application.[19] Adequate understanding of the condemnation expressed by criminal punishment requires analysis at both levels.

Assume, for example, that Spike is tried, convicted, and punished for his assault on Mother Beneficence. This process expresses condemnation at both levels of analysis. The legal system expresses condemnation of the first type at the institutional level of analysis by defining assault as a criminal offense and by prescribing criminal punishment. Modern criminal codes might include some offenses that are primarily regulatory and relatively trivial, but the core rules of the criminal law proscribe violations of person and property, expressing widely accepted moral standards within the society.[20] By setting minimally acceptable standards of morally relevant social behavior that correspond at least roughly with widely accepted moral precepts and by prescribing punishment for violations, a penal code provides an official representation of an important component of the conventional public morality. Thus, provisions prohibiting certain types of behavior as criminal offenses express condemnation of those types of conduct as contrary to the conventional morality.

In addition to proscribing specified types of conduct as criminal violations of the conventional public morality, the penal code prescribes certain forms of punishment for those who engage in the proscribed conduct under conditions of culpability. In this manner, the forms of punishment typically applied to those who violate the core rules of the criminal law become the paradigmatic symbols of moral condemnation within the conventional public morality represented by the criminal law. Execution and imprisonment, for example, take on special significance as symbols of moral condemnation in a society that relies on these modes of punishment for serious crimes.

Criminal punishment expresses the second through fifth types of condemnation at the level of the specific application of this institution to a particular person at a particular time for a specific offense. Society applies the institution to the defendant through the processes of conviction, sentencing, and execution of the sentence. By convicting Spike of this particular assault, the jury expresses condemnation of the second type in that it reaffirms the more abstract institutional condemnation of this type of conduct.[21] Condemnation of the third type extends not only to the general type of behavior proscribed by the offense definition, but also to this particular instance of that prohibited type. Thus, the

---

19 Kurt Baier, *Is Punishment Retributive?* 16 Analysis 25, 25–32 (1955).

20 MPC at Part II; Herbert Morris, On Guilt and Innocence 33 (Berkeley: Univ. of Calif. Press, 1976).

21 Robert Schopp, *Wake Up and Die Right: The Rationale, Standard, and Jurisprudential Significance of the Competency to Face Execution Requirement,* 51 La. L. Rev. 995, 1031, 34 (1991).

jury's verdict expresses condemnation of Spike's attack on Mother Beneficence as well as of the general category of assaultive behavior.

A jury might exculpate Spike under the insanity defense if he acted while suffering a severe psychological disorder. Excuses, including the insanity defense, prevent conviction, but they undermine neither the institutional condemnation of the general category of conduct proscribed by the offense definition, the jury's ratification of this systemic condemnation, nor the jury's condemnation of this particular assault. Rather, excuses provide the jury with a method of saying, "We condemn assaultive behavior in general and this specific instance of it, but you did not commit this offense as a responsible agent." Thus, the insanity defense exculpates defendants who do not merit condemnation as persons who have violated the law as accountable agents. In contrast, conviction and punishment of a fully culpable defendant convey the fourth type of condemnation in that it condemns the defendant as one who has violated the law as a fully accountable agent by the standards of this criminal justice system.

The fifth and final type of condemnation expressed by conviction and punishment in clear cases addresses the defendant as morally blameworthy for wrongful conduct. Absent a finding of severe psychological disorder or some other disability giving rise to an excusing condition, the jury would condemn Spike as morally blameworthy. That is, Spike is not only appropriately called to account by systemic standards, he is also morally blameworthy in the eyes of the jury.[22]

In summary, the paradigmatic case of conviction and punishment of a fully culpable defendant for committing a criminal offense and violating a widely accepted moral standard expresses condemnation of five different types at two levels of analysis. First, the offense definition condemns a certain type of conduct at the institutional level by proscribing that type of behavior and prescribing criminal punishment. The second through fifth types of condemnation occur at the level of specific application. The second involves the jury's ratification of the institutional condemnation of the general category of behavior proscribed by the offense definition, and the third conveys the jury's condemnation of this particular instance of the prohibited type. Although both the second and third types of condemnation are expressed by a direct application of the institution, the second type reaffirms the institutional condemnation of the general category of behavior proscribed by the offense definition, and the third type conveys the jury's condemnation of this particular instance of the prohibited type. Fourth, the conviction condemns the defendant as one who violated the criminal law as an accountable agent by systemic standards. Fifth, it condemns the defendant as morally blameworthy for wrongful behavior.

---

22 *Id.* at 1034–5.

2.3.2   Hard Cases for Moral Condemnation

In clear cases of unjustified offenses by fully culpable offenders, such as Spike's assault on Mother Beneficence, all five types of condemnation converge in that they clearly apply to this defendant for this offense. Difficult cases arise when circumstances that do not give rise to legal defenses undermine one or more of these five types of condemnation. Juries may struggle, for example, when they encounter a defendant who committed an unjustified and unexcused offense under conditions of great stress or provocation because the jurors may consider the fifth type of condemnation inappropriate. Suppose, for example, that Smith punches Jones in the nose in response to a prolonged series of malicious insults by Jones. Many jurors might think that Jones got what he deserved and that Smith is not blameworthy for the assault, although the provocation would not establish a legal justification or other defense. These jurors would find the fifth type of condemnation undeserved in such a case. Furthermore, jurors who endorse the systemic condemnation of assault as a general category of behavior might deny that this particular instance of that type merits condemnation, considering the third type of condemnation inappropriate as well.

When the official penal code diverges from the widely held conventional morality regarding certain types of behavior, the jury may also consider the second type of condemnation inappropriate in that they might wish to refrain from ratifying the official proscription of conduct of that type. Arguably, certain statutes criminalizing fornication, cohabitation, or possession of marijuana or obscene materials fall into this category in that they express condemnation at the institutional level toward a type of conduct that many jurors may not consider appropriate for moral condemnation. If jurors who encounter circumstances such as these accept an obligation to apply the law as they are instructed by the judge, they may convict the defendants although they do not intend to express condemnation of this type of conduct. In certain cases of conscientious civil disobedience, the jurors may consider the behavior acceptable and the defendants unusually praiseworthy. Thus, although all five types of condemnation apply in clear cases with fully culpable offenders such as Spike, punishment may not accurately express condemnation of the second, third, or fifth type under certain circumstances.

In contrast to the second, third, and fifth types of condemnation, the first type, involving condemnation at the institutional level of the general category of conduct, inheres in any institution of criminal punishment because the criminal justice system serves as the official representation of the conventional public morality for that society.[23] Thus, it expresses condemnation of a certain type of conduct by the standards of that official conventional morality when it

---

23 *See infra* § 3.3 for further discussion of the criminal law as representing a conventional public morality.

defines that type of behavior as an offense and prescribes the paradigmatic forms of criminal punishment such as incarceration and execution.

Many, if not all, criminal justice systems condition conviction and punishment on retributive requirements of guilt, culpability, responsibility, or desert. These institutions, including the contemporary American system, establish criteria of accountability as necessary conditions for conviction and punishment.[24] The fourth type of condemnation, directed toward the defendant as an accountable agent who has violated the criminal law, inheres in conviction and punishment by these retributive systems because they require accountability by systemic standards as a necessary condition for conviction and punishment. Thus, condemnation of the first and fourth types inheres in criminal conviction and punishment by a retributive system.

In summary, the core rules of the criminal law set minimal standards of public morality in a particular society by prohibiting certain categories of behavior and prescribing punishment for offenses. A penal code represents an official statement of an important part of the conventional public morality. Proscription of a category of behavior and prescription of punishment for it expresses institutional condemnation of that type of conduct from the perspective of that conventional morality. The paradigmatic methods of punishment employed by the criminal justice system assume symbolic significance in that they come to represent systemic condemnation. Clear cases of wrongful conduct by fully culpable actors also elicit condemnation of four types at the level of specific application, but only the first (systemic) and fourth (accountability) types of condemnation inhere in all cases of legal punishment by retributive criminal justice systems.

2.3.3　Moral Condemnation and Justification Defenses

Dudley, in contrast to Spike, deserves praise rather than condemnation because he risked injury in order to rescue the innocent Mother Beneficence. In order to understand the nature of justification as a defense that renders Dudley inappropriate for conviction and punishment, consider his case in light of the condemnation inherent in criminal punishment and the reasons why that condemnation is not appropriate for him. It seems immediately obvious that Dudley does not merit the fifth type of condemnation in that he is not morally blameworthy for

---

24 MPC at §§ 2.01, 2.02, 4.01; Rethinking at §§ 6.6, 10.3. Note the minimal sense of "retributive"as used here. A system is retributive in this sense if it limits criminal punishment to those who commit offenses while meeting specified conditions of accountability that serve to render the offense appropriately attributed to the person as a accountable agent. It does not require that the punishment be of similar quality to the harm caused by the offense or that punishment be thought of as restoring a moral balance. *See* Schopp, *supra* note 21, at 1020–7 (discussing this sense of retributivism).

his act. Many would contend that he is praiseworthy for exposing himself to risk in order to rescue Mother Beneficence. This fifth type of condemnation is not inherent in criminal punishment, however, and defendants who are not appropriate for such condemnation sometimes lack a legal defense for their conduct. Some defendants qualify for punishment by systemic standards despite being inappropriate for the second, third, and fifth types.

The first and fourth types of condemnation are inherent in criminal punishment, however, rendering conviction and punishment of defendants who do not merit these types of condemnation unjustified. The first type addresses the general category of behavior proscribed in an offense definition rather than a particular act or actor. The fourth type condemns specific defendants who violate proscriptions of the criminal law in their capacities as accountable agents by systemic standards. Dudley is a fully accountable agent who qualifies for no recognized excuse and who fulfilled all offense elements in the definition of assault. Dudley purposely caused bodily injury to Spike. It initially appears, therefore, that Dudley qualifies for the fourth type of condemnation. This appearance is deceptive, however, because the first and fourth types of condemnation interact in a manner that significantly affects Dudley's case. The resolution to Dudley's case requires examination of this relationship between the first and fourth types of condemnation.

Any particular act may constitute an instance of many different types of action. Dudley's act of punching Spike, which exemplifies the type of conduct proscribed by the offense definition for assault, also constitutes an instance of the types defined as moving one's arm, swinging one's hand, rescuing Mother Beneficence, and many others. Dudley's act exemplifies both the type proscribed by the offense definition for assault and the type described by the justification defense usually referred to as "defense-of-others." This defense applies to those who exercise force necessary to prevent the unjustified use of force by another person against a third party.[25] Thus, Dudley's conduct exemplifies many types of action, only some of which are subject to the first type of condemnation inherent in offense definitions.

The objective elements of an offense definition identify the proscribed type of action by describing certain conduct, circumstances, or results.[26] These ele-

---

25 MPC at § 3.05; Defenses at § 133; Alvin Goldman, A Theory of Human Action 10–15 (Princeton: Princeton Univ. Press, 1970). Act-types are general descriptions of certain act-properties that humans can exemplify at a particular time and place. For example, raising one's hand, standing up, and asking a question are all act-types. Act-tokens are specific instantiations of those types by a particular person at a particular time. For example, Smith's raising his hand at a particular time is a token of the act-type defined as "raising one's hand." Similarly, Dudley's punching Spike in the nose at a particular time is a token of the act-type defined by the MPC's definition of assault as "purposely, knowingly, or recklessly causes bodily injury to another" MPC at § 211.1(1)(a).
26 Defenses at § 11(a).

ments specify the properties that render an act an instance of the proscribed type. Homicide statutes, for example, forbid acts of the type defined by the property "causes the death of another human being."[27] Justification defenses recognize exceptions to the general prohibitory norms underlying the offense definitions in that they identify certain conditions under which conduct exemplifying these properties remains acceptable according to the conventional public morality. The defense provided for the use of force in the defense of others, for example, provides exceptions from the general prohibitory norm underlying the assault and homicide statutes for acts that fulfill the offense elements for these crimes in circumstances that render such conduct necessary to protect another person from the use of unlawful force by a third party.[28]

General prohibitory norms are principles of the conventional public morality that proscribe certain categories of behavior. These prohibitory norms do not, however, exhaust the conventional public morality. Other principles might address positive obligations, including, for example, obligations to exercise reasonable care to avoid harming other people or their property and to protect the innocent. The fully articulated conventional public morality would include all of the principles of public morality represented by the law of a particular society and the relationships among them. These would include the complete set of prohibitory norms underlying the criminal offense definitions of the penal code as well as a variety of other widely endorsed moral principles officially represented by the law. These principles provide good reasons to act or refrain from acting. Criminal offense definitions take the form of behavioral directives representing prohibitory norms that provide decisive reasons to refrain from certain types of behavior under most conditions. Justification defenses identify unusual circumstances in which other principles of the conventional public morality provide countervailing reasons of sufficient strength to override the prohibitory norms underlying a particular offense definition.

Dudley, for example, struck Spike in circumstances in which the principle that one ought to protect the innocent from harm overrode the prohibitory norm that one ought not cause physical harm to other human beings. The general prohibitory norm that supports the offense definition for assault provides good reasons, and usually decisive reasons, to refrain from violating the assault statute, but in these circumstances, the principle that one ought to protect the innocent from harm gave rise to overriding reasons to exercise force against Spike. Thus, Dudley's conduct exemplified the type of behavior prohibited by the offense definition for assault, but it also exemplified the type of conduct exempted from punishment by the defense-of-others statute that applies when conduct that vio-

27 MPC at § 210.1(1).
28 *Id.* at § 3.05; Defenses at § 133.

lates the assault statute does not violate the fully articulated conventional public morality.

The fourth type of condemnation condemns the actor as one who violated the criminal law as an accountable agent. In order to qualify for this type of condemnation, one must meet two conditions; first, one must violate the criminal law, and second, one must do so in one's capacity as an accountable agent by systemic criteria. If justifications recognize exceptions to the prohibitory norms represented by offense definitions, then actors like Dudley, who qualify for justification defenses, do not fulfill the first condition because they do not violate the fully articulated conventional public morality represented by the criminal law.

Both justifications and excuses preclude criminal punishment because they render the fourth type of condemnation inappropriate. This interpretation does not render justification and excuse indistinguishable, however, because each undermines this type of condemnation in a different manner. While justified defendants do not violate the fully articulated conventional public morality, excused defendants violate that morality, but they do not do so in their capacity as accountable agents.

In short, excuses exempt certain actors from condemnation and punishment because their conduct that violates the directives of the criminal law is not attributable to them in their capacities as accountable agents by systemic criteria. Justifications preclude condemnation and punishment of actors not because of the merit or accountability of the actors but because these defenses exempt certain subsets of generally proscribed categories of conduct from the condemnation expressed at the institutional level by the offense definition. Thus, justified actors do not violate the fully articulated conventional public morality represented by the law.

2.4   Knowledge and Justification Revisited

2.4.1   *Moral Condemnation, Prohibitory Norms, and Unknowingly Justified Defendants*

If justified defendants have not violated the fully articulated morality represented by the law, then they are immune from punishment for the same reason that precludes punishment of those who simply fail to meet the objective offense elements for any criminal offense. Individuals in either category have not engaged in behavior forbidden by the integrated set of provisions constituting the criminal law. Fletcher correctly argues that unknowingly justified defendants do not merit special exemptions from the general prohibitory norms.[29] Justification defenses do not exempt defendants, however; they exempt categories of behavior. Justification defenses qualify the behavioral directives represented by a variety of assault and homicide statutes by exempting conduct that violates these provisions in identified circumstances from the prohibition contained in the offense definitions and from the condemnation and punishment authorized by those statutes. The integrated behavioral directive contained in the assault and defense-of-others provisions reads roughly "Do not cause bodily injury to another human being, unless such conduct is necessary to prevent that other human being from using unlawful force against a third person." It does not read "Do not cause bodily injury to another human being unless you are altruistically motivated."

Compare the unknowingly justified defendant to the malicious actor who performs legal activity for vicious reasons. Suppose the Smith family runs a small laundry that barely makes enough profit to sustain the family. Jones owns a highly profitable chain of commercial laundries that have made him wealthy. Jones opens another store across the street from the Smith laundry purely for the satisfaction of driving them out of business. Jones successfully does so through the legal business advantages derived from greater volume and capital. Jones, like the unknowingly justified defendant, acts from pure malice, but he is immune from conviction and punishment and from the type of condemnation inherent in legal punishment because he has not performed any act prohibited by the fully articulated conventional public morality.

Most citizens might believe that Jones should not have engaged in such behavior. Thus, Jones's conduct might violate the conventional *social* morality in the sense that most citizens would disapprove of his behavior toward the Smiths. A conventional *public* morality, however, has three properties. First, it is conventional rather than critical in that broad popular support rather than critical defensibility by appeal to some moral principles determines its content. Second, it represents broadly held moral standards of good, evil, right, and wrong. It does not include, for example, nonmoral beliefs about prudence or aesthetics. Third, it is public in the sense that it addresses only those aspects of morality that are widely thought to fall within the public jurisdiction and, thus, to be the proper subject of law.

The conventional social morality may support a variety of obligations that fall beyond the scope of the conventional public morality because they address aspects of social life that are considered inappropriate for legal regulation. Most citizens might endorse general obligations to treat strangers with courtesy and family with kindness, for example, but hold that these obligations fall beyond the scope of legal enforcement. Similarly, most members of society might hold that people ought not indulge in heartlessly competitive business

---

29 *See supra* § 2.2.

practices, such as those practiced by Jones against the Smiths, but that law should not attempt to enforce this particular standard. We infer the conventional public morality from the law because it consists of that portion of the conventional morality that is relegated to the jurisdiction of legal institutions.

Some might suggest that Jones differs from unknowingly justified defendants in that he has not violated any general prohibitory norm represented by an offense definition. One who violates a general prohibitory norm, these critics would contend, does not deserve the advantage afforded by the exception unless he acts while aware of it. To say that a certain class of acts are excepted from a prohibitory norm, however, is just to say that these acts are not prohibited. If justifications recognize exceptions to general prohibitions, then acts that fall into these categories, like the evil but legal acts of Jones, are not legally prohibited. One cannot consistently say that justification defenses recognize exceptions to general prohibitory norms and that conduct falling within the scope of the justifications violates those norms. Thus, a person whose conduct falls within the scope of a justification, like a person who performs no conduct violating an offense definition, conforms to the fully articulated conventional public morality.

Suppose, however, that one were to define justification defenses in a manner that included the knowledge requirement in the description of the exceptions to the general prohibition. Fletcher contends that justifications have objective and subjective elements. Justification defenses exculpate, on this view, because the defendant had good and sufficient reasons for violating the general prohibitory norm.[30] Fletcher describes the prohibitory norm generated by integrating the general prohibition against homicide with the self-defense justification as "Thou shalt not kill unless thine own life or limb is in great danger."[31] Consider the alternative formulation, "Thou shalt not kill unless *you know* that thine own life or limb is in danger."

2.4.2 *Justification Defenses with Subjective Elements*

If one defines justifications purely in terms of objective circumstances and, further, contends that justifications create exceptions to prohibitory norms and that these justifications are available only to defendants who are aware of those justificatory circumstances, then one faces the difficult task of explaining why the general prohibition applies to some acts that are explicitly excepted from it. By drafting the defense in a manner that includes both objective circumstances and the knowledge requirement in the description of the exempted subclass, however, one avoids this predicament because acts fall into the excepted subclass only if the defendant knows of the justificatory circumstances.

---

30 Rethinking at 576.
31 *Id.* at 457.

A thorough evaluation of this proposal requires further elaboration of the role of the fourth type of condemnation in light of the prospective and retrospective functions of criminal offense definitions. These provisions operate prospectively by providing directives to citizens, which impose obligations of compliance on citizens and describe the types of conduct individuals must avoid in order to fulfill those obligations.[32] When courts apply these directives retrospectively as criteria for criminal conviction and punishment, they must determine whether the defendants performed prohibited acts for which they may fairly be held accountable. Fletcher contends that prohibitory norms and justifications that create exceptions to these norms serve the prospective function, while excuses address only the retrospective function by exculpating those defendants whose conduct cannot fairly be attributed to them as accountable agents.[33]

Fletcher frames prohibitory norms as directives prohibiting conduct such as killing or stealing. These directives address objective offense elements without culpability elements.[34] They prohibit certain categories of acts defined by properties specified as conduct, circumstances, or results. Thus, they direct citizens to refrain from performing any specific acts of the type defined by the objective offense elements in the definition of the criminal offense. Individuals who use these norms as guidelines for voluntary compliance must evaluate contemplated behavior in order to determine whether it would constitute an instance of a prohibited type. People act in furtherance of their goals or desires by pursuing action-plans, which consist of a set of acts intended to achieve some end. Stated intuitively, they pursue an action-plan in order to achieve some end.[35]

Dudley, for example, punches Spike and restrains him in order to protect Mother Beneficence and facilitate Spike's arrest. Dudley's action-plan consists of the set of acts he selects to achieve his purpose and the decision to engage in that set of acts. The set includes acts that are intended or anticipated as part of the action-plan. Dudley's intended acts include punching Spike, holding Spike on the ground, and yelling "call the police" to a bystander. If Dudley anticipated that yelling to the bystander would startle the bystander but did not yell for the purpose of startling that person, then startling the bystander was an anticipated but not intended component of the action-plan. Acts described as intended and anticipated in the terminology of action-theory correspond roughly to acts performed purposely and knowingly in the MPC.[36]

---

32 *Id.* at 456–7.

33 *Id.* at 456–7, 491–2. Presumably the norms and justifications serve both functions because they provide courts with criteria of exculpation when they apply.

34 *Id.* at 456. "[T]hou shalt not do X where 'doing X' may stand for 'killing,' 'stealing,' 'raping,' and so forth."

35 Robert F. Schopp, Automatism, Insanity, and the Psychology of Criminal Responsibility 92–3 (Cambridge: Cambridge Univ. Press, 1991).

36 *Id.* at §§ 4.2, 4.3.

Had Dudley wanted only to rescue Mother Beneficence and not to facilitate Spike's arrest, he might have chosen to yell at Spike rather than punching him on the expectation that doing so would frighten Spike, causing him to run away. In most circumstances, actors select action-plans to act upon from a wide array of potential action-plans because they believe that the intended and anticipated acts that comprise the plan selected are more likely than those in any available alternative plan to satisfy their complex set of wants and goals.

Offense definitions serve the prospective function of the criminal law by altering the desirability of prospective action-plans. The objective offense elements proscribe certain act-types such as causing the death or bodily injury of another human being. The moral condemnation inherent in the proscription as well as the prospect of punishment for performing acts of the proscribed types reduce the probability that actors will select action-plans that include instances of these types as intended or anticipated components. Although actors select action-plans on the basis of the intended and anticipated acts that constitute these plans, the actual results may differ from those intended or anticipated due to error or luck.

In their prospective role as directives regarding future behavior, offense elements address action-plan selection rather than actual conduct. The conduct performed by a particular individual is the product of action-plan selection, predictive accuracy, and luck, but information regarding predictive errors and luck is not available to the deliberating agent during the process of action-plan selection.[37] Thus, the directives represented by objective offense elements are most accurately understood as instructions regarding action-plan selection. As applied to the prospective function, homicide statutes express the directive "Do not act on action-plans that include intended or anticipated acts that cause the death of another human being."[38]

Action-plans rather than acts most accurately represent actors as decision-making agents because action-plans represent the wants, intentions, and expectations of the actors, while acts diverge from action-plans due to error or luck. Culpability elements define a required relation between the conduct forbidden by the objective offense elements and the decision maker as represented by the action-plan. A purposeful culpability element applies to an act directly representing the actor's wants and intentions, while a negligent culpability element represents a less direct relationship between the decision maker's action-plan and the proscribed conduct. Thus, an actor who causes the death of another person by acting on an action-plan that includes killing that person as an intended

---

37 Information about general accuracy or the probability of errors in these circumstances may be available, but not information regarding the actual errors or luck that will affect the outcome of this decision.

38 Schopp, *supra* note 35, at § 4.2 (discussing the relationship between purposeful, knowing, or reckless homicide and intended or anticipated acts on action-plans).

action commits murder, while one who causes the death of another by acting on an action-plan that would have included killing the other person as an anticipated act if the actor had deliberated with due care commits negligent homicide.[39]

Failure-of-proof defenses regarding the culpability element exculpate the defendant by demonstrating that the act that exemplified the proscribed type lacked the relation to the action-plan required by the offense definition and, thus, that this offense cannot be attributed to the actor as an accountable agent.[40] By undermining the required relation between the actor as an accountable agent and the proscribed conduct, these defenses undermine the fourth type of condemnation discussed previously, which condemns the actor as one who violates the criminal law in his capacity as an accountable agent by systemic standards. Excuses undermine the fourth type of condemnation by undermining the actor's status as an accountable agent, at least as applied to this offense. The insanity defense, for example, exculpates those who fulfill all offense elements while suffering severe psychological dysfunction, which renders them incapable of functioning as accountable agents regarding this conduct.[41] In short, excuses and failure-of-proof defenses regarding the culpability elements preclude the fourth type of condemnation by defeating the attribution of this offense to this person as an accountable agent. For this reason, both categories of defenses are primarily relevant to courts engaged in the retrospective function of the law.

Justifications, in contrast, address both the prospective and retrospective functions. Justifications serve the retrospective function in that they exempt a subset of acts from the general prohibition underlying the offense definition, identifying circumstances in which courts should exculpate defendants who fulfill all offense elements. These defendants do not qualify for the fourth type of condemnation because they have not violated the fully articulated conventional public morality as represented by the integrated set of offense definitions and justification defenses stated purely as conduct, circumstances, and results. Unknowingly justified defendants would violate the fully articulated norms if the exceptions created by justification defenses contained both objective elements and a knowledge requirement. These defendants would not qualify for the exceptions provided by justification defenses drafted in this manner because they lacked the requisite knowledge.

---

39 *Id.* at § 4.2. One who acts on an action-plan including homicide as an intended action performs that action purposefully, fulfilling the requirements of the murder statute. One who acts on an action-plan that would have included the homicide as an anticipated act if the actor had exercised due care in selecting the action-plan causes the death through lack of due care, that is, negligently.

40 *Id.* at 106–7; Defenses at §§ 22, 62(b).

41 Schopp, *supra* note 35, at ch. 6.

Although unknowingly justified defendants were not aware of good and sufficient reasons for violating the general norm, such reasons were available. That is, circumstances provided good and sufficient reasons for violating the norm, but these defendants were not aware of and did not act for those reasons. In these cases, the available reasons justified the acts that exemplified the proscribed act-types, but the actors' action-plans did not reflect or rely upon these reasons. If, for example, Dudley failed to notice that Spike was attacking Mother Beneficence and attacked Spike only for the purpose of stealing Spike's wallet, then Dudley's conduct would have exemplified the act-type described as rescuing another person from an unlawful use of force, but his action-plan would not reflect that act-type as intended or anticipated. His action-plan would consist of the plan to punch Spike in order to rob him.

A justification defense with a knowledge requirement would direct the defense toward the defendant's action-plan by limiting its scope to those who acted on an action-plan that included acts representing the justificatory reasons as anticipated or intended components. The action-plan represents the actor as a decision maker, however, providing the foundation for attributions of accountability, culpability, and blameworthiness. The action-plan and the manner in which it is selected are critical to excuses and failure-of-proof defenses because these defenses address the attribution of the offense to the actor as an accountable agent by systemic standards of accountability. Thus, a penal code that drafts justification defenses with knowledge requirements conflates the role of justifications with those of excuses and failure-of-proof defenses by directing the justification defenses toward the action-plan and the attribution of the offense to the actor as an accountable agent rather than toward modifications of general prohibitory norms.

In adjudicating a claim of justification under a justificatory provision including a knowledge requirement, a court would have to ask two questions: first, was X's act A justified? and second, was X justified in performing A? The first question addresses the reasons available in the situation for performing A in order to appraise the social acceptability of the act from the external point of view. The second question addresses the reasons that X was aware of in order to appraise X's decision to engage in the conduct from the internal point of view.[42] A successful claim of justification under this type of provision would require both external and internal justification.

Although intuitively clear cases of fully justified actors involve defendants such as Dudley who perform actions that are justified from both the internal and external points of view, justification defenses should not require internal justification based on justificatory knowledge for at least three reasons regarding

---

42 I use the terms "external" and "internal" partially to avoid widespread ambiguity regarding the meaning of "subjective" and "objective" in the discussion of justification defenses.

the retrospective function. First, as explained above, doing so conflates the role of justifications with those of other defenses by directing the inquiry toward the actor's action-plan and the attribution of conduct to the actor as an accountable agent. Second, although internal justification is relevant to the fifth type of condemnation, which addresses the moral blameworthiness of the fully culpable actor for performing the offense, this type of condemnation is not inherent in legal conviction and punishment. Internal justification would constitute one aspect of a comprehensive moral evaluation, but blameworthiness from this perspective is neither necessary nor sufficient for accountability by the systemic standards of the conventional morality represented by the criminal law.[43] Third, a knowledge requirement would serve primarily to extend liability to some defendants who would otherwise avoid criminal punishment only through luck, but attempt liability applies to these individuals.[44] Although unknowingly justified defendants may not merit exemption from liability, attempt liability can provide liability within the conventional morality embodied in the criminal law, and moral evaluation involves the fifth type of condemnation already discussed rather than the first and fourth types, which are inherent in criminal conviction and punishment.

While these considerations render the knowledge requirement inappropriate for the retrospective function, it is simply unnecessary and redundant for the prospective function. Justification defenses and the general prohibitions they modify serve the prospective function of the criminal law by providing norms for voluntary compliance. Individuals who rely on these guidelines in directing their conduct select action-plans intended to avoid behavior that violates the fully articulated norms. The fully articulated norm regarding homicide with the self-defense exception as formulated without the knowledge requirement directs the individual to refrain from acting on action-plans that include acts that cause the death of another human being unless those acts qualify as self-defense.

A knowledge requirement in a justification defense is redundant for the prospective function because all acts in an action-plan are anticipated or intended, rendering it impossible for an actor to act prospectively on an action-plan including an act of self-defense without realizing that it is an act of self-defense. That is, any prospective act of self-defense in an action-plan must be anticipated or intended as an act of self-defense in order to be part of the action-plan as an act of self-defense. Thus, adding a knowledge requirement adds nothing to the norm as applied to the prospective function because the norm directs actors regarding action-plans that include only acts defined by properties of which the actors are aware whether or not the knowledge requirement

---

43 *See supra* § 2.3.1.
44 MPC at § 5.01; Defenses at § 122(d).

is included. Simply stated, the knowledge requirement is redundant for the prospective function because the process of action-plan selection addresses only anticipated and intended acts.[45]

In summary, excuses, failure-of-proof defenses, and justification defenses undermine the grounds for the moral condemnation inherent in criminal punishment. Justifications preclude this condemnation in a different manner from the other defenses. Excuses and failure-of-proof defenses render this condemnation inappropriate by defeating attribution of the offenses to the defendants as accountable agents, while justifications preclude this condemnation by exempting the actor's conduct from the general proscription. If the justificatory provisions creating those exceptions are drafted purely in terms of conduct, circumstances, and results, then limiting the defense to knowingly justified actors permits condemnation ostensibly for accountable violations of the norms directed toward actors who have not violated the complete set of norms constituting the fully articulated conventional public morality. Alternately, justifications drafted with a knowledge requirement avoid this problem, but the requirement is redundant for the prospective function of the norms, and it needlessly conflates justifications with other defenses when applied retrospectively.

The approach to the controversy regarding unknowingly justified defendants advanced here relies upon a theoretical framework emphasizing the moral condemnation inherent in legal punishment, the distinction between external and internal justification, and an interpretation of criminal offenses grounded in action-theory. In order to support these organizing principles for the analysis of justification defenses, the next section applies these principles to the previously identified difficult cases regarding unknowingly justified actors and putative justification. The following sections apply these principles to the remaining controversial issues and difficult cases, contending that this form of analysis clarifies the parameters of legal justification defenses.

2.4.3 Hard Cases and the Knowledge Requirement

First, consider the difficult cases involving unknowingly justified or putatively justified defendants such as Ann, Anna, and Alice. These cases elicit troubling intuitions because the actors are neither unambiguously guilty like Spike nor fully justified like Dudley. Recall that Ann, Anna, and Alice attack other persons. Ann is unknowingly justified, while Anna acts from the mistaken belief that she is justified. Alice realizes that circumstances justify her attack, but she

---

45 That the action-plan includes only anticipated and intended acts while the knowledge requirement addresses knowledge rather than anticipation does not establish a significant difference between the two. Prospectively, both approaches require awareness that the act is highly likely to be generated, while retrospectively both require that the actor expected that the act that was actually generated would be generated. Schopp, *supra* note 35, at § 4.2.

acts out of hate. Arguably, common intuitions would hold Anna but not Ann or Alice justified[46]

The type of condemnation inherent in punishment and the distinction between internal and external justification are central to understanding these cases. Although it might seem intuitively wrong to say that Ann and Alice were justified in acting as they did, their acts were externally justified in the circumstances. Both Ann and Alice were morally blameworthy for acting on malicious motive, but this addresses the fifth type of condemnation involving moral blameworthiness, which is not inherent in criminal punishment. Neither is eligible for the critical fourth type of condemnation because neither violated the fully articulated conventional public morality. The justificatory circumstances provided external justification for their actions, bringing that behavior within the scope of a justification defense recognizing an exception to the general prohibitory norm.

Alice, but not Ann, was internally justified in the sense that she was aware of the justificatory circumstances that exempted her conduct from the general norm. Thus, Ann would be vulnerable to attempt liability, but Alice would not because attempt liability attaches to those whose conduct would constitute crimes if the circumstances were as the actors believed them to be.[47] Ann's attempt liability constitutes the legal system's device for holding her liable for acting in an internally unjustified manner in circumstances that fortuitously render her action externally justified. Such attempt liability increases convergence between legal liability and common moral intuitions.

Although Alice behaves in a manner that demonstrates reprehensible character, she does not engage in conduct prohibited by the conventional public morality. The criminal law does not address character independent of prohibited conduct. Arguably, most plausible theories of political morality would define character unaccompanied by conduct as falling beyond the scope of the public jurisdiction.[48] Alice, like the malevolent launderer Jones, would be morally blameworthy but not subject to condemnation for any offense contained in the conventional morality embodied in the criminal law. Not surprisingly, common intuitions sometimes reflect the conventional social morality rather than the narrower conventional public morality institutionalized in the criminal law.

Anna, contrary to some people's intuition, lacks legal justification because she violated a prohibitory norm in the absence of justificatory circumstances that would support an exception. The intuitive notion that Anna was justified by her reasonable but mistaken belief that justificatory conditions applied reflects

---

46 *See supra* §§ 1.1.4 (Ann and Anna), 2.2 (Alice).
47 MPC at § 5.01(1)(a).
48 *See infra* § 3.3 for further discussion of the conventional public morality in the context of liberal political morality.

a judgment of internal justification that addresses both her lack of moral blame-worthiness and the attribution of the violation to her in her capacity as an accountable agent by systemic standards. Her lack of moral blameworthiness is relevant to the fifth type of condemnation of an offender as morally blame-worthy, which is not inherent in criminal punishment. Hence, the fact that she does not qualify for that type of condemnation does not in itself preclude con-viction and punishment.

Anna's reasonable mistake regarding justification is relevant to the fourth type of condemnation, however, in that it undermines the attribution of her pro-hibited act to her in her capacity as an accountable agent. That is, the circum-stances that led to her reasonable but erroneous belief that she was justified pre-vented her from selecting her action-plan in light of the relevant information.[49] Thus, her action-plan did not include an unjustified offense, as defined by the fully articulated conventional public morality, as an anticipated or intended component of the plan. Factors that undermine the fourth type of condemnation by virtue of defects in the action-plan, the process of action-plan selection, or the required relation between action-plan and proscribed conduct exculpate the actor, but they do not justify the action. Putative justification provides internal but not external justification, supporting excuse but not a justification defense.

This analysis also accommodates Greenawalt's case involving the forest ranger who burns a section of forest because he reasonably but erroneously believes that doing so is necessary to save the town. Greenawalt contends that one ought to be justified in making the best choice in light of all available infor-mation. Indeed, we might suppose the ranger places himself at some danger in carrying out his decision. The ranger is justified in burning the forest, and he is praiseworthy for accepting personal risk in order to carry out his plan. While he is justified in burning the forest, however, burning the forest is not justified. That is, the ranger is internally justified by the reasons to which he has access, but the act of burning the forest is not externally justified by all the reasons there are. Some unknown causal factor, such as wind conditions, rendered his action unnecessary to save the town and, hence, unjustified. He was internally justified in acting, however, because he was not aware of this factor at the time he was confronted with the decision. In this way, the ranger resembles Anna who was also confronted with a decision in the absence of full information.

The ranger may elicit even stronger intuitive approval than Anna because the story indicates that the ranger is morally praiseworthy for fulfilling what he rea-

---

49 In this section, I discuss only reasonable mistakes regarding justification. Those who commit unjustified offenses due to reasonably mistaken beliefs are blameworthy for neither the pro-scribed conduct nor the mistake. Reckless or negligent mistakes regarding justification raise more complex issues regarding blameworthiness for the mistake and for offenses with reck-lessness or negligence as culpability elements. *See* MPC at § 3.02(2); Defenses at § 184; *see infra* §§ 4.5.3, 4.5.4 regarding unreasonable but nonculpable mistakes.

sonably understood to be his responsibility at some risk to himself. His moral praiseworthiness renders inappropriate the fifth type of condemnation, however, and this is not the type that inheres in legal conviction and punishment. Once one recognizes the distinctions between internal and external justification and between moral blameworthiness and systemic legal accountability, one can describe the ranger as systemically accountable because he possesses the required capacities and as internally justified and praiseworthy for performing acts that are not externally justified. Although the ranger is an accountable agent by systemic standards, his externally unjustified act is not appropriately attributed to him in this status because his reasonable error resulted in his selecting an action-plan on which the intended acts were justified. These conditions preclude the fourth type of condemnation in a manner that grounds excuse rather than justification. Thus, the ranger is excused from legal liability, and he is morally praiseworthy for his conscientious decision and effort.

The final difficult case regarding the knowledge requirement involves *X* and *Y* who attack one another out of mutual mistakes, generating a conflict between two putatively justified actors. Each actor is internally but not externally justified. Interpreted in this manner, these cases create no problem of conflicting justifications because each lacks the external justification that supports a justification defense although each may be eligible for excuse.

2.5   The Social Matrix and the Incompatibility Thesis

2.5.1   Assisting Justified Acts

Fletcher contends that justifications modify prohibitory norms, creating a matrix of related social responsibilities. Third parties may assist justified acts, and they may not resist or interfere with these acts.[50] This claim seems intuitively plausible in that justified acts are legally permissible acts, and there is no obvious reason why one may not assist another in performing a legal act or why one may interfere with a legal act. Dudley illustrates the positive aspect of this matrix in that he justifiably assists Mother Beneficence in her justified exercise of self-defense. Any third party who interfered with Mother Beneficence and Dudley by entering the fray in support of Spike would have violated the negative aspect that proscribes interference with justified conduct such as that of Mother Beneficence and Dudley.

The incompatibility thesis holds that two parties in violent conflict with one another cannot both be justified.[51] The incompatibility thesis can be understood

---

50 *See supra* § 1.1.5.

51 *See supra* § 1.1.5. Some conflicts can involve additional parties who participate as principals in more complex conflicts or as assistants to the primary parties, but I will use this simple formulation. In addition, we must understand the thesis as limited to illegal conflicts, with legal contests such as boxing matches or football games falling beyond the scope of the claim.

as a corollary of the negative aspect of the social matrix. Each of two parties in violent conflict interferes with the other; if either is justified, then the other interferes with justified conduct and cannot be justified according to the social matrix. Therefore, no more than one party in the conflict can be justified.

This thesis apparently works well when applied to Spike's attack and the resulting conflict. Mother Beneficence is justified, but Spike is not. Dudley assists Mother Beneficence by interfering with Spike, creating a second conflict in which Dudley is justified but Spike is not. Should some third party misunderstand the situation and intervene to protect Spike from Dudley, that person could not be justified because she would interfere with Dudley who is justified. She may, however, qualify for an excuse if she innocently misinterpreted the situation.

When combined with the requirement that the justified defendant act with justificatory knowledge, the social matrix encounters difficulty with cases in which Z knowingly assists the unknowingly justified X in killing Y. If X lacks justification because he lacks justificatory knowledge, then it seems that Z is both justified and unjustified. Z is justified in that she acts with knowledge of the justificatory circumstances, and she is unjustified in that she assists in X's unjustified killing of Y.[52]

The distinction between internal and external justification allows one to resolve this type of problem regarding the social matrix. X's killing of Y is externally justified by all of the relevant reasons that actually apply, although X is not internally justified by the reasons of which he is aware. Although the act that X actually performs is a member of an exempted subset of behavior generally proscribed by the prohibitory norm, he acts on an action-plan that includes an act of the proscribed type as an intended act. X's action-plan renders him morally blameworthy because the plan represents X as an accountable agent. The criminal law ordinarily distributes punishment for committing proscribed conduct as an accountable agent, however, not for being a person who acts on reprehensible motives. In this matter, X resembles the malevolent launderer Jones who engaged in legal conduct for malicious motives. X remains vulnerable to attempt liability, which applies to those who act on action-plans intended to produce proscribed conduct. Attempt liability expresses the systemic condemnation of such action-plans and of those who act on them.

Z is both internally and externally justified. Her action-plan exemplified the exempted subtype that X actually performed (justifiably killing) rather than the proscribed type of conduct (unjustified killing) that X intended. The apparent contradiction regarding Z's action is illusory because she is internally justified by the reasons of which she is aware, and she is externally justified by all rele-

---

52 *See supra* § 1.1.7, case 4.1.

vant reasons. She assisted *X* in the externally justified act he actually performed rather than in the internally unjustified act he intended.

This resolution of *Z*'s case demonstrates why third parties may justifiably assist justified acts. This third-party permission arises from the external justification of the act, and not from the original actor's internal justification in performing the act. The third party who assists another in performing a justified act stands in a position analogous to an accomplice to a legally permissible act.[53] That is, the third party behaves as an accomplice to an act that exemplifies an exempted subtype of the generally proscribed behavior and that, therefore, does not violate the conventional public morality. These third parties do not qualify for the fourth type of condemnation because they have neither committed nor assisted legally proscribed conduct. Their intentions and motives determine whether they qualify for attempt liability or moral blame.

2.5.2   *The Duty Not to Interfere and the Incompatibility Thesis*

In addition to the right to assist justified acts, the complete social matrix includes the duty not to resist or interfere with justified acts and the associated incompatibility thesis. Critics attack the duty not to resist or interfere and the incompatibility thesis by advancing difficult cases that constitute putative counterexamples to the duty and to the thesis in that two or more parties are arguably justified in interfering with one another in a violent confrontation. If one accepts both parties' action as justified, these cases defeat the duty not to resist justified action because each party is justified in acting in a manner that interferes with the other's justified action, and they defeat the incompatibility thesis because both parties to a violent confrontation are justified.

In one case, the defendant Young came to the aid of an apparent mugging victim who was actually struggling with two police officers attempting to complete a lawful arrest. One of the police officers was injured in the ensuing struggle, and Young was convicted of criminal assault.[54] Greenawalt advances this case as one involving a violent conflict among justified actors. The police were justified in making a lawful arrest and in resisting Young's interference with that arrest. Yet, Young was justified in intervening in what he reasonably believed to be a mugging because, surely, society wants to encourage rather than condemn the willingness of citizens to protect one another from mugging.[55]

Young was not justified in interfering with a lawful arrest, and this is the type of action that his conduct actually exemplified. Yet, Young acted on an

---

53 MPC at § 2.06(2)(3).

54 People v. Young, 11 N.Y.2d 274, 183 N.E.2d 319, 229 N.Y.S.2d 1 (1962), *rev'g* 12 A.D. 262, 210 N.Y.S.2d 358 (1961).

55 Kent Greenawalt, *On the Perplexing Borders of Justification and Excuse,* 81 Colum. L. Rev. 1897, 1919–20 (1984).

action-plan that included as an intended act an act of rescuing a mugging victim but not an act of interfering with an arrest. Young's conduct exemplified the act-type proscribed by the offense definition for criminal assault, but the intended act on his action-plan exemplified the exempted subtype represented by the justification for defense of others. The intuitive judgment that Young does not deserve condemnation for acting as he did reflects his action-plan, which represents him as an accountable agent, providing the appropriate focus for attributions of desert. Thus, Young was internally justified in acting on his action-plan, although his resulting action was not externally justified.

Young was not culpable for his unjustified act, either by the standards of ordinary critical morality or by the standards of the conventional morality represented by the criminal law. He is not a proper subject of the fourth type of condemnation inherent in criminal punishment because his reasonable mistake regarding justification prevents attribution of his externally unjustified offense to him as an accountable agent. This reason for withholding condemnation supports the excuse of putative justification based on nonculpable mistake rather than justification, however, rendering the apparent conflict between mutually justified actors illusory. The police officers were both internally and externally justified in pursuing the lawful arrest and in resisting Young's interference in that arrest. The police officers and Young were internally justified, but only the officers were externally justified. Thus, the case represents a conflict between the justified use of force and excusable force. This case demonstrates that it distorts the social matrix attributed to justification defenses to say that only one *party* to a violent conflict can be justified. More than one *party* to the conflict can be internally justified, but this matrix precludes the possibility of conflicting externally justified *acts*.

Certain prison escape cases also present difficult challenges to the social matrix and to the incompatibility thesis. Courts and commentators disagree regarding the application of justification defenses to prison inmates who escape from incarceration in order to avoid impending violence.[56] If one contends that these defendants are justified under the general justification available to those who choose the lesser evil, these cases seem to violate the incompatibility thesis in that prison officers who attempt to prevent these escapes act in pursuit of their legal responsibilities and within the scope of the justificatory defense available to those who use force in law enforcement.[57] This interpretation arguably justifies both sides of a violent conflict.

This apparent conflict between two justified parties arises only in limited conditions. If the prisoner can avoid the violence that constitutes the greater

---

56 *See, e.g.,* David Dolinko, *Intolerable Conditions as a Defense to Prison Escapes,* 26 U.C.L.A. L. Rev. 1126 (1979); Fletcher, *supra* note 5.

57 MPC at §§ 3.02, 3.07(1), (3). The MPC includes "believes" language, but in light of the previous discussion of putative justification, I treat these provisions as requiring necessity.

evil by fleeing from a cell or common area to the custody of the officials, the conflict does not arise. Under those circumstances, only flight *to* the officials is justified by the defense, and the officials fulfill their duty by accepting custody of the prisoner. The difficult conflicts arise when the prisoner can avoid the violence only by escaping *from* the custody of officials.

One might argue that the officials should be excused rather than justified in their use of force. According to this line of argument, the prisoner's justified escape constitutes legal activity under an exception to the norm proscribing escape. The officials who exercise force in resisting this escape do so under the reasonable but mistaken belief that the escape is unlawful, and, thus, they fall under the excuse provided for putative justification. This interpretation may strike many readers as inadequate for two reasons. First, it apparently licenses escalating violence by the justified escapees as they exert the force necessary to accomplish their justified ends and to protect themselves from the excused but unjustified force directed at them by the officials. Second, it seems inadequate to say that the officials engage in legally wrongful but excusable conduct when they act in pursuit of the responsibility with which the legal system charges them.

Alternately, one might argue that the escapees should be excused rather than justified.[58] This interpretation also encounters difficulties, however, because the justificatory choice-of-evils defense appears to apply most clearly to at least some of these cases in that the escapees commit relatively less serious escape offenses in order to prevent more serious homicides or sexual assaults. Such escapes to avoid homicide or sexual assault seem to merit exculpation, even if the escapees act without the disability or extreme fear that would ordinarily ground excuse. In short, it is difficult to explain why defendants should be excused rather than justified in circumstances in which they lack the disability that usually grounds excuse and in which the specific defense that most accurately applies is the justificatory defense for choice of the lesser evil rather than an excuse.[59]

Finally, one might deny the incompatibility thesis, contending that both parties are justified, but this position legitimizes mutual violence, apparently violating the matrix that purports to establish a set of compatible rights and duties. Although this interpretation frustrates the criminal law's function of preventing violent confrontation, however, the criminal law pursues a complex set of purposes, and there is no reason to assume that any possible interpretation can completely satisfy all of them. The criminal law is intended to prevent crime and to limit punishment to culpable offenders, for example, and certain

---

58 Fletcher, *supra* note 5.
59 Some commentators would argue that duress is the most appropriate defense and that coercion provides the disability. *See infra* ch. 5 for discussion of duress.

defenses and procedural devices designed to promote the latter goal may frustrate the former.[60] Furthermore, the potential for mutually justified violence in prison escape cases interpreted in this manner does not arise from a defect internal to the theoretical formulation of justification defenses. Rather, it reflects a tension between these defenses and the provisions that license arrest and detention.

The social matrix and the incompatibility thesis appropriately apply to justification defenses defined in terms of actual necessity, with nonculpably mistaken belief regarding necessity giving rise to excuse for putative justification. Statutes authorizing the use of force by officers in arrest, detention, or escape prevention ordinarily apply to any lawful arrest or detention.[61] Lawful arrest by a law enforcement officer ordinarily requires reasonable grounds to believe that the subject has committed a crime.[62] Thus, although justification defenses require actual necessity, authorization to use force in law enforcement requires only reasonable belief regarding the justificatory conditions. These provisions collapse external justification into internal justification by authorizing arrest on the basis of reasonable belief. That is, they create an exception to the general prohibitory norm against the use of force, but they do so on the basis of the officer's reasonable beliefs regarding the grounds for arrest. By virtue of these provisions, arresting officers qualify for exceptions to the general prohibitory norms on the basis of internal rather than external justification. Potential cases of mutual justified violence during prison escapes reflect this contrast between justification defenses grounded in necessity and arrest authorized by the arresting officers' reasonable beliefs.

These conflicts between externally justified justification defenses and internally justified exercises of force in law enforcement are not unique to prison escape cases. Suppose, for example, that *X* sees terrorist *Y* bringing a bomb into a crowded building in a baby carriage. *X* knocks *Y* down and rushes from the building with the carriage in order to prevent harm to the other occupants when the bomb detonates. Police officer *Z* witnesses *X*'s conduct and attempts to stop and arrest *X* in the building. *X* is justified in her assault on *Y* and in taking *Y*'s property from the building by the justificatory defenses addressing defense of others and choice of evils, but *Z* is also authorized in exercising force against *X* in making an arrest based on reasonable belief. This conflict between legal acts reflects the potential tension between externally justified justification defenses and internally justified arrest.

---

60 One might plausibly argue, for example, that the insanity defense limits punishment to culpable offenders at the expense of creating a loophole through which some guilty defendants escape punishment and continue to commit crimes. Similarly, one might contend that restrictions on searches, seizures, and confessions limit the state's ability to secure convictions and prevent crime.
61 MPC at §§ 3.07(1), (3).
62 Criminal Law at § 5.10(a).

These cases suggest that justification defenses create a matrix of social responsibility, but the claim that others may assist justified acts and may not interfere with such acts misstates the parameters of the matrix. Consider the clear case of force justifiably exercised by Dudley against Spike. Suppose that as Dudley approaches Spike and raises his fist to strike, Spike immediately ducks, falls to the ground, and surrenders. Alternately, suppose Officer Fife steps between Dudley and Spike, restraining and arresting Spike. In each case, Spike or Officer Fife interferes with Dudley's justified use of force by evading it or by rendering it unnecessary and therefore unjustified.[63]

Neither Spike nor Officer Fife would have been justified if they had intervened by hitting Dudley. Dudley's justification defense does not preclude others from justifiably interfering with Dudley's conduct; rather, it precludes their interfering through force directed against Dudley. Dudley's defense renders lawful his otherwise illegal use of force, and, therefore, Dudley's use of force does not carry the justificatory significance of unlawful force. That is, it does not justify responsive conduct, such as defensive force, that would otherwise have been illegal. Others remain free, however, to interfere with Dudley's justified conduct through actions authorized by statute (Fife's arrest of Spike) or through behavior that is not forbidden (Spike's ducking).

In short, justification defenses do no preclude others from resisting or interfering; rather, they eliminate any justificatory significance that the actor's conduct would otherwise have had regarding ordinarily illegal means of resisting or interfering. Because Dudley's use of force against Spike was justified, it does not justify the use of otherwise unlawful force by Spike or Fife against Dudley. Dudley's justification defense does not, however, preclude interference by means that do not rely on Dudley's force for their justification. Thus, justified actors can sometimes come into mutually justified violent conflict with law enforcement officers precisely because the officers' use of force draws its justification from statutory authorization and the officers' beliefs rather than merely from the actors' behavior.

Just as the justification defenses do not categorically preclude resistance, they do not categorically legitimize assistance. Although Dudley is justified in assisting Mother Beneficence in defending herself, he may not do so through any means he pleases. Spike's attack would not have justified Dudley in ramming the bus he was driving into Spike and ten innocent bystanders. Similarity, if X were shooting at Y from a rooftop, Z would be justified in loaning Y a rifle with which to shoot back in self-defense but not in blowing up the building and its occupants. Y's justification does not authorize Z in assisting Y through any

---

63 I Oxford English Dictionary 1462. To interfere is "to come into collision or opposition, so as to affect the course of"; "to interpose, take part, so as to affect some action." Interference implies opposition but not necessarily violence.

means possible; rather, it renders Y's use of defensive force legal and therefore precludes accomplice liability for Z's assistance in that conduct. Y's justification defense prevents Z's otherwise legal conduct from becoming illegal merely by virtue of the fact that it constitutes assistance to Y's use of force. In contrast, any act performed by Z for the purpose of promoting an illegal use of force by Y would elicit accomplice liability.[64]

In summary, justification defenses represent exceptions to prohibitory norms, establishing a revised matrix of social responsibility including the following privileges and duties. First, Z may assist Y in a justified exercise of force against X without becoming liable merely by virtue of having assisted. Second, if Z resists or interferes with Y's justified exercise of force through otherwise illegal means, Z may not justify that conduct by appealing to Y's justified use of force. Stated differently, neither does conduct justified by a justification ground accomplice liability for those who assist through otherwise legal behavior, nor does it provide justification for those who resist or interfere with the conduct through otherwise illegal conduct.

2.5.3 Hard Cases and the Revised Matrix of Social Responsibility

Dressler challenges the incompatibility thesis with two additional types of hypothetical cases. The first involves only innocent parties. A dam collapses, sending a torrent of water rushing down a valley toward a town populated by a thousand innocent people. B can save the innocent inhabitants of the town only by immediately detonating an explosion that will redirect the water away from the town but toward the innocent C who is farming by himself in the next valley. B must decide whether to detonate the explosives causing the death of the innocent C or to refrain from doing so, resulting in the deaths of the thousand innocent townspeople. C accurately perceives the entire situation and sees B reach for the detonator. C realizes that he can save his own life only by shooting B before B detonates the explosion. Arguably, this case violates the incompatibility thesis because the lesser-evils defense justifies B in detonating the explosion, and self-defense justifies C in shooting B in order to prevent B from killing C.[65]

A mechanical application of the revised social matrix as interpreted above encounters no difficulty with this case. The lesser-evils defense justifies B's

---

64 MPC at § 2.06.
65 This case represents an elaboration of the type listed as case 5.4 and introduced into the contemporary justification debate by Joshua Dressler, *New Thoughts about the Concept of Justification in the Criminal Law: A Critique of Fletcher's Thinking and Rethinking,* 32 U.C.L.A. L. Rev. 61, 89–90 (1984). Although some jurisdictions except homicide from the lesser-evils defense, neither the MPC nor Robinson accept this exception. MPC at § 3.02; Defenses at § 124.

action, rendering it legal. Self-defense justifies force only in response to unlawful exercises of force, and B's justified act does not fall into this category.[66] The revised social matrix prohibits C's shooting of B in that C's ordinarily unlawful act of shooting another person can draw no justification from B's justified act. No conflict of justified acts occurs here because B is justified while C is not. In order to appreciate the force of this example, however, one must understand it as a proposed intuitive counterexample to the social matrix as a component of conventional public morality. Should a society require that an innocent party refrain from resisting the sacrifice of his life to save others? Can a plausible conventional public morality hold that an innocent party acts wrongfully rather than justifiably in attempting to prevent others from sacrificing his life?

Consider a modified version of this case. This revised story is identical to the original with one exception. A third party D rather than C perceives the situation and must decide whether to allow B to redirect the water, killing the oblivious C, or to shoot B, saving C but accepting the deaths of B and a thousand townspeople. What would justify D in rescuing C at the expense of 1,001 innocent lives? All parties are innocent victims of a natural disaster. The decision apparently involves an unavoidable choice between one innocent life and 1,001, with no additional morally relevant factors to consider. If D would not be justified in rescuing C at the expense of 1,001 lives in the revised case, what legally recognized justificatory significance lies in the mere fact that the roles of D and C reside in the same person in the original story?

Although the framework advanced here accommodates this case without generating an instance of legally justified violent conflict, the intuitive discomfort elicited by the case remains. The proposed resolution is theoretically consistent, but it seems unfair to C. Clear cases of fully justified violence, such as Dudley's conduct toward Spike, demonstrate both internal and external justification, and this justification is symmetrical. A symmetrically justified act treats all parties justly, all things considered. That is, no individual suffers undeserved injury.[67] Dudley's conduct elicits intuitive consensus both because Mother Beneficence is an innocent victim who merits rescue and because Spike deserves what he gets. Some cases such as this one involving B and C or those addressing self-defense against innocent aggressors elicit ambivalent intuitive responses because some party suffers undeserved injury regardless of the choice made.

Perhaps an ideal moral world would be free of undeserved injury, but justification defenses, and the criminal law generally, pursue a more modest aim. According to the theory advanced in this book, justification defenses exculpate

---

66 MPC at §§ 3.02, 3.04.
67 Symmetrical justification arguably rules out windfall benefits as well, but cases involving justification defenses rarely raise this issue.

defendants who do not merit the fourth type of condemnation because they do not violate the fully articulated conventional public morality. Many acts result in undeserved injury to some party without violating any legal norm. The malicious launderer Jones, for example, inflicted undeserved harm on the Smith family without violating any legal norm.[68] Benevolent as well as malevolent actors sometimes inflict undeserved injury without violating any legal norm. Suppose *X* drives legally and carefully along a residential street but hits a child who darts into the street from between two cars in a manner that would prevent the most skilled and careful driver from avoiding her. *X* causes bodily harm to the innocent child without fulfilling the culpability requirement for criminal assault or falling below the standard of reasonable care for tort liability.

The law allows conduct that causes injury to innocent parties for several reasons. Proscribing conduct that might accidentally harm innocent people despite due care would require massive restrictions on individual liberty and economic activity such as driving and manufacturing. Laws prohibiting all intentional infliction of suffering on others would require severe sacrifice of other important values. Proscribing true harmful statements about others, for example, would entail a marked limitation of free expression. Finally, some circumstances simply do not provide an alternative course of action that does not injure some innocent party. The justification defense provided for defendants who choose the lesser evil explicitly addresses such cases.

In short, some justified violations of criminal offense definitions elicit ambivalent intuitive responses because the justification is asymmetrical, involving undeserved harm to some party, but other legal acts elicit similar intuitive responses for the same reason.[69] Justification defenses, like other legal provisions, sometimes fail to provide symmetrical justification for many reasons, including those discussed. Although it may result in harm to an innocent third party, conduct that fulfills a recognized justification defense, like conduct that violates no offense provision, fails to qualify for the fourth type of condemnation because it does not violate the fully articulated conventional public morality.

Clearly, the conventional public morality represented by the revised social matrix demands much more fortitude of *C* in the original story than it demands of *D* in the revised version because *C* must refrain from saving his own life, while *D* must refrain from saving *C*'s life. Should *C* and *D* both refrain from shooting, most observers would count *D* as responsible but *C* as heroic. Fortitude and heroism address character, praiseworthiness, and evaluation of actors, however, rather than external justification of acts. This case raises important

---

68 *See supra* § 2.4.1.

69 Perhaps the most troubling cases are those, such as the flood case described previously, in which events create circumstances in which some innocent parties must suffer and other innocent parties must decide how to direct that loss.

issues that a fully satisfactory conventional public morality must address, but these are not issues of justification and exceptions to prohibitory norms. These issues involve evaluation of actors and the appropriate role of legal concepts such as excuse and mitigation in the social response to individuals who encounter extraordinarily demanding circumstances. Chapter 5 returns to these issues.

Dressler's second case involves two parties competing for scarce and vital resources to which neither has a prior claim. *G* and *H* survive a shipwreck and find themselves adrift at sea with no means to stay afloat except a single plank floating in the water. The plank is barely large enough to support one person. Each person can survive only by attaining sole possession of the plank, and neither has any prior claim to it nor any prior duty to the other. Either can release the plank, in which case the party who releases will die and the other will live. Alternately, both can hold on, leading to the death of both because the plank will not float with their combined weight. Finally, each can attempt to take the plank from the other. Arguably, either is equally justified in securing and defending the plank from the other, despite the fact that doing so assures the death of the other. This interpretation justifies both sides of the violent confrontation.[70]

This case raises a variety of technical issues. If either party takes the board from the other, the former will knowingly cause the death of the latter. If both hold onto the plank, however, both will die. It seems, therefore, that each party causes both deaths merely by holding onto the board and can avoid committing homicide only by releasing the plank, sacrificing his own life. Yet, neither has any obvious obligation to sacrifice for the other. Perhaps fairness would suggest that both parties should hold onto the plank, understanding that it will not support both, because one person will probably become exhausted before the other, and that person will drown, leaving the plank to the other, who can survive.

This story elicits conflicting intuitions, but it provides no reason to favor one party over the other. It seems, therefore, that either both parties are justified in holding onto the plank or in fighting for sole possession or else neither party is so justified. If one thinks neither party is justified, this case raises no concern for the original or revised social matrices or for the incompatibility thesis. If one thinks both parties are justified, the justification arises from the desperate circumstances and the lack of preferable alternatives rather than from the unjustified conduct of the other because any circumstances justifying one must also justify the other as they encounter identical conditions. That is, if both par-

---

70 This case is an elaboration of the type listed as case 5.3, § 1.1.7, and introduced into the contemporary debate by Dressler, *supra* note 65, at 88. I set aside the alternative of both letting go and stipulate that no form of sharing can succeed.

ties are justified, then they do not justify otherwise illegal conduct by appeal to each other's justified behavior. Thus, this case remains consistent with the revised social matrix, which precludes justification of otherwise illegal conduct by appeal to another party's justified conduct.

If one thinks that both parties are justified, this case constitutes a counterexample to the original incompatibility thesis, which denies that both parties in violent conflict can be justified. Notice, however, that the term justification has wide and narrow senses in this area of discourse. In the narrow sense, a justified act is an otherwise illegal one that is rendered permissible by a justification defense. In the wide sense, a justified act is one that is permissible in light of all legally relevant considerations. Conduct justified in the wide sense includes but is not limited to conduct justified in the narrow sense. Certain acts are justified in the wide but not the narrow sense, for example, because they are authorized by statute or simply because they are not forbidden by any offense definition. Officer Fife's intervention between Spike and Dudley is justified by statutory authorization. Jones's conduct in driving the Smith family laundry out of business is legally justified in the wide sense that it does not violate any law. The parties who compete for the plank in this case are justified in the wide sense if at all, in that they do not appeal to justification defenses to justify their conduct. Thus, their conduct is consistent with the revised social matrix.

The negative aspect of the original social matrix, which precludes interference in justified conduct, generates the incompatibility thesis as a corollary. The revised social matrix precludes justification in the narrow sense of otherwise illegal conduct by appeal to the behavior of other parties that is justified in the narrow sense. That is, one cannot establish a justification defense by finding justificatory significance in another's conduct when that conduct is justified by a justification defense. Self-defense, for example, legitimizes the use of force only in response to unlawful aggression.[71] The prison escape cases provide examples of potential conflict between the prisoner's conduct, which is justified in the narrow sense by appeal to the choice among evils, and the official's conduct, which is justified in the wide sense by the authorizing statute. Athletic contests such as boxing matches or football games exemplify conflicts among actors who are justified in the wide sense in that they engage in legally authorized athletic events. None of these cases violates the revised social matrix because they do not justify otherwise illegal conduct by appeal to another's behavior that is justified by a justification defense.

One can imagine bizarre circumstances that arguably exemplify violent conflicts between parties justified in the narrow sense. Suppose, for example, that *M* and *N* simultaneously pull knives and launch unprovoked and unlawful

---

71 MPC at § 3.04; The choice-of-evils defense appeals to the harmful affects avoided rather than to lawful or unlawful conduct; *see id.* at § 3.02.

attacks at each other in an elevator. Both are victims of unlawful attacks they cannot avoid. Both can protect themselves only through defensive violence. Both were engaged in illegal conduct at the moment that the other attacked, but neither provoked the other's attack through that illegal behavior.[72] Both engaged in unlawful assaults at the moment they initiated their attacks, but these assaults immediately became mutually justified exercises of defensive force because each was the subject of the other's unprovoked assault. If this constitutes a case of mutually justified self-defense, it serves as a counterexample to the incompatibility thesis, but it remains consistent with the revised social matrix because both parties justify their conduct by appeal to the other's illegal assault. This case remains difficult to interpret because the aggressive acts constitute unprovoked assaults and externally justified self-defense simultaneously. Thus, the manner in which one interprets the case depends on the category one adopts as controlling. Plausible cases of violent conflict between parties justified in the narrow sense do not seem to arise.[73]

In short, the revised social matrix accommodates the troubling cases. One can identify certain conflicts in which both parties are justified in the wide sense, but it is difficult to find clear cases of mutually justified violence in the narrow sense, and it is this narrow sense that is directly relevant to the theory of justification defenses because only these cases involve the justificatory force of justification defenses and conduct that falls within their scope. It is not clear, however, that the incompatibility thesis fulfills an independent function in the theory of justification defenses. The original social matrix generates the incompatibility thesis as a corollary and can address the relevant cases in terms of the duty not to resist justified conduct without appeal to the thesis.[74] The revised social matrix accommodates the relatively clear cases, and the difficulty encountered with certain cases such as those involving G and H (contesting for the plank) or M and N (attacking in the elevator) reflects ambivalent intuitive judgments regarding justification. The revised social matrix addresses these cases without appeal to the incompatibility thesis.

2.6   Conclusion

This chapter advances a theoretical framework for the analysis of the general category of justification defenses as part of an integrated system of criminal law. The theory calls upon the notion of a conventional public morality represented by the law, the condemnation inherent in conviction and punishment, the prospective and retrospective functions of justifications, and the distinctions

---

72 *Id.* at §3.04(2)(b)(i).
73 Having said this, however, I am confident that at least one of my more perverse colleagues will concoct one.
74 *See supra* § 1.1.5 discussing the incompatibility thesis as a corollary of the original matrix.

between internal and external justification, symmetrical and asymmetrical justification, and wide and narrow justification in order to clarify the analysis of this category of defenses. Courts rely on justification defenses retrospectively in order to identify conduct that is exempt from the condemnation inherent in the conviction and punishment authorized by offense definitions for conduct that violates the general prohibitory norms represented by the objective elements of those offense definitions. Individuals rely on these defenses prospectively when they select action-plans in order to avoid those that include acts prohibited by the fully articulated conventional public morality represented by the law.

Those who act within the scope of justification defenses do not merit the condemnation inherent in criminal punishment. Legal conviction and punishment ordinarily expresses condemnation of five types at two levels of analysis, but only the first type of condemnation, expressed at the institutional level by the proscription of certain act-types as criminal offenses, inheres in every institution of legal punishment. Specific applications of punishment in a retributive system also express condemnation of the actors who have violated the fully articulated conventional public morality as accountable agents by systemic standards. Justification defenses exempt certain defendants who do not merit this type of condemnation because their actions do not violate the fully articulated conventional public morality.

Excuses, in contrast, exculpate those who violate the public morality but not in the capacity of accountable agents. Some excused defendants lack the capacities required to qualify as accountable agents, while others lack the knowledge that would provide the opportunity to apply these capacities to the decision to perform the proscribed conduct. This latter group's action-plan selection is internally justified by the reasons they are aware of, although their conduct is not externally justified by all the relevant reasons that apply.

Justification defenses apply only to conduct that is externally justified and, thus, is not prohibited by the fully articulated conventional public morality. Justified behavior is permissible because it is not forbidden, although the actors who perform such conduct may be blameworthy if they are not internally justified. Putative justification excuses those actors who are internally justified in the selection of their action-plans, which represent them as moral agents.

Justification defenses establish a revised matrix of social responsibility in that neither does conduct justified by a justification defense ground accomplice liability for those who assist through otherwise legal behavior, nor does it provide justification for those who resist or interfere through otherwise illegal conduct. This revised social matrix does not logically preclude the possibility of violent conflict in which both parties are justified in the wide sense, but it is very difficult, and perhaps impossible, to devise plausible cases in which two or more parties in violent conflict are justified in the narrow sense.

The resolution of certain cases takes a form that is logically consistent but intuitively unappealing because the justification is asymmetrical in that one party suffers some undeserved injury. Discussion of these cases that is limited to justification defenses fails to adequately address their morally salient features. The entire discussion of the technical grounds for liability and justification in the plank case, for example, seems to miss an important aspect of the dilemma faced by these parties. How can society demand of *G* and *H* that they refrain from struggling for their lives in these circumstances? Can any social institution reasonably require that people sacrifice their lives or allow others to sacrifice them in order to save others? This case, like that of *C* (in the flood case), raises questions regarding the reasonable limits on the demands any social institution can make on individuals. Chapter 5 returns to some of the troubling cases, such as those involving *C, G,* and *H*. That chapter proposes an interpretation of duress as an exculpatory claim of a type separate from justification or excuse, and it addresses the remaining difficult cases from Chapter 2 as well as some that arise in Chapters 3 and 4 in the context of self-defense.

Although the conceptual framework advanced in this chapter has relied heavily on the nature of the condemnation inherent in criminal conviction and punishment in a conventional public morality, it does not propose any substantive theory of public morality because clarification of the nature and parameters of the general category of justification defenses does not require such a theory. Analysis of the specific justification defense of self-defense, in contrast, requires criteria of justification reflecting a substantive theory of political morality. Thus, Chapter 3 advances a theory of self-defense in a liberal society.

3

Self-defense

Mother Beneficence and Dudley raise the specific justification defenses of self-defense and defense of others, respectively. These defendants present intuitively and legally clear cases because they represent a standard form in which a competent and culpable aggressor (A) attacks an innocent victim (V), and V or a third party defends V by exercising necessary and proportionate force against A.[1]

Section 1.2.1 identifies three difficult tasks that a comprehensive theory of self-defense must address. First, a satisfactory account must accommodate cases that elicit ambivalent intuitive responses and raise substantial doubts about justification because they diverge from the standard form. These cases might involve, for example, innocent aggressors (IAs), innocent bystanders (IBs), or innocent shields (ISs). Second, a satisfactory theory must present and defend appropriate parameters for the defense. It must explain, for example, the proper role, if any, for a duty to retreat and for requirements of imminence and proportionality. Third, a satisfactory account must provide a theoretical foundation that explains and justifies the defense in a manner that accommodates the difficult cases and the prescribed parameters.

This chapter pursues two projects. First, it advances a substantive theory of self-defense addressing the important problematic concerns listed above. This account integrates the central features of current legal doctrine with justificatory principles found in liberal political philosophy. Second, this chapter advances a methodological thesis in that it interprets the law of self-defense in light of the broader and more abstract principles of political philosophy represented by the legal rules. On this approach to legal analysis, the structure and content of the law reveal underlying principles of political morality. These prin-

---

1 For the sake of convenience, I employ the following conventions. Capital letters such as V or A represent specific parties in hypothetical cases. I refer to general categories of actors in the text by spelling out the terms including "victims," "aggressors," etc. Innocent aggressors are identified as such in the text and represented by IA in hypotheticals. Thus, any aggressor represented as A is a culpable aggressor.

ciples inform a theory that addresses self-defense as morally justified individual action and as morally justified law. This method produces an analysis of the American law of self-defense as the law of self-defense in a liberal society.

This approach compliments the analytic structure in Chapter 2 in the following manner. Chapter 2 develops an account of the general category of justification defenses as a type of defense that exempts certain conduct from the expression of condemnation inherent in criminal conviction and punishment by a legal system representing a conventional public morality. Chapter 2 does not, however, provide any content to that public morality. This chapter advances a theory of self-defense as a component of the conventional public morality of a liberal society. Thus, the broader theory of liberal political morality provides a substantive moral theory that justifies self-defense and generates the appropriate parameters within which the exercise of defensive force qualifies for an exemption from the expression of condemnation that ordinarily applies to those who violate the assault and homicide statutes.

Section 3.1 examines some contemporary scholarship regarding self-defense in order to delineate the central issues, the competing theories, and the remaining points of contention. Section 3.2 presents some hypothetical cases illustrating the two types of interests at stake in circumstances giving rise to claims of self-defense. Section 3.3 provides a normative structure for the analysis of self-defense in a liberal society, and Section 3.4 advances an account of self-defense as individual action justified by the principles of liberal political morality reflected in contemporary American law. Section 3.5 discusses self-defense as a legal defense in a liberal society. Finally, Section 3.6 summarizes and concludes the argument.

3.1   Contemporary Theories

3.1.1   Self-defense and the Social Order

Fletcher identifies two dominant theoretical approaches to self-defense law. The first interprets self-defense as a choice among evils in which victims must compare the harm caused by effective self-defense with the injury avoided and select the path that will minimize net harm. In making this determination, however, victims may discount to some unspecified degree the value of harm to the aggressor's interests. Although Fletcher represents the lesser-evils model as currently dominant in Anglo-American law, he endorses the second approach, which justifies self-defense as a means of protecting and vindicating autonomy.[2] He contends that this theory currently prevails in Germany and the Soviet Union and that it was widely accepted in early Anglo-American law.

2 Rethinking at 857–60.

According to this theory, victims may exercise the defensive force necessary to protect autonomy. Although Fletcher does not offer a precise analysis of autonomy, he describes it as a prelegal concept that shapes and supports the law, and he contends that attacks upon legally protected rights and interests give rise to a right to use force in self-defense.[3] He advances the concept of *Right (Recht)* as morally sound law and contends that victims are justified in using force to defend against violations of any rights or interests protected by morally sound law. These rights and interests are part of the *Right,* and, thus, attacks on them are violations of the entire social order. Victims are justified in using force to protect these rights and interests because by doing so they protect the *Right.* There is no requirement of proportion because maintaining the social order justifies any force necessary to defend a legally protected right or interest.[4]

Although Fletcher does not present a complete explication of his conception of autonomy, it appears to be inextricable from *Right,* and the two are apparently related in the following manner. Morally sound law creates a justifiable social order and protects certain individual rights and interests. Personal autonomy constitutes a broad general right on the part of individuals to exercise those specific rights and interests allocated to them within this justifiable social order. Aggressors who violate these rights and interests attack their victims and the social order. Victims or third parties may justifiably exercise the force necessary to protect specific rights or interests, the autonomy of the victims, and the larger social order.

According to this view, victims may exercise force in self-defense against innocent aggressors because the justification lies in the protection of victims and the social order, not in the aggressors' culpability. Victims may exercise all necessary force without regard for proportion because the justification for their action does not lie in the balance of harms. Defensive force protects the social order, and *Right* should never yield to wrong.[5] For the same reason, victims have no duty to retreat before exercising force in self-defense.[6] Compassion and concern for the humanity of aggressors may, however, temper the manner in which they should exercise defensive force.

Although Fletcher addresses most cases of self-defense under this justificatory doctrine, his theory reflects the historical roots of the defense in that it

---

3 *Id.* at 860–8.

4 *Id.* at 862–4; George Fletcher, *The Right and the Reasonable,* 98 Harv. L. Rev. 949, 964–71 (1985); George Fletcher, *Punishment and Self-Defense,* 8 Law & Phil. 200, 208–11 (1989). The theory attributed here to Fletcher is derived from several of his writings, some of which were not directed primarily toward self-defense. While it is intended as an accurate representation of Fletcher's position, it may include some claims that he would not endorse.

5 *Right and Reasonable, id.,* at 968–71; *Punishment, id.,* at 209–10.

6 *Rethinking* at 865–6.

addresses certain cases under a related excuse. This excuse reflects the historical doctrine of *se defendendo* and applies only to defendants who have killed
aggressors in order to save their own lives or those of their closely related family members. This defense is premised on the contention that threats to one's
life elicit an involuntary response in self-protection. Under such circumstances,
it is often said that the victims had no alternative or no real choice, and, therefore, that we ought not punish them for doing what anyone would have done.
In contrast to justified self-defense, *se defendendo* carries a duty to retreat
before exercising deadly force because it applies only when victims have no
alternative.[7]

Fletcher addresses two additional types of difficult cases through this
excuse. First, if victims who kill innocent shields while protecting themselves
from aggressors are appropriately exculpated, they should be excused rather
than justified.[8] Second, putative self-defense may be excused but not justified.
Putative self-defense occurs when victims exercise force against others under
the reasonable but mistaken belief that the others are attacking. Fletcher denies
that mistaken beliefs can justify action but contends that they may provide the
basis for excuse.[9]

Fletcher provides a comprehensive theory, and perhaps for this reason it
invites several criticisms. First, it generates intuitively problematic results in
certain circumstances because it disregards almost entirely the culpability or
interests of aggressors. Innocent aggressors, like culpable ones, are subject to
any force necessary to protect victims' rights and the social order. In addition,
Fletcher contends that justified conduct is right conduct, rather than merely tolerable.[10] Yet, it seems at least plausible to argue that injuring an innocent
aggressor in order to prevent a similar injury to an innocent victim is tolerable
rather than morally superior or mandated. It is not clear why it would be unacceptable for innocent victims to sacrifice their own interests to those of innocent aggressors or for third parties to refuse to injure innocent aggressors in
order to prevent harm to innocent victims. In these circumstances, people must
choose between innocent parties with no obvious grounds for preferring one
over the other.

Fletcher treats culpable and innocent aggressors similarly insofar as he
allows the victim to engage in justified self-defense against either, but the victim who kills an innocent shield is excused rather than justified. On this view,
innocent aggressors are treated as if they are more similar to culpable aggressors than they are to innocent shields. Yet, it is difficult to find morally relevant

---

7 *Id.* at 856–7.
8 George Fletcher, *The Right to Life*, 13 Ga. L. Rev. 1371, 1387–8 (1979).
9 Rethinking at 762–9; *Right and Reasonable, supra* note 4, at 971–80. *See supra* § 2.4 regarding putative justification.
10 *See supra* § 2.1.

reasons for differentiating in this manner among innocent aggressors and shields. Victims' interests are susceptible to similar injury by the acts or presence of culpable aggressors, innocent aggressors, or innocent shields. When attacked by culpable aggressors, however, victims must choose between innocent parties and culpable ones, while victims threatened by innocent aggressors or shields must choose among innocent parties.

These concerns are exacerbated because this theory imputes no duty of retreat or proportion. This approach would recommend grossly disproportionate injuries in certain circumstances because it grants no role to the consequentialist balancing of harms. Thus *V* may shoot a fleeing apple thief who is in the process of stealing a single apple from *V*'s grove if that is the only means by which *V* can prevent the violation.[11] While Fletcher contends that compassion and concern for humanity should temper *V*'s decision to exercise this right to engage in self-defense, it is not clear that this resolves the problem. If he intends this qualification to carry such force that *V* would not be justified in causing the disproportionate harm, then the theory subtly incorporates a proportionality requirement without providing a foundation for that provision in the broader theory. If, in contrast, he contends that *V* would be justified in exercising disproportionate force, then the intuitively problematic examples remain unaddressed.

Finally, the theoretical basis for this approach is not entirely clear. The central concepts are autonomy, *Right,* and the social order, but the precise relationship among these considerations remains troublesome. Concentration on autonomy suggests that individual rights and self-determination are of primary importance, while the social order emphasizes the larger system in which these individual rights are embedded. In many circumstances, one may reasonably expect these two levels of analysis to converge, but in certain situations, they might diverge. Suppose, for example, that *V* can prevent *A* from violating her rights only by shooting *A* in circumstances in which doing so is likely to precipitate a riot.

In summary, Fletcher's theory provides a comprehensive approach that addresses the historical roots of self-defense as both justification and excuse. In addition, the emphasis on victims' rights and the social order provides a plausible account of many standard cases and explains why innocent victims may justifiably inflict more severe injuries on aggressors rather than absorbing less serious harm from aggressors. It encounters difficulty when dealing with innocent aggressors and shields, however, particularly when victims can avoid injury only by inflicting markedly disproportionate harm on those persons. This concern arises from the failure of the theory to attribute any explicit force to the aggressors' culpability or to the consequentialist weighing of harms.

11 Rethinking at 871.

3.1.2   Self-defense and Distributive Justice

Recent work addressing self-defense as a problem in distributive justice explicitly addresses the balance of harms and aggressor culpability.[12] On the distributive theory of self-defense, an innocent victim can justify the exercise of force against a culpable aggressor as a decision to distribute unavoidable harm to the party who culpably created the situation in which someone must suffer the injury. This distributive theory is less comprehensive than Fletcher's in that it addresses only the standard cases in which an innocent victim can save her life only by killing the culpable aggressor. The core of this approach is the harm distribution principle (HD), which holds roughly that when harm is inevitable and will be of equal severity regardless of who suffers it, then distribute it to the party who culpably caused the harm to be inevitable.[13]

HD includes a proportionality principle in that it only authorizes defensive force when the severity of the harm will remain roughly equivalent regardless of who suffers it. It also includes an implicit duty to retreat before exercising force because it authorizes only the distribution of inevitable injury.[14] HD is grounded in the formal principle of justice, which demands that one treat like cases alike and unlike cases differently in proportion to their morally relevant differences. When inevitable harm must be distributed, culpably causing that inevitable harm provides a morally relevant difference between victims and aggressors, justifying victims in distributing the injury to the aggressors.[15] Although culpability plays a central role in this theory, self-defense is not justified as a form of punishment. Rather, the culpable aggressor substantially worsened the victim's circumstances by creating conditions in which at least one of the parties must suffer some injury. The aggressor owes the victim restitution for this loss, and the victim is justified in rectifying her situation by directing the injury toward the aggressor.[16]

The distributive theory integrates a consequentialist concern for selecting the lesser harm with consideration of the culpability of the parties in that it allows one to allocate unavoidable harm to the culpable party but does not endorse infliction of disproportionate harms. In this manner, it avoids some of

---

12 This discussion of the distributive approach draws primarily on the work of Phillip Montague and B. J. Smart. Montague explicitly designates his theory as a distributive one, while Smart presents his approach as rectificatory.

13 Phillip Montague, *Self-Defense and Choosing between Lives,* 40 Phil. Stud. 207, 216 (1981); Phillip Montague, *Punishment and Societal Defense,* 2 Crim. Just. Ethics 30, 32 (1983); Phillip Montague, *The Morality of Self-Defense: A Reply to Wasserman,* 17 Phil. & Pub. Aff. 81, 81–2 (1988).

14 *Choosing, id.* at 216; *Societal Defense, id.* at 31–2; *Morality, id.* at 81–8.

15 *Choosing, supra* note 13, at 215–16; *Morality, supra* note 13, at 82, 88.

16 B. J. Smart, *Understanding and Justifying Self-Defense,* 4 Int'l J. Moral & Soc. Stud. 231, 237–42 (1989). Montague presents his theory as one of justified distribution rather than restitution.

the intuitive difficulties encountered by either the lesser-harms approach or a culpability-based approach in their pure forms. The distributive theory is intuitively plausible in that it grants significance to proportion and treats innocent aggressors and shields differently than guilty aggressors. In addition, it is consistent with most law and applied morality in that it attributes weight both to consequences and to principles of responsibility.

Despite these assets, the distributive theory does not provide a fully satisfactory approach because it does not address nonstandard cases such as those involving innocent aggressors or shields. Neither does it address cases of culpable aggression in which the degree of injury caused will vary significantly according to which party suffers it. Thus, it fails to accommodate cases in which it seems intuitively plausible that victims might be justified in inflicting disproportionate harm on culpable aggressors. Suppose, for example, that *V* can prevent *A* from breaking *V*'s arm only by killing *A*. Reasonable people might differ regarding the justification of *V*'s killing *A,* but the distributive theory simply fails to address cases that do not meet the condition of equivalent harms.

Although the distributive theory addresses both the balance of harms and culpability, it does not fully satisfy either consequentialist or desert-based concerns. The consequentialist theorist would compare the total amount of harm caused by available actions, but this theory compares the injury avoided by the victim to that inflicted on each culpable aggressor, thus allowing the victim to cause a much greater amount of harm than she avoids in cases involving multiple aggressors. Similarly, on a desert-based approach, it is not clear why an innocent victim is justified in distributing unavoidable harm to a culpable aggressor only when the amount of injury will be equal regardless of who suffers it. Thus, the distributive theory neither provides a priority ordering between consequentialism and culpability nor explains how to integrate these two principles in difficult cases.

Finally, the distributive theory addresses only self-defense as a justification, omitting the cases that arguably provide grounds for excuse. The *se defendendo* excuse applies to cases in which it seems intuitively that the victims are not justified, yet should not be punished. Suppose, for example, that *V* can prevent her own murder only by killing *A* and two innocent bystanders. The distributive theory simply fails to address such cases.

Commentators have criticized each of the various principles proffered as the theoretical foundation for self-defense, rejecting each as insufficient to accommodate the practice. We should not be surprised to learn that such a complex aspect of law and social morality cannot be explained by reference to a single principle or purpose. We need a complex theory that explains how various important principles and purposes of the legal system combine to support an integrated theory of self-defense. A fully satisfactory theory of self-defense must address the use of defensive force as individual action and as morally jus-

tified law. Sections 3.2 to 3.4 examine hypothetical cases, current legal doctrine, and liberal principles of political philosophy in order to develop an
account of self-defense as individual action justified by the liberal principles of
political morality embodied in the law. Section 3.5 integrates this analysis with
certain formal features of a system of law in order to derive an account of
morally justified self-defense law from a liberal perspective.

3.2   Legal Defenses and Individual Interests

The dominant approach to self-defense in contemporary American criminal
law as represented by the MPC allows one to exercise force against another
person in self-defense when that force is immediately necessary for the purpose
of protecting oneself from the use of unlawful force by that other person. The
victim may exercise deadly force in self-defense, however, only when such
force is necessary to protect herself against death, serious bodily injury, kidnapping, or compelled sexual intercourse. Any force that creates a substantial
risk of death or serious bodily injury qualifies as deadly force.[17] Clear cases of
justified self-defense under these provisions occur when innocent victims kill
aggressors in circumstances such that doing so was the only available means of
preventing the aggressors from unlawfully killing them. Similarly, victims justifiably injure aggressors when doing so is necessary to prevent the aggressors
from exercising unlawful but not deadly force against the victims. Consider the
following example.

(SD1) *V* is walking home from work one night when an assailant steps from a doorway
and grabs her arm and purse. *V* kicks *A* and hits him with her umbrella, running away
when *A* releases his grip in order to protect himself from the umbrella.

The MPC also provides a general justification defense for innocent parties
who encounter circumstances in which they must choose among harmful alternatives. The code provides this justificatory defense for actors who engage in
behavior that would ordinarily constitute an offense when that conduct is necessary to avoid a greater harm or evil.[18] Known as the "necessity," "lesser-
evils," or "choice-of-evils" justification, this defense applies to cases such as
the following one.

(NE1) A bicyclist suffers a fall on a lonely country road, disabling her bicycle and seriously injuring herself. As night falls and the temperature drops, she breaks into an empty
farmhouse because doing so is necessary to call for help and prevent hypothermia.

---

17 MPC at §§ 3.04(1), (2)(b), 3.11(2). Recall that the issue of necessity versus belief in necessity
    has been addressed *supra* at § 2.4.
18 *Id.* at § 3.02.

The necessity defense would exculpate the bicyclist because breaking into the house was necessary to prevent the potentially fatal hypothermia, although she would remain liable to the owner of the house for compensatory damages under civil law.[19] Although SD1 and NE1 present clear cases of the self-defense and necessity justifications respectively, consider case SD2.

(SD2) *V* takes a book to a bench in the park, fully intending to sit there and read all afternoon; *A* approaches with a baseball bat, orders *V* to stay on the bench until 3:00 P.M., and threatens to hit *V* with the bat if but only if *V* tries to leave before 3:00.[20] When noise distracts *A*, *V* makes her escape by grabbing the bat and hitting *A*, breaking his leg.

In SD2, *A* threatened no injury to *V*'s concrete interests.[21] *V*'s hitting *A* was not necessary to avoid personal injury, property damage, or the loss of the opportunity to do anything that *V* actually wanted to do. *V* had planned to stay on the bench until after 3:00 P.M. independently of *A*'s threat. The only injury *V* suffered from *A*'s threat was the violation of her sovereignty over her own bodily movement.[22] *A*'s threat injured *V* only insofar as it deprived *V* of the discretion to decide for herself either that she would stay on the bench until 3:00 P.M. or that she would change her mind and leave. NE1 provides a standard necessity case in which the bicyclist suffers threat of injury to her concrete interests in avoiding illness and death, but she encounters no threat to her sovereignty because natural events can infringe upon concrete interests, but they cannot violate sovereignty. The farmhouse owners suffered temporary injury to their concrete property interests, but compensation cures this injury, and their right to compensation vindicates their sovereignty over their property. Had the owners never received compensation because the bicyclist was never found or died

---

19 *Id.* at § 3.01(2); The Law of Torts 147–8 (W. P. Keeton ed., St. Paul, Minn.: West Pub. Co., 5th ed. 1984).

20 In specifying that he will injure *V* if but only if *V* moves, *A* may seem like an unusually precise thug. *A* is not uncommon, however, among the growing criminal subclass of the unemployed philosopher/mugger.

21 By "concrete" interests, I mean those involving one's material or physical concerns. In the current ordinary sense, "concrete" means "combined with or embodied in matter, actual practice, or a particular example; existing in a material form as an actual reality, or pertaining to that which so exists. Opposed to abstract." I Oxford English Dictionary at 504. In this book, concrete interests are those that involve the holders' physical, material, or financial well-being as opposed to their political standing or status. An earthquake or a declining market, for example, could severely impair the concrete interests of property holders without affecting their legitimate rights in their property. Conversely, zoning laws that prohibited members of certain racial groups from buying homes in certain neighborhoods would undermine the political standing of all members of that group, although these laws may have no effect on the concrete interests of the individual members of that group who lack the financial resources or desire to buy in that area.

22 By "sovereignty," I mean *V*'s right to exercise discretion or authority over a specific domain. This concept will be developed further in the discussion of liberalism in § 3.3.1.

despite the break-in, the fact that they had a legal claim would vindicate their standing under the law as the parties who hold the right of sovereign control over their property.

In a standard self-defense case such as SD1, *A* threatens both concrete interests and sovereignty. The threat to or violation of each constitutes an independent injury, but the violation of sovereignty differentiates these clear cases of self-defense from many applications of the necessity defense. *A*'s culpable offense against *V* violates some aspect of *V*'s sovereignty and subjugates *V* to *A*, imputing lesser standing to *V*. Norms requiring that *V* tolerate such an intrusion would effectively ratify that violation and the imputation of lesser standing, undermining *V*'s equal status. Thus, the appropriate norm of self-defense for any particular legal system reflects not only the need to define the conditions under which private persons may protect their own concrete interests in the absence of immediate state assistance, but also the importance of personal sovereignty and equal standing to the political philosophy represented by that social system. A political philosophy vesting fundamental value only in maximizing the concrete well-being of the citizenry, for example, might collapse self-defense into the general justification defense, requiring that individuals always act in the manner expected to minimize the net harm to concrete interests. In contrast, a political system vesting significant value in individual self-determination must develop defenses that grant corresponding weight to violations of sovereignty as well as to the balance of concrete harms.

3.3   The Normative Structure

As a specific justification defense, self-defense identifies certain circumstances in which the conventional public morality underlying the criminal law provides an exception to the prohibitory norm represented by the homicide and assault statutes. Individuals who fulfill the material elements of these offense definitions do not merit the condemnation inherent in criminal conviction and punishment because their conduct does not violate the fully articulated conventional morality. The principles of political morality represented by a particular legal system explain and justify the parameters of justified self-defense in that conventional morality. In the United States and other legal systems representing the western liberal tradition, a satisfactory theory of justified self-defense must articulate the broad general principles of liberal political morality and explain the role of self-defense in a complex set of legal institutions instantiating these principles.

For the purpose of this book, I set aside two issues. First, I do not claim to defend liberal political theory as the most defensible political morality or the criminal justice systems currently operating in the United States as ideal legal institutions. I assume only that liberal political morality and a criminal justice system reflecting these principles could provide a defensible form of political organization. Presumably, those who hold that such institutions are necessarily indefensible will find little significance in the role of any particular component such as self-defense specifically or justification defenses generally. Second, I do not defend any particular liberal theory as the most defensible form of liberalism. Rather, I articulate broad general properties of mainstream contemporary liberal political theory that provide a philosophical foundation for legal systems such as those established in liberal democracies.

3.3.1   Political Liberalism

Theorists who advance variants of liberal political theory differ regarding both their precise theoretical formulations and the structure of political institutions they endorse.[23] For the purpose of this book, I discuss two broad categories of liberal political morality. First, structural liberalism addresses the structure of basic political institutions in a liberal society, reflecting principles of political justice that are compatible with a number of more general moral theories.[24] Second, substantive liberalism constitutes a subset of structural liberalism in which substantive moral principles common to the liberal political morality and to the more general moral theory provide an intrinsic connection between the political and more general theories.[25] I make no attempt to provide an exhaustive survey of contemporary liberalism, nor do I claim that the structural and substantive categories provide the most illuminating account for all purposes.[26] Rather, this account provides a useful framework for the analysis of justification defenses in a liberal society.

Structural liberalism describes and defends basic institutions of political justice that provide a structure for a fair system of social cooperation among individuals who endorse a variety of comprehensive moral doctrines. Those who endorse various comprehensive moral doctrines can differ with one another regarding a number of important moral issues, principles, and obligations, yet converge on certain principles of political morality such that they can support mutually compatible liberal political institutions.[27] These institutions

---

23 *See generally* Will Kymlicka, Liberalism, Community, and Culture (New York: Oxford Univ. Press, 1989).

24 *See, e.g.,* John Rawls, Political Liberalism (New York: Columbia Univ. Press, 1993).

25 *See, e.g.,* Joel Feinberg, Harm to Self (New York: Oxford Univ. Press, 1986); Joseph Raz, The Morality of Freedom (New York: Oxford Univ. Press, 1986). Feinberg and Raz each advance theories of substantive liberalism, although Feinberg emphasizes more heavily autonomy as a right to personal sovereignty, and Raz emphasizes autonomy as an ideal development of the autonomous virtues.

26 *See, e.g.,* Jean Hampton, *Retribution and the Liberal State,* 5 J. Contemp. Legal Issues 117 (1994). Hampton provides an alternative account for a different purpose.

27 Rawls, *supra* note 24, at Lect. I, §§ 1–3. Rawls refers to religious, moral, or philosophical comprehensive doctrines. I refer to all of these as moral doctrines in order to include those systems

establish and protect public and nonpublic domains of jurisdiction. Citizens participate in and influence the public domain through political institutions that instantiate the shared principles of political morality and protect the individual's discretion to pursue a broad range of moral principles within the nonpublic domain.[28] Thus, the political structure protects individual self-determination in each domain.

Competent adults participate in the political process as citizens with equal standing in the public sphere. Political institutions respect individual self-determination by allowing each competent adult equal standing in the political process by which citizens collectively determine the limits of their own liberty and the boundaries of the public jurisdiction. John Rawls identifies the capacities required to exercise a sense of justice and develop a conception of the good as the criteria of competence that render the individual eligible for the status of equal citizenship.[29] These capacities allow each to participate in the political process and exercise an equal set of basic liberties. This equality of standing in political institutions provides the basis for mutual respect among citizens and for self-respect as a member of the political process by each.[30]

Although liberal societies can differ regarding the precise boundaries of the public domain, they maintain some substantial sphere of nonpublic life beyond the reach of government jurisdiction. This nonpublic sphere allows each person the opportunity to develop and pursue a conception of the good consistent with that person's comprehensive moral doctrine through individual decisions and voluntary relationships with others. Thus, each competent adult defines a life of his or her own through the manner in which he or she exercises sovereign discretion in the nonpublic sphere and participates as an equal citizen in the public domain.[31] In short, liberal political morality respects individual self-determination by providing for equal standing as a citizen in the political process in the public sphere and by protecting each citizen's equal domain of nonpublic jurisdiction within which that individual exercises sovereign discretion.

A political structure grounded in liberal principles of political morality differs from a mere political compromise insofar as its citizens adopt a variety of comprehensive moral doctrines, each of which recognizes as morally valuable the principles of political morality embodied in liberal political institutions. Thus, citizens can differ regarding their comprehensive moral doctrines and conceptions of the good life, yet they can share common principles of political

---

or aspects of systems that people rely on to address moral questions regarding how we ought to live.
28 *Id.* at Lect. I, § 6.
29 *Id.* at Lect. I, §§ 3.3, 5.
30 *Id.* at Lect. V, § 7, Lect. VI, § 6.
31 *Id.* at Lect. I, §§ 5, 6.

morality that bind the political society.[32] Those who endorse this liberal political morality that emphasizes distinct public and nonpublic domains and the
equal standing of competent citizens in the public sphere are structural liberals
in the sense that their liberal principles address the basic structure of political
institutions.

Structural liberals can vary significantly in the content of their comprehensive moral doctrines and in the manner in which their comprehensive doctrines
support structural liberalism. Utilitarians, for example, might vest instrumental
moral value in liberal political institutions if they accept plausible empirical
hypotheses about human psychology and social institutions, leading to the
inference that liberal political institutions are likely to maximize utility. Similarly, those who hold a religious view that vests fundamental value in freely
accepting a particular religious doctrine as God's word might support liberal
political institutions as providing the freedom of conscience necessary to allow
such free acceptance of that doctrine.

In contrast to the instrumental value recognized by the Utilitarians and religious adherents just described, substantive liberals recognize an intrinsic relationship between liberal political morality and their comprehensive moral doctrine. Substantive liberals are structural liberals who vest fundamental value in
individual autonomy as a moral value that provides a common foundation for
liberal political institutions and for those aspects of their comprehensive moral
doctrine that govern the nonpublic domain. Thus, the public and nonpublic
spheres each reflect respect for individual autonomy in their respective domains
of the person's life. Joel Feinberg, for example, develops a complex conception
of autonomy as a right to self-determination, a set of virtues, an ideal development of these virtues, and a set of capacities.

At the level of political structure, the substantive liberal endorses structural
liberalism in which the status of equal citizenship in the democratic political
process respects autonomy as a right to self-determination in the public sphere.
The protected nonpublic domain provides the opportunity for each competent
adult to exercise the right to self-determination in the nonpublic sphere and to
pursue autonomous virtues by defining his or her life as an extended personal

---

32 *Id.* at Lect. IV, §§ 3, 8, Lect. VIII, § 5. Consider, in contrast, circumstances in which a society
   might agree on liberal political institutions as a mere political compromise. Suppose a region
   was populated in roughly equal proportions by members of three different religious groups,
   each of which endorsed as part of its comprehensive religious doctrine a political theocracy in
   which all were required to adhere to that religion in all matters. If the members of each group
   realized that they would not be able to enforce the theocracy they believed they ought to establish, they might agree to liberal political institutions as a means of protecting themselves from
   the establishment of a theocracy by one of the other religions. They would accept these institutions only as a lesser evil, however, recognizing no moral value in them, and all would stand
   ready to abandon liberal political institutions as valueless if circumstances developed that
   allowed the theocracy they favored.

project. Finally, the capacities for a sense of justice and a conception of the good that provide the basis for equal standing as a citizen in liberal political institutions correspond roughly to the autonomous capacities that enable that individual to exercise autonomy as a right to self-determination and pursue a life reflecting the autonomous virtues.[33]

The substantive liberal emphasizes the right to self-determination as a value that integrates the public and nonpublic domains. Although structural liberals might differ regarding the parameters of the nonpublic spheres they endorse and regarding their reasons for doing so, they support distinct public and non-public domains. Substantive liberals join other structural liberals in protecting the right to self-determination as a right to equal standing in the political process of the public sphere, and they vest fundamental value in self-determination as personal sovereignty in the nonpublic domain.[34] On this view, the non-public domain provides the autonomous individual with a sphere of personal sovereignty within which he exercises discretionary authority analogous to the political sovereignty of nations. This right to self-determination extends to a domain of central self-regarding life decisions through which each individual defines and pursues a life, providing the opportunity for each to develop the autonomous virtues. Respect for personal autonomy as sovereignty requires respect for the individual's unfettered choice in those matters that fall within the nonpublic domain because they do not infringe on the legitimate interests of others.[35]

For the substantive liberal, sovereignty is a fundamental value in that it is categorical, underivative, and noncompensable. It is categorical in the sense that discretionary authority within the domain of sovereignty is not subject to review, compromise, or limitation by government. Any claim of authority by the government to review and approve decisions within the protected domain would violate sovereignty, regardless of whether that authority was ever exercised. The mere acknowledgment of authority to review and approve under-mines the discretionary control that constitutes sovereignty. Various matters

---

33 Feinberg, *supra* note 25, at 28–31; *compare* Rawls, *supra* note 24, at Lect. I § 3.3, Lect. VIII, § 3 regarding the capacity for a sense of justice.

34 The fundamental value for autonomy does not entail structural liberalism as a political philos-ophy. Some who endorse the fundamental value of autonomy in the comprehensive doctrine might, for example, endorse social anarchism as the preferred form of political organization. Others might endorse social anarchism in principle but hold that in practice, social anarchism lacks the effective structure required to prevent domination by the powerful. Thus, they might endorse structural liberalism as the form of political organization most likely to protect auton-omy in practice. For the purpose of this book, I define substantive liberalism as a subset of structural liberalism. That is, substantive liberals vest fundamental value in autonomy in their comprehensive doctrines, and they endorse structural liberalism as the theory of political morality that protects and promotes autonomy. Thus, the value for autonomy provides an intrin-sic connection between the comprehensive doctrine and the political morality.

35 Feinberg, *supra* note 25, at 52–70.

may fall beyond the scope of the individual's sovereignty because, for example, they directly affect the legitimate interests of others. If a decision falls within the domain of individual sovereignty, however, respect for that person's right to self-determination precludes any intrusion.[36] Sovereignty is underivative in that substantive liberals value it independently of any instrumental purpose it may serve.[37] Finally, it is noncompensable in that others cannot justify intruding into a clearly competent individual's sphere of sovereignty by providing other benefits, such as increased well-being in return.[38]

While Feinberg presents the fundamental nature of sovereignty as part of the very concept, Rawls vests similar weight in self-determination by granting lexical priority over other benefits to a set of basic liberties. This set includes the political liberties to vote and be eligible for public office; freedom of speech, assembly, conscience, and thought; freedom of the person and the right to hold personal property; and freedom from arbitrary arrest and seizure.[39]

Feinberg advocates a sphere of personal sovereignty that encompasses all primarily and directly self-regarding critical life-decisions.[40] At this level of generality, the domain of sovereignty is identical for all competent adults. Similarly, Rawls contends that the basic liberties are the same for all members of society. He argues that the fundamental rights and liberties define the individual's standing in the public sphere and provide the basis for self-respect as well as for respect by others. On Rawls's view, self-respect is inextricable from respect within a community of shared interests that confirms one's endeavors and standing.[41] At this fundamental level, self-determination and equality converge because government must treat persons with respect as beings capable of directing their own lives. It does so by according to each equal citizenship and participation in the political process as well as a sphere of personal sovereignty that equals that enjoyed by other members of the community and that identifies the person as a member in full standing of that community.[42]

Although structural liberals who are not substantive liberals might endorse personal sovereignty in the nonpublic domain as either derivative or underivative, they join substantive liberals in protecting individual sovereignty in the

---

36 *Id.* at 54–5.
37 They may also vest instrumental value in sovereignty in that, for example, they might hold that respect for an individual's sovereignty promotes that person's ability to develop the autonomous virtues and pursue the ideal. The point here, however, is that the value of sovereignty is not merely instrumental for the substantive liberal.
38 Feinberg, *supra* note 25, at 57–62.
39 Rawls, *supra* note 24, at Lect. VIII, § 6; John Rawls, A Theory of Justice 61, 243–51 (Cambridge, Mass.: Harvard Univ. Press, 1971).
40 Feinberg, *supra* note 25, at 52–7.
41 Rawls, *supra* note 24, at Lect. V, § 7, Lect. VIII, § 6; Rawls, *supra* note 39, at 202, 440–6, 544–6.
42 *Id.;* Ronald Dworkin, Taking Rights Seriously 272–4 (Cambridge, Mass.: Harvard Univ. Press, 1968).

nonpublic domain from political interference. Structural liberals must recognize sovereignty as categorical and noncompensable because any intrusion into an individual's nonpublic domain undermines the central distinction between public and nonpublic morality that enables structural liberals to converge on common principles of political morality despite differences in their comprehensive doctrines.

Any attempt to justify political intrusion into an individual's domain of sovereignty would have to appeal to some moral principle as sufficient to override the shared principles of political justice. That is, the shared principles of political morality provide good reasons to maintain distinct public and nonpublic domains. Any justification for transgressing that boundary by subjecting an individual's nonpublic domain to political intrusion must appeal to some other source of morally relevant reasons as outweighing those shared principles. This appeal would effectively endorse that alternate source of morally relevant reasons as superior to the shared principles and to any other moral principles that were not accepted as sufficient to override the shared principles.

Suppose, for example, that a particular society includes the competent adult's right to accept or reject health care in the nonpublic domain. Smith refuses a prescribed course of treatment, deciding to accept approaching death rather than extending life at the expense of extremely debilitating side-effects. If a court ordered the treatment on the grounds that it would maximize the happiness of all those who cared about Smith, it would effectively endorse a utilitarian comprehensive doctrine as a source of reasons sufficient to override the shared principles of political morality. This appeal to the principle of utility would undermine the public–nonpublic distinction, endorse the utilitarian comprehensive doctrine, and violate the equal standing in the political society of Smith as well as of all those who held comprehensive doctrines that were not deemed sufficient to override the shared principles. Compensation with some other benefit, such as free health care, would not cure the imputation of lesser standing. Thus, structural liberals must treat individual sovereignty within the nonpublic domain as categorical and noncompensable, although they might hold that Smith made the wrong decision according to their comprehensive doctrines.

In summary, contemporary liberal political theory supports political institutions that provide a fair system of social cooperation among citizens who may endorse a variety of comprehensive moral theories. These institutions respect individual self-determination within distinct public and nonpublic domains of jurisdiction. This requires a relationship between the individual and the government in which the government accords equal respect to all persons by recognizing equal standing in the democratic political process and by protecting a sphere of sovereignty within which each individual can direct his or her own life and develop self-respect as a member of a community of equal, sovereign citizens. Although substantive liberals vest a more comprehensive value in autonomy as a value fundamental to both the public and nonpublic spheres, they share with other structural liberals at least the following important commitments. They endorse liberal political principles and institutions as morally valuable, rather than merely as political compromise. They maintain distinct public and nonpublic domains, and they protect the equal citizenship of competent adults in the public sphere as well as the sovereign control of each citizen within the nonpublic sphere.

The rule of law is central to this political philosophy in that law in a liberal society defines and protects the boundaries of the public and nonpublic domains and regulates the conduct of individuals and of the government in the public sphere. Constitutional law limits the scope of government power, preventing the government from directly intruding into the individual's domain of sovereignty and prohibiting the government from distributing social resources in a manner that imputes lesser status or worth to some persons than to others. Certain areas of law, such as the law of contracts, wills, and family associations, facilitate the ability of individuals to order their voluntary associations.

Criminal law protects personal sovereignty and equal status by proscribing, preventing, and punishing actions by some citizens that violate the rights and interests of others. Thus, the criminal law not only maintains the conventional public morality that orders cooperative social interaction, it also articulates the contours of the individual's sphere of sovereignty by defining certain types of intrusions as crimes.[43] When a liberal state enforces the criminal law, it not only maintains the public order and safety through deterrence and restraint, it also vindicates the sovereignty of the victim by punishing and condemning conduct that violates that person's right to self-determination.

3.3.2   The Criminal Justice System in the Liberal Society

The criminal law proscribes certain types of conduct and prescribes punishment for those who are convicted of engaging in those types of conduct under conditions of culpability as defined by the code. By doing so, the criminal law guides social behavior through several different mechanisms. Most obviously, it is intended to prevent criminal conduct through incapacitation and deterrence.[44] Perhaps more importantly, however, it serves as an official representation of an important part of the conventional public morality. As such, it articulates boundaries of acceptable behavior in the public sphere, providing guidelines for vol-

---

43 Some types of activity might be criminalized for other reasons. Perjury, for example, is proscribed in order to promote the effectiveness of the legal system, and securities regulations are designed to promote effective functioning of the economy. Crimes such as those against person and property, however, help to define the individual's sphere of autonomy by forbidding others from intruding into those areas.
44 Criminal Law at § 1.5.

untary compliance by those who accept a responsibility to conform to that conventional morality. To the extent that the criminal law converges with standards widely held among citizens, it is likely to be accepted as representative of the conventional public morality, thus reinforcing those standards and helping to shape them.

Insofar as it represents, reinforces, and shapes the conventional public morality, the expressive function of the criminal law may influence behavior more effectively than does the attempt to direct conduct through enforcement.[45] Recall from Chapter 2 that the criminal law expresses condemnation of five types at two different levels of analysis. The criminal law expresses condemnation of certain types of conduct at the institutional level by formulating criminal offense definitions in a manner that prohibits those types of conduct as criminal and authorizes punishment of those who are convicted of violating those prohibitions. At the level of application, conviction for a particular offense reaffirms the institutional condemnation of conduct of this type, condemns this particular instance of that type, condemns the defendant as one who has violated the prohibition represented by an offense definition under conditions of accountability by systemic standards, and condemns that defendant as morally blameworthy.[46]

The criminal justice system reaffirms the standing of both the defendant and the victim through the appropriate expression of condemnation. It reaffirms the standing of the defendant as a competent citizen of the political sphere insofar as the requirements of criminal responsibility limit criminal liability to those who violate the criminal law in their capacities as competent agents. That is, by trying and convicting the defendant in the criminal process rather than resorting, for example, to the civil commitment process of the mental health system, the legal system treats the defendant as a citizen who possesses the capacities required for equal standing in the political sphere.[47]

Criminal conviction and punishment of the defendant vindicates the standing of the victim in the political institutions. Criminal conduct against private persons injures their concrete interests, such as those in safety and property, and it violates their protected domain of sovereignty by interfering with their discretionary control. The crime places the victim and the aggressor in a relationship of relative inequality such that the aggressor violates the victim's sov-

---

45 Joel Feinberg, *Doing and Deserving* 95–118 (Princeton: Princeton Univ. Press, 1970). The enforcement process serves both as a direct tool of coercive behavior control and as a means of communicating the expressive function. Thus, to a certain extent, enforcement constitutes one means of expression.

46 *See supra* § 2.3.

47 Robert F. Schopp, *Sexual Predators and the Structure of the Mental Health System: Expanding the Normative Focus of Therapeutic Jurisprudence,* 1 Psychol., Pub. Pol'y, & L. 161, 177–80 (1994).

ereignty in order to promote his own interests, imputing lesser standing or importance to the victim. Even unsuccessful attempts express the offenders' disregard for their victims' standing. By convicting and punishing the criminal, the criminal justice system repudiates the imputation of lesser standing inherent in the crime, reaffirming the status of the victim. Conviction and punishment communicate public repudiation of the aggressor's violation of the victim's sphere of sovereignty and public vindication of the victim's standing as an equal citizen of the political society.[48] In contrast, when the state refuses or neglects to prosecute and punish violations against certain classes of citizens, such as prostitutes or transients, this refusal or neglect effectively ratifies the imputation of inferior status to these parties.

On this view, the government can violate an individual's sovereignty either directly or indirectly. It can do so directly through state action that transgresses the individual's right to self-determination by violating political freedoms or that imputes inferior status to some through treatment that marks them as less important or worthy of respect than others. Constitutional law protects citizens from such direct violations. Second, the government can indirectly violate the individual's standing as an equal, sovereign person by acquiescing in criminal violations against that person by another. Insofar as the criminal law defines and protects the contours of the nonpublic domain, government derogates one person's standing indirectly when it subjects that person's sovereignty to violation by another by virtue of the manner in which it defines, enforces, or fails to enforce the criminal law.

3.3.3 Justification Defenses

Recall from Chapter 2 the interpretation of the criminal law's offense definitions and justification defenses as an official representation of the conventional public morality. Offense definitions represent general prohibitory norms of the conventional public morality, but in contrast to those underlying norms, they take the form of relatively specific behavioral directives. That is, if one thinks of a conventional public morality as a set of widely accepted moral principles regarding conduct that falls within the public jurisdiction, then the general prohibitory norms consist of general principles proscribing certain categories of conduct as wrongful according to that conventional public morality. In a liberal society, these might include, for example, general principles proscribing conduct that physically harms other persons, violates their property rights, or infringes on their legitimate sphere of personal discretion.[49]

---

48 Feinberg, *supra* note 45, at 104.
49 *See supra* § 2.3.

Legal offense definitions take the form of more specific behavioral directives, intended to give more definite notice to citizens and to constrain the lati-
tude of legal decision makers. The offense definitions prohibiting various types
of homicide and assault, for example, all provide more specific behavioral
directives representing the general prohibitory norm stating the conventional
moral principle that one ought not physically harm other persons.

In certain unusual circumstances, violations of offense definitions under
conditions of accountability do not warrant condemnation. Justification
defenses serve as corrective devices, preventing conviction and expression of
condemnation in these circumstances. Specific justification defenses, including
self-defense, address relatively well-defined types of circumstances in which
conduct fulfills the material elements of offense definitions but does not warrant the condemnation ordinarily directed toward behavior of that type. The
necessity defense serves as a residual defense that applies to conduct that violates an offense definition in conditions that do not qualify for any specific justification defense but that render condemnation unjustified.[50]

Thus, a criminal code containing typical assault and defensive force provisions would represent a conventional public morality in roughly the following
manner. The offense definition for assault, along with other offense definitions,
such as those in the homicide statutes, would instantiate a general principle that
one ought not cause physical harm to other human beings. The statutes allowing the use of force in defense of self or others would represent the principle
that one may exercise physical force against another when doing so is necessary to prevent that other person from exercising unlawful force against an
innocent person. The integrated conventional public morality would hold that
one ought not cause physical harm to another person *unless* doing so is necessary to prevent the unlawful use of force against another person or to serve
some overriding principle in the conventional morality. Thus, in these circumstances, it would grant priority to the principle endorsing protection of the
innocent over the principle prohibiting the use of force.

The criminal law would contain a series of specific offense definitions and
justification defenses designed to instantiate these general principles in the
form of specific behavioral directives addressing homicide, assault, self-
defense, defense of others and property, the use of force in law enforcement,
and so on. These specific provisions might include various clauses regarding
proportion, retreat, imminence, or other considerations intended to accurately
represent the conventional public morality in light of practical considerations
such as the need for relative generality, decidability, predictability, and simplic-
ity as well as concern for error preference. Sections 3.4 and 3.5 develop a theory of justified self-defense in a liberal society. This theory draws upon liberal

---

50 *See supra* § 2.3.

principles of political morality in order to provide the justificatory foundations for the exercise of defensive force and to define the appropriate parameters such as those addressing proportion, retreat, or imminence.

3.4 Self-defense as Justified Conduct in a Liberal Society

When an innocent victim exercises force in self-defense against a fully responsible aggressor, the victim protects both her concrete interests and her right to self-determination, rejecting the imputation of inequality inherent in the unlawful aggression. Just as punishment for some attempted crimes can be justified at least partially as a vindication of the victim's sovereignty, self-defense can be justified as protection of sovereignty in cases such as SD2 that involve violations of the right to self-determination without apparent threat to concrete interests. The claim here is not that self-defense is a form of punishment or a down payment on punishment, but rather that in a system of law representing a liberal political philosophy, both self-defense and punishment reflect a deeper value for the equal status of persons as autonomous individuals with their own spheres of personal sovereignty.

On this view, any culpable criminal activity constitutes a serious transgression against the victim. An aggressor who commits even a minor crime not only threatens some minor concrete interests of the victim, he also violates the victim's sovereignty over some aspect of her life that is included in the protected domain of self-determination that partially defines the standing of a citizen in that society. If the state did not defend the victim's right to self-determination against culpable violations by prosecuting and punishing those who committed offenses against her, it would indirectly violate her sovereignty and equal standing by acquiescing in the offense and passively ratifying the imputation of lesser standing. Similarly, if the criminal law refused to recognize the victim's right to protect her own right to self-determination when state protection was unavailable, it would effectively require that she acquiesce in this violation of her sovereignty and imputation of lesser standing.

By initiating criminal activity in a manner such that the victim can prevent violation of her sovereignty only through the use of defensive force, the aggressor creates a situation in which either he or the victim must suffer some injury to interests that ordinarily merit legal protection. The victim's decision to protect her sovereignty through the exercise of force is not comparable, however, to a choice regarding which party will absorb equal and unavoidable injury.[51] By engaging in a criminal violation of the victim's sovereignty, the aggressor steps outside of the domain of central, self-regarding life decisions within

---

51 This liberal position differs in this regard from the distributive theory described in § 3.1.2.

which he can claim a right to freedom from interference. The victim's exercise of defensive force against the aggressor does not, therefore, violate his right to self-determination. In these circumstances, the victim must choose either to allow violation of her sovereignty or to inflict injury on the aggressor's concrete interests.

On the liberal theory, others cannot intrude into a competent person's right to self-determination for her own good because sovereignty is noncompensable. If a theory rejected paternalistic intrusions into a person's sovereignty but protected an aggressor's concrete interests at the expense of the victim's right to self-determination by forbidding her exercise of defensive force against that aggressor, it would effectively ratify the aggressor's imputation of lesser standing to the victim. It would do so by treating the aggressor's concrete interests but not the victim's as sufficient to limit the victim's right to self-determination. Thus, the liberal theorist must allow the exercise of defensive force against an aggressor, even if the injury to that aggressor exceeds the setback to concrete interests the victim would have absorbed had she refrained from exercising force in self-defense.

The priority of the victim's sovereignty over the aggressor's concrete interests carries weight at the level of harm and at the level of risk. At the first level, the victim has no obligation to respect a requirement of proportion regarding concrete injuries; if she can protect herself from sustaining a black eye only by breaking her assailant's leg, for example, she has no obligation to absorb the black eye merely because a broken leg is disproportionate to a black eye. A victim may take any action against an aggressor necessary to prevent a culpable violation of her sovereignty by that aggressor because he steps outside his protected sphere when he attacks her. His sovereignty is not at stake, and her sovereignty takes priority over his concrete interests, just as it does over her own.

When a victim faces intrusion by an aggressor, she must decide how much force is necessary and sufficient to protect herself from that intrusion. As with any human decision, she might err, and the decision she makes reasonably includes a weighing of error preference. If the victim uses more force than necessary, she might harm the aggressor more than necessary to protect herself. If she uses less force than necessary, she might fail to dissuade the intrusion, possibly increasing the danger to her own interests. If, for example, V awakens during the night to find that A is climbing in through V's window, V might hit A in the head with a baseball bat, or V might yell "stop or I'll brain you." If V does the former when the latter would have sufficed, V might severely injure A unnecessarily, but if V does the latter when the former was necessary, V might be severely injured (suppose A is armed and starts shooting). Just as A's culpable intrusion takes A beyond the bounds of his protected sphere and justifies V in protecting her sovereignty at the expense of harm to A's concrete interests, it also justifies V in granting priority to her right to self-determination regarding the error preference. Risk of intrusion into V's sovereignty takes priority over risk of unnecessary harm to A's concrete interests; thus, V is justified in taking action necessary to repel the intrusion in a manner that places any risk of unnecessary injury on A.[52]

A similar analysis precludes a duty to retreat. A victim would have a moral duty to retreat from a place she legitimately occupied in order to avoid injuring a culpable aggressor in self-defense only if that aggressor's concrete interests took priority over her sovereignty and concrete interests. In short, victims are constrained by the principle of necessity, but not by requirements of retreat or proportion regarding either harm or risk.

This interpretation justifies defensive force by appeal to considerations that differ markedly from those addressed by lesser-harms or forfeiture theories. In contrast to the lesser-harms position, this theory justifies victims in injuring aggressors by appeal both to the fundamental nature of the value for sovereignty in a liberal society and to the bounds of each individual's domain of protected choice. The noncompensable nature of the liberal right to self-determination gives priority to victims' sovereignty over aggressors' concrete interests, and culpable transgressions move aggressors beyond the boundaries of their protected domains, presenting victims with a choice between their sovereignty and the aggressors' concrete interests. When faced with this choice, victims may justifiably choose any necessary injury to the aggressors' concrete interests as the lesser sacrifice of important moral value. In doing so victims opt for the lesser evil although they inflict greater harm to aggressors' concrete interests than those aggressors would have inflicted on their victims' concrete interests.[53]

Some theorists contend that aggressors forfeit some right such as the right to life or bodily safety. Other writers reject forfeiture theories of self-defense because such theories seem to allow retaliation when the threat is over and to place the attacker outside the law's protection as an outlaw; yet we generally do not allow retaliation when the threat has terminated, and the law continues to protect the attacker from some conduct, including unnecessarily severe

---

52 In some extended sense, any circumstances present some risk. On the account presented here, V is justified in sacrificing A's interests rather than subjecting herself to any realistic risk of harm created by A's culpable intrusion. Notice, however, that in most plausible cases, the principle of necessity provides substantial protection for A, because A can render the use of any force unnecessary simply by discontinuing the threat and acknowledging the wrong through surrender and compensation. Merely halting the attack may not suffice, particularly in contexts involving repeated aggression. I will not pursue this issue here.

53 Writers often use "lesser-evil" and "lesser-harm" interchangeably, but if "harm" is understood as a setback to concrete interests, then the two must be distinguished because a lesser harm can constitute a greater evil. In a liberal society, a violation of sovereignty without substantial injury to concrete interests (e.g., SD2) may constitute a lesser harm but a greater evil as a greater violation of important moral value. The liberal who vests noncompensable value in personal sovereignty will hold that any violation of V's sovereignty by A constitutes a greater evil than does any necessary injury to A's concrete interests by V.

force.[54] On the account advanced here, defensive force is justified by the priority of the victim's sovereignty over the aggressor's concrete interests, not by
forfeiture. Aggressors do not forfeit their sovereignty because their right to
self-determination never extended to actions that intrude into victim's protected domains. Although victims may protect their sovereignty at the expense
of aggressors' concrete interests, justified self-defense does not include unnecessarily severe defensive force because gratuitous injury would result in a net
sacrifice of well-being without protecting the fundamental value for sovereignty.

The significance of sovereignty and equal standing in the liberal theory of
self-defense differentiates self-defense from actions taken in response to threatening natural events. When natural events endanger two parties equally, neither
has any obvious justification for shifting the loss to the other. Suppose, for
example, that a flood is threatening two farms and that *B* can avoid the damage
to his farm only by blasting the riverbank in a manner that will redirect the flood
entirely toward *C*'s farm. *B* and *C* hold equal status, and neither is responsible
for the natural event posing the danger to *B*. *B* has no grounds for violating *C*'s
interests or sovereignty to protect *B*'s own. When the danger to *B* is much
greater than the danger to *C* (for example, the bicyclist case NE1), *B* can choose
to infringe on *C*'s interests but must compensate *C* because *C* retains equal
standing with *B*. Under these circumstances, *B* can justifiably infringe on *C*'s
concrete interests without violating *C*'s right to self-determination because *B*
must choose between concrete injuries of disparate magnitude, and *C*'s right to
compensation vindicates *C*'s sovereignty.

Sovereignty and equality of status under the law are properties of political
relationships among persons. Natural events threaten concrete interests, but
they do not threaten sovereignty or equality of status. Thus, two responsible but
not culpable moral agents who encounter dangerous natural events must balance the respective harms to their concrete interests with no basis for weighing
one party's interests over the other's. Contrast the clear self-defense case (SD1)
in which culpable action by *A* threatens *V*'s right to self-determination and concrete interests, providing a justificatory reason for *V* to favor her own sovereignty and interests over *A*'s concrete interests.

Cases involving innocent aggressors resemble standard self-defense cases in
that the threats to the victims' interests issue from human sources rather than
from natural events. In the standard case, however, *A*'s culpable violation
against *V* justifies both *V*'s use of defensive force against *A* and the law's simul-
taneous condemnation of *A*'s violation against *V* and ratification of *V*'s use of
force against *A*. Legal institutions justifiably differentiate between *A*'s use of

---

54 Hugo Bedau, *The Right to Life*, The Monist 550, 567–70 (1968); Fletcher, *supra* note 8, at
    1380–3.

force and V's because A culpably creates the circumstances in which V must exercise force against A's concrete interests in order to protect her sovereignty. Innocent aggressors threaten their victims' concrete interests, but they do not undermine sovereignty because they do not culpably deny the relationship of equal standing between the parties. The aggressor may be one who through no fault of his own does not realize that his conduct threatens the victim or one who believes that his harmful behavior is necessary and justified. The small child with the gun he thinks is a toy exemplifies the first type of innocent aggressor, and the paranoid individual who shoots a policeman under the delusional belief that the policeman is a terrorist who is about to blow up the building exemplifies the second type.

Individual sovereignty plays a complex role in the relationships among aggressors, victims, and the social institutions within which they interact. By infringing on V's right to self-determination, A subjugates V's interests to his own and denies V's standing as a person who enjoys a sphere of sovereignty equal to that of all others in society, including A. In contrast, innocent aggressors threaten their victims' concrete interests, but they do not undermine their victims' sovereignty or their standing as equals. In order to understand why innocent aggressors do not erode their victims' sovereignty or standing, one must consider the relationship among sovereignty, equal standing, and self-respect. Each competent adult enjoys equal standing with all other competent adults in a liberal society by virtue of commanding equal citizenship in the political process and a domain of personal sovereignty identical to that held by others.[55] Each such person participates in a community of equally sovereign persons and draws self-respect partially from this participation as an equal in a community of shared values.[56]

Innocent aggressors are not culpable for their transgressions because they suffer some disability or lack of information that prevents them from participating in the community as fully functioning members. For purposes of criminal liability, these innocent aggressors are excused by virtue of infancy, insanity, nonculpable mistake, or some similar excuse. When courts exculpate defendants by virtue of infancy or insanity, for example, they reaffirm the characterization of these defendants' conduct as offenses, but they exclude these defendants from the class of responsible persons who are appropriately held liable for criminal conduct.[57] By excluding these defendants from the class of

---

55 The domains are equal at the abstract level of principle. They may differ, for example, in how much property the individual owns or controls. This chapter discusses the significance of sovereignty and equal respect for self-defense by competent adults. Cases involving infants or incompetent adults as victims, bystanders, or shields raise additional issues that space limitations prevent me from examining here.

56 Rawls, *supra* note 39, at 440–6; Joel Feinberg, Rights, Justice, and the Bounds of Liberty 151 (Princeton: Princeton Univ. Press, 1980).

57 Excuses exclude these defendants from the class of responsible agents for this particular act but not necessarily for all actions.

responsible agents, the courts effectively remove them from the community of sovereign persons whose equal standing provides one source of self-respect for each. Thus, violations by these individuals do not impute lesser standing in the community to the victims because these aggressors have been excluded from the category of persons who participate in that community as equals.

Many agents from outside the community of equals, including natural events, nonhuman animals, and innocent aggressors, can limit one's practical ability to choose within the range usually protected by the right to self-determination. Legally sanctioned intrusions carry special significance, however, because law provides the official representation of the conventional public morality. Direct legal intrusions impute lesser standing to the subject, and indirect legal intrusions ratify similar imputations by others. In contrast, legal rules that prohibit such intrusions and mark them as illegitimate repudiate the imputation of lesser status, reaffirming the standing of the victims and the bounds of their sovereignty. Thus, excused transgressions by innocent aggressors injure their victims' concrete interests, without undermining the victims' sovereignty or status as equals in the community.

The victims of these innocent aggressors encounter difficult choices among concrete interests with no grounds for disregarding those of the innocent aggressors. These victims may kill innocent aggressors rather than forfeit their own lives because they have no obligation to sacrifice their concrete interests for those of the innocent aggressors. They must retreat if they can do so safely, however, because the considerations of sovereignty and equal status that bar a duty to retreat from culpable aggressors do not apply. Victims who can avoid killing innocent aggressors by absorbing a less severe and compensable injury themselves ought to do so because this choice would produce the lesser concrete harm among innocent parties. Victims can claim subsequent compensation because they have no obligation to sacrifice their concrete interests to those of the innocent aggressor.

Cases involving innocent shields (*IS*s) raise issues closely related to those involved in the *IA* cases. Consider the following examples.

(IS1): A stalks *V* for the clear purpose of killing *V.* Upon realizing that *V* has a gun and intends to kill *A* in self-defense, *A* grabs an innocent person (*IS*) and holds *IS* between *V* and himself for the purpose of discouraging *V* from shooting at *A* and for the purpose of using *IS* as a shield who will absorb the bullet if *V* fires. Can *V* fire at *A,* knowing that *IS* as well as *A* is highly likely to be killed?

(IS2): A stalks *V* for the purpose of killing her, and *V* can save herself only by grabbing *IS* and holding him in front of her while she reaches for her gun and shoots *A*. Here, as in IS1, *V* can save herself only by causing the death of both *A* and *IS.*

These two hypotheticals share the following common features: the culpable *A* initiates the danger; *IS* is entirely innocent; *V* can save herself only by causing the death of both *A* and *IS*. To many people, it seems intuitively clear that *V* may justifiably kill *A* but not that *V* can justifiably cause the death of *IS*. Although *V* can save herself only by causing the death of *IS* in either case, it is not at all clear that *V* is equally justified (or unjustified) in both cases. IS1 differs from IS2 only insofar as *A* holds *IS* while *V* shoots *IS* in IS1 and *V* holds *IS* while *A* shoots *IS* in IS2.

A simple lesser-harms calculation apparently precludes *V* from saving herself in either case, because she would be trading one culpable life and one innocent one for a single innocent life. If one disregards the life of *A*, then *V* must decide between innocent lives in both hypotheticals. If one frames the issues in this manner, there is no clearly superior action for *V*, but again, both cases appear to turn on the same choice. Yet, at least some readers will find intuitively that *V* seems more justified (or less unjustified) in IS1 than in IS2.

Consider IS1 first. *A*, *V*, and *IS* all stand to suffer the same concrete loss, in that each faces death. Under the approach advocated here, *V* can justifiably infringe *A*'s concrete interests in order to protect her sovereignty from the threat that *A* culpably created. *V* and *IS* stand equally as two innocent lives. *A* culpably violates both of their spheres of sovereignty in order to threaten *V*'s life, forcing *V* to choose between *IS*'s life and her own. Although *A*'s culpable aggression markedly distorts *A*'s relationship with *V* and *IS*, it does not alter the relationship of equality between *V* and *IS*. Thus, *V* has no justification for redirecting *A*'s threat away from her and toward *IS*. As to the relationship between *V* and *IS*, *A*'s threat resembles a natural event in that *V* has no grounds for favoring her own interests by shifting a comparable loss from either source to another innocent party. *V* would be justified, however, in saving her life at the cost of a compensable and significantly less severe injury to *IS* because by doing so she would choose the lesser of concrete harms and *IS* could claim compensation from either *V* or *A*. In short, the victim in IS1 encounters circumstances justifying self-defense against *A* but not justifying her in shifting comparable losses from herself to *IS*.

Although *V* can save herself only by causing the death of *IS* in either case, the interpretation advanced here supports the intuitive inclination to say that IS1 and IS2 do not present morally equivalent circumstances. The explanation lies in the violation of *IS*'s sovereignty. In IS1, *A* violates the sovereignty of both *V* and *IS*, forcing *V* to choose between the two innocent lives. In IS2, in contrast, it is *V* who violates *IS*'s sovereignty, imputing a lesser status to *IS* than to herself. Although *V* is an innocent victim of *A*, *V* and *IS* do not stand as comparable parties in IS2 because *V* is a victim of *A* and a victimizer of *IS*, but *IS* is a victim of both *A* and *V*. *V* has an obligation not to violate *IS*'s sovereignty for her own benefit in IS2.

This account of self-defense relies heavily on the significance of the victim's sovereignty and equal standing in order to justify defensive force. At first glance, this theory might appear to call into question the justification of the exercise of defensive force by seriously impaired victims. That is, if an individual suffers substantial impairment of the psychological capacities that qualify one for equal standing in the public domain and sovereignty in the nonpublic domain, does this failure to qualify for equal standing and sovereignty undermine the justification for the use of defensive force by those individuals?

Suppose, for example, that the fully culpable *A* attempts to molest the moderately retarded *V* as she walks home from the park after a softball game. As *A* grabs *V* and attempts to pull her into his car, *V* hits *A* with her softball bat and runs away, leaving *A* lying on the ground with a fractured kneecap. Set aside two plausible but inadequate approaches. First, one might argue that *V* would lack the capacities required for criminal responsibility and, thus, that she would qualify for an excuse. *V* might qualify for an excuse, but this response fails to address the question regarding the justification of her actions, and it leaves open the possibility that she might be liable in tort. Second, one might argue that *V*'s conduct is justified by a simple balancing of harms to concrete interests in that *A*'s attempt to force *V* into his car creates a risk of death or serious bodily injury. This balancing of harms to concrete interests might suffice to justify *V*'s use of force, but insofar as it frames the assault as one that threatens only concrete interests, it understates the severity of the attack. This approach treats *V* as merely a repository for concrete interests, suggesting that her incompetence disqualifies her from any standing other than that of a sentient being.

V's impairment prevents her from engaging in the process of practical reasoning to a level of competence that would enable her to participate fully in the public domain as an equal and to exercise sovereignty over self-regarding decisions in the nonpublic domain. This impairment might justify the state in finding her incompetent to stand trial or not criminally responsible if she were charged with a crime. Similarly, it might justify a court's decision to declare her incompetent for person and property and to appoint a guardian. For each specific legal purpose, a court must determine whether *V*'s impairment renders her incompetent or not responsible by the criteria established for that particular legal function.

Although *V*'s impairment can justify the state in subjecting her to treatment for specific purposes that departs from the manner in which it must treat unimpaired citizens, it does not justify the state in depriving her of protection under law. *V*'s impairment justifies state intrusion for the purpose of protecting her interests precisely because her interests remain worthy of state protection, despite her inability to pursue them independently. *A*'s attack on the incompetent *V* violates her standing as one who retains a domain of protected interests that commands restraint from other citizens and protection from the state. If the state refused to prosecute, convict, and punish those who committed criminal offenses against *V*, it would ratify the violations of her standing represented by those offenses. Similarly, if the state refused to recognize *V*'s standing to defend her protected interests in the absence of immediate state assistance, it would acquiesce in A's violation of V's standing.

In summary, self-defense must be construed in light of the broader political philosophy underlying the legal system. In a liberal society that respects the individual's standing as a citizen and right to self-determination, any culpable criminal conduct infringes on the victim's concrete interests and violates her sphere of self-determination as well as her standing in the public jurisdiction. The aggressor imputes an unjustified imbalance of standing by culpably violating the victim's protected domain, and according to a political philosophy that vests fundamental value in the individual's right to self-determination, any violation of standing constitutes an injury to a fundamental interest. Liberal principles of political morality justify the victim in exercising any force necessary, therefore, to defend her protected domain against the culpable aggressor. She has no obligation to observe rules of proportion or retreat regarding the aggressor. She must not violate the standing of an innocent party, however, and she must retreat rather than injure an innocent aggressor or third party. She has no obligation to allow an innocent aggressor to injure her and no justification for shifting the threat from herself to an innocent third party. Under certain circumstances, one can justify shifting lesser and compensable injuries.

3.5   Self-defense as Morally Justifiable Law

Some critics might find this position wanting for at least two reasons. First, this theory apparently allows a victim to kill an apple thief.[58] By rejecting the principle of proportionality as a limit on the victim's exercise of force against culpable aggressors, this position allows severe violence when it is the only available means of preventing relatively minor transgressions. In addition to raising intuitive doubts, this conflicts with predominant law, which establishes a requirement of rough proportionality by establishing a series of rules for the use of deadly and nondeadly force in response to various types of threats to person or property.[59] Second, it may make unreasonable demands of impartiality in cases of innocent aggressors, shields, or bystanders. It may seem intuitively unreasonable to hold, for example, that victims are not justified in protecting their lives at the expense of innocent parties. Can we realistically require such sacrifice to spare strangers? This section addresses the first objection, and Chapter 5 addresses the second in the context of the discussion of duress and other difficult cases from Chapter 2.

Consider the common intuitive response to the contention that one may justifiably kill an apple thief. Envision A stealing an apple from V and V shooting

---

58 Rethinking at 871. Certain variations of the apple thief cases fall under self-defense or defense of property. Fletcher addresses these issues together as necessary defense, and the MPC addresses them in related provisions at §§ 3.04, 06.

59 MPC at §§ 3.04–06.

A because it is the only available means of preventing the theft. It seems likely that most people will imagine *V* as a farmer or vender and *A* as a child grabbing the apple and running away with it. If *A* is a child, however, the culpability condition is not met or, at least, it is in question. On the view advanced here, therefore, *V* should treat the case as one involving an innocent aggressor. If we replace the child with an adult, why would an adult engage in such activity? The most probable answer seems to be that this particular adult needs the apple very badly; that is, *A* is starving. If *A* is starving, however, the culpability condition again comes into question. When we fully describe the apparently counterintuitive cases, *A* is likely to take on characteristics that render the transgression less than fully culpable due to incompetence or circumstantial pressure.

Now complete the story carefully to establish a fully innocent victim, a fully culpable aggressor, and conditions that render the shooting necessary to stop the theft. Suppose *V* is an elderly farmer who grows apples in an orchard and sells them at the local market. *A* is the local bully who walks up to the farmer's stall at the market and takes the apple. When the farmer says, "Stop, that is my apple," the bully responds, "Tough, old lady, what are you going to do about it?" The farmer, who is old, frail, and less than arm's length away from the bully takes a gun from under her apron and shoots him.[60] Does this victim shooting this apple thief provide the intuitively clear case of an immoral act that we usually accept as an intuitive counterexample? When completed with details that render *A* fully culpable and the shooting actually necessary to stop the culpable violation of *V*'s sovereignty without submitting *V* to additional risk, it does not seem counterintuitive to say that *V* was justified.

Law, however, cannot adopt to each individual case and detailed hypothetical. The role of law requires that legal rules prohibit or justify relatively broad categories of conduct. The principle of legality mandates that "conduct is not criminal unless forbidden by law which gives advance warning that such conduct is criminal."[61] Penal statutes must take the form of relatively broad proscriptions or exceptions that provide notice, address an unpredictable variety of factual circumstances, and allow relatively consistent application across time and circumstances. These rules represent the conventional public morality of the society at a level of generality sufficient to reinforce that morality, guide individual conduct in conformity with the law, and guide decisions of officials in the enforcement of the law.

Officials who make and enforce the law must consider error preference, just as individual citizens must. A general rule of law allowing citizens to apply as

---

60 The significance of the description of *V* as "frail and less than arm's length away" is not that *V* was afraid she would be attacked, but rather that she could not take out the gun and use it only as a threat because *A* could easily take it from her; i.e., doing so would have put *V* at increased risk. Recall the discussion of the priority of sovereignty at the levels of harm and risk in § 3.4.
61 Criminal Law at § 3.1.

much force as necessary to prevent culpable violations of their sovereignty would call upon individuals in highly stressful situations to make two complex determinations with little or no opportunity for evidence gathering or reflection. They would have to make instant appraisals of culpability and necessity. The rough rule of proportion represented by the dominant contemporary approach to the justified use of defensive force can be understood as an attempt to guide these decisions according to the moral principles presented here with adjustments for practical limitations and defensible error preferences.

The MPC allows defensive force when it is immediately necessary to prevent an aggressor from using unlawful force. The code limits the use of deadly force, however, to situations in which it is necessary to prevent the aggressor from subjecting her to deadly force, kidnapping, or compelled sexual intercourse.[62] Although the code does not require retreat before using nondeadly force in self-defense, it does prohibit the use of deadly force when safe retreat is available. This retreat requirement does not apply, however, when the attack that justifies self-defense with deadly force occurs in the victims's dwelling or place of work.[63] The commentaries do not provide a comprehensive justification for these rules regarding proportionality and retreat, but they suggest that the rationale for both is primarily consequentialist in that they represent a decision to accept some relatively minor injuries and violations of rights in order to avoid loss of life. These comments assert that protecting human life enjoys a high priority among societal values, and they represent this value as the cornerstone of a lesser-harms rationale.[64]

A strictly consequentialist approach based on a preference for lesser concrete harms would apply proportionality and retreat requirements to all applications of force in self-defense unless there were good reasons to think that other considerations such as deterrence would support different rules as promoting lesser harm in the long run. Fletcher's theory, in contrast, would allow any force necessary to repel the aggression without regard for proportion or retreat because "right need never yield to wrong."[65]

The approach advanced in this chapter explains these requirements in a more satisfactory manner than either Fletcher's theory or the lesser-harms rationale apparently advocated in the commentaries. It does so by appealing to the primary importance of personal sovereignty adjusted for the necessary generalization of legal rules and a preference for nonfatal errors. The argument advanced in Section 3.4 contends that the innocent victim is justified in exercising any force necessary to repel a culpable aggressor without regard for pro-

---

62 MPC at § 3.04. The issue regarding necessity versus belief in necessity has been addressed *supra* § 2.4.
63 *Id.* at § 3.04(2)(b).
64 *Id.,* comments at 47–8, 52–7.
65 Rethinking at 865.

portion or retreat. In order to avoid tragic errors, however, a law based on such a rationale could require safe retreat before exercising deadly force. Such a rule would qualify the practical priority of sovereignty in order to prevent fatal errors produced by inaccurate judgments of necessity or culpability.

This account does not endorse the high priority for protecting human life without regard for culpability that the MPC commentaries suggest. Rather, the priority accorded the protection of human life varies according to culpability, and an innocent person's right to self-determination takes priority in principle over the culpable aggressor's life when deadly force is necessary to protect the sovereignty of the innocent victim. It is not clear, however, that the code consistently endorses the priority for protection of life asserted in the commentaries. The MPC allows deadly force in self-defense when necessary to prevent kidnapping or compelled sexual intercourse. The code's authors may have considered these crimes to be among those that carried the most serious risk of deadly injury. It is at least as plausible to contend, however, that the severity of these crimes lies in the extreme degree to which they deprive the victims of the opportunity to exercise their right to self-determination. Offenders who commit these crimes exercise a degree of physical control over their victims that almost completely deprives them of personal discretion. By doing so, these crimes strike at the heart of the fundamental value for individual sovereignty.

Similarly, the dwelling-place exception to the retreat rule recognizes the importance of the sovereign person's ability to retain control of the single place in the world that is most clearly his or her own, not necessarily in the sense that the individual holds title to it, but rather in the sense that it is the place in which that person's decisions and actions are least susceptible to intrusion from the requirements of others.[66] Although a small minority of jurisdictions recognize a cohabitant exception that requires individuals to retreat before exercising deadly force when attacked in their own homes by cohabitants, most do not.[67] The liberal theory explains why location in the home carries special legal protection for the defendant but not for the attacking cohabitant. As a protected domain in which the autonomous individual is shielded from unnecessary intrusion by government or other individuals, the home provides the opportunity for each to exercise sovereignty and develop the autonomous virtues through the pursuit of personal projects and central relationships. Individuals who defend themselves from attacks in their homes protect this important function, but assailants, including cohabitants, extend beyond their own sphere of sovereignty and violate that of the victim in a manner that creates a particularly salient threat to the victim's autonomy. Thus, those who exercise defensive

---

66 This explanation does not address the workplace exception nearly as satisfactorily, but the MPC is equivocal about the legitimacy of that exception. MPC at § 3.04 and comments at 55–7.
67 Criminal Law at § 5.7(f).

force in their homes injure only the concrete interests of their assailants in conditions in which that injury is necessary in order to repulse a particularly severe assault upon their sovereignty.

In short, this analysis can accommodate the intuitively plausible proportionality and retreat requirements of the MPC without sacrificing the principled priority of individual sovereignty over the balancing of concrete harms.[68] These requirements represent practical qualifications of the basic principles, and they are grounded in error preference, the formal properties of law, and plausible hypotheses regarding human propensity to err.[69]

Arguably, the law ought to be revised to remove these rough rules of proportionality and retreat from the substantive standards. On this view, it would be more consistent with the underlying moral principles to legalize any force necessary to defend oneself from culpable attack without exposing oneself to undue risk. Procedural devices such as the burden of persuasion could address these matters of error preference by requiring that the defendant carry that burden by showing that the force used was necessary in light of the risk in the circumstances. Addressing error preference procedurally would enhance the expressive function of the criminal law by allowing formulation of the substantive provisions in a manner that more nearly approximated the conventional public morality represented by the criminal law. Resolution of this issue extends beyond the scope of this book because it depends partially on empirical hypotheses regarding the likely effects of such procedural rules.

3.6 Conclusion

The moral justification of self-defense reflects broad underlying principles of public morality. In a liberal society that vests fundamental value in the individual's right to self-determination and recognizes each sovereign person's equal

---

68 Some statutes limit self-defense (or deadly force) to cases in which *V* is threatened with imminent harm. The MPC does not require a threat of imminent harm, but it does require that the defensive force be immediately necessary to prevent the threatened harm. MPC at § 3.04(1). The MPC's position is consistent with the position advanced in this chapter because force that is not immediately necessary may not be necessary at all, given *V*'s fallibility in predicting future events. Recall, however, that *V* would not be required to postpone defensive force against *A* if doing so would increase the risk to *V*. It would not be consistent with the position advanced here for the law to require imminence of harm because such a provision would preclude defensive force necessary to protect sovereignty merely because some delay would occur between the opportunity to exercise force and the unjustified injury. It is conceivable that an imminence requirement might be defensible as a concession to error preference similar to that which grounds the rough proportionality rules. It seems unlikely, however, that an imminence rule would serve this purpose more effectively than the "immediately necessary" clause. *See infra* § 4.4.2.

69 The MPC's requirement that victims refrain from using deadly force when they can retreat in complete safety applies in relatively few cases if it is interpreted as written. Only rare circumstances will place a person in serious danger of unlawful attack, yet allow retreat with complete safety.

standing, any culpable criminal conduct infringes on the victim's concrete interests and violates her sphere of sovereignty. The aggressor imputes inequality of standing by culpably violating the victim's protected domain, and in a liberal society any violation of sovereignty constitutes an injury to a fundamental interest. The victim may exercise any force necessary, therefore, to protect her sphere of self-determination against an aggressor whose culpable conduct extends beyond his own protected domain. She has no obligation to observe rules of proportion or retreat against an aggressor, but she must consider the interests of innocent aggressors or shields and must not violate the sovereignty of an innocent party.

Certain common legal provisions requiring retreat or rough proportionality may be justifiable as qualifications of the basic moral principles in light of the formal properties of law, defensible error preferences, and reasonable hypotheses regarding human propensity to err. These provisions should remain open to revision, however, if evidence either undermines the empirical hypotheses that support them or demonstrates that procedural devices can adequately address these considerations.

Certain difficult cases remain because some actors exercise force in circumstances that deviate from the standard form demonstrated by Mother Beneficence and Dudley. In some of these cases, the use of force seems intuitively to be justified, yet it remains difficult to accommodate under reasonable legal rules of self-defense. Others involve circumstances that seem to justify neither the actors' exercise of force nor their punishment. Cases of the latter type arise, for example, when A threatens V with severe harm in circumstances in which V can prevent that harm only by killing A and innocent hostages. On the analysis advanced in Section 3.4, V is justified in killing A but not in killing the innocent parties. Yet, some people will find it unreasonable to hold V liable to criminal sanctions if she defends herself by causing the death of A and the hostages. Although traditional common law excused some of these defendants under the doctrine of *se defendendo,* this approach has proven difficult to explain and justify.

Chapter 4 examines a series of contentious cases involving the exercise of defensive force by battered women against their batterers. Some of these cases raise difficult issues regarding the interpretation and application of the underlying principles of political morality as embodied in legal justification defenses. Chapter 5 addresses the defense of duress in the context of a series of difficult and related cases raised in Chapters 2 through 4 that seem to challenge the traditional distinction between justification and excuse.

4

Self-defense and Battered Women

Chapter 2 advances an account of the general category of justification defenses as addressing conduct that fulfills all material elements of an offense definition but does not warrant condemnation by the standards of the fully articulated conventional public morality. Chapter 3 completes the normative framework by providing substantive moral principles, and it interprets self-defense as a justification defense in a legal system representing liberal principles of political morality. Chapter 4 applies this analysis to a set of cases that have been particularly troubling to accommodate in a satisfactory manner through the application of ordinary self-defense doctrine. These cases address claims of self-defense by battered women who have exercised deadly force against their mates who have battered them.[1]

Although these cases raise a variety of complex issues, the emphasis on expert testimony regarding the battered woman syndrome calls particular attention to the significance of the defendants' mental states for the distinction between justification and excuse. Despite the focus of justification defenses on categories of conduct that are exempted from general prohibitory norms, many justification provisions require reasonable belief regarding the justificatory conditions rather than their actual occurrence. These battered women's cases often emphasize the putative relevance of the battered woman's syndrome to the reasonableness of the defendants' beliefs regarding the necessity of defensive force. By virtue of this emphasis on the defendants' psychological processes, these cases deviate from the standard form of self-defense in a manner that requires clarification of the parameters of and the justification for contemporary self-defense provisions as specific justification defenses.

---

1 *See supra* § 1.2.2.

Although expert testimony regarding the battered woman syndrome has gained wide acceptance in the courts, the empirical foundation and legal significance of this syndrome remain obscure.[2] The judicial opinions and the commentary demonstrate the practical significance of rigorous theoretical analysis of criminal law doctrine. Much of the doctrinal and applied controversy regarding these cases arises directly from the failure of legislatures and courts to maintain a clear and consistent formulation of important conceptual issues, including the distinction between justification and excuse.

This chapter examines the empirical support for the battered woman syndrome and the relationship between the syndrome and self-defense doctrine in order to establish the appropriate interpretation and integration of these clinical and legal frameworks in circumstances in which battered women exercise deadly force against their batterers. This analysis pursues both practical and theoretical agendas. Practically, it examines the appropriate role of evidence regarding the syndrome and the battering relationship in these cases. Theoretically, it addresses several controversial concerns arising in the theory of self-defense doctrine and in the broader theory of justification defenses. Finally, it demonstrates the importance of these theoretical considerations in resolving the applied questions that become particularly cogent when battered women exercise deadly force against their batterers.

Section 4.1 briefly describes the most common type of contemporary self-defense provision and the differences between this formulation and the interpretation of self-defense endorsed in Chapter 3. Section 4.2 briefly describes the battered woman syndrome and its putative relevance to self-defense, and Section 4.3 reviews and evaluates empirical research regarding the battered woman syndrome. Section 4.4 analyzes the relevance of the syndrome for the common contemporary provisions formulated in terms of "reasonable belief." Section 4.5 considers these cases and the putative relevance of the syndrome under the approach to self-defense developed in this book, and Section 4.6 concludes the chapter.

4.1　Self-defense Doctrine

The parameters and variations of contemporary self-defense provisions are discussed extensively elsewhere. Roughly, individuals may exercise force in self-defense only when they reasonably believe that doing so is necessary to protect themselves from the imminent use of unlawful force by others.[3]

---

2 Holly Maguigan, *Battered Women and Self-defense: Myths and Misconceptions in Current Reform Proposals,* 140 U. Pa. L. Rev. 379, 452 (1991); Elizabeth M. Schneider, *Describing and Changing: Women's Self-defense Work and the Problem of Expert Testimony on Battering,* 9 Women's Rts. L. Rep. 195, 200–1 (1986).

3 Criminal Law at § 5.7; Defenses at §§ 131, 132.

Most jurisdictions impose a proportionality requirement by limiting deadly defensive force to circumstances in which the actor reasonably believes it necessary to defend against the imminent use of unlawful force threatening death or serious bodily injury.[4] Some jurisdictions adopt the MPC provision requiring only belief, rather than reasonable belief, and others limit the defense to cases of actual necessity, disregarding entirely the defendants' beliefs regarding that necessity.[5] The MPC imports a reasonableness requirement, however, by allowing liability for negligent or reckless homicide for those who exercise deadly defensive force on the basis of negligently or recklessly held beliefs about the necessity of using such force.[6] A large majority of jurisdictions require reasonable belief in the necessity of exercising deadly force, either explicitly or through provisions similar to those of the MPC.[7]

Although some jurisdictions require retreat before exercising deadly defensive force, the majority do not, and those that do usually provide a dwelling-place exception for persons who are attacked in their own homes.[8] Thus, for most cases of self-defense by battered women, involving attacks occurring in the home, the defendant has no duty to retreat.[9] The imminence requirement takes several forms. Some jurisdictions require an imminent attack, while others require an immediate attack or that the defensive force be immediately necessary.[10]

The analysis of self-defense contained in the previous two chapters and this one differs from this mainstream approach in two important respects. First, it interprets any justification defense, including self-defense, as requiring actual necessity rather than belief or reasonable belief in the necessity to engage in the ordinarily criminal activity. Putative self-defense involving a mistaken belief in the necessity of defensive force would provide an excuse rather than a justification, and it would require a nonculpable, rather than a reasonable, mistake.[11] Second, self-defense would include no proportionality requirement in principle, although self-defense law might incorporate a proportionality provision as a concession to error preference. Consistent with the contemporary majority rule, it would not require retreat.[12]

---

4 Criminal Law at § 5.7(b); Defenses at § 131(d).
5 MPC at § 3.04(1); Defenses at §§ 121(c), 184(a), (b).
6 MPC at § 3.09.
7 Criminal Law at §§ 5.7(b), (c).
8 MPC at § 3.04(2)(b)(ii)(1); *id.* at § 5.7(f). Only a small minority of jurisdictions recognize a cohabitant exception to the dwelling-place exception.
9 Maguigan, *supra* note 2, at 419–20.
10 Criminal Law at § 5.7(d); Defenses at § 131(c); *id.* at 414–16.
11 *See supra* § 2.4 and *infra* § 4.5.
12 *See supra* §§ 3.4, 3.5.

4.2   The Battered Woman Syndrome and Self-defense

4.2.1   The Battered Woman Syndrome

The dominant conception of the battered woman syndrome as described in court opinions and by commentators is that advanced by Lenore Walker.[13] It includes interpersonal and intrapersonal components. The interpersonal component takes the form of the cycle of violence, which reportedly consists of a three-part repetitive pattern of interaction consisting of periods of gradual tension building, acute violence, and loving contrition. During the third phase the batterer apologizes for the acute violence and promises that it will not recur. Although courts and commentators describe all three phases, some battering relationships include only part of the cycle.[14] Repeated episodes of abuse within an ongoing relationship constitute the only common interpersonal factor across all cases.

Courts and commentators have generally emphasized the intrapersonal component of the syndrome when explaining the significance of the syndrome for these cases. They contend that the recurring cycle of violence promotes a predictable set of psychological responses in the victims of battering. This set includes most prominently depression, decreased self-esteem, and learned helplessness. This last trait consists of a perception of oneself as helpless to alter the battering relationship. People who suffer learned helplessness reportedly perceive themselves as having little or no ability to affect their own lives in general or the battering in particular. Courts and commentators have emphasized the significance of learned helplessness in explaining the relevance of expert testimony regarding the syndrome to claims of self-defense.[15]

For the sake of clarity and consistency I follow the common practice of the courts and commentators in reserving "battered woman syndrome" or "the syndrome" for the set of intrapersonal psychological characteristics including depression, decreased self-esteem, and learned helplessness. I refer to the interpersonal pattern involving repeated episodes of abuse within an ongoing relationship as the "battering relationship" or the "pattern of battering."

---

13 Lenore Walker, The Battered Women Syndrome (New York: Springer Pub. Co., 1984); Lenore Walker, The Battered Woman (New York: Harper & Row, 1979); State v. Kelly, 478 A.2d 364, 369–73 (N.J. 1984). *Kelly* is often cited as the leading case addressing the relevance of the syndrome for self-defense, so I use it to illustrate the most commonly accepted view.
14 State v. Kelly, 478 A.2d 364, 371 (N.J. 1984); Kit Kinports, *Defending Battered Women's Self-defense Claims,* 67 Or. L. Rev. 393, 397 (1988); Battered Woman Syndrome, *id.* at 95–7.
15 State v. Kelly, 478 A.2d 364, 377 (N.J. 1984); People v. Torres, 488 N.Y.S.2d 358, 361–2 (Sup. 1985); State v. Allery, 682 P.2d 312, 315–16 (Wash. 1984); Battered Woman Syndrome, *supra* note 13, at 86–94, 147; Kinports, *id.* at 398, 416; Stephen J. Schulhofer, *The Gender Question in Criminal Law,* 7 Soc. Phil. & Pol'y 105, 119–22 (1990).

4.2.2   *The Putative Relevance of the Battered Woman Syndrome to Self-defense*

Courts and commentators have argued that expert testimony regarding battered woman syndrome provides juries with important information regarding several aspects of self-defense. Although commentators disagree about the relative frequency of confrontation and nonconfrontation cases, they agree that some cases involve circumstances in which the defendants exercise violence in the absence of an imminent overt attack. Some contend that expert testimony regarding the syndrome explains how these defendants could reasonably believe that attacks were forthcoming and that defensive force was necessary despite the absence of immediate violence. Some courts and commentators discuss a special ability to perceive subtle clues of forthcoming violence as part of the syndrome, arguing that this aspect of the syndrome renders the perception of imminent violence reasonable despite the lack of external indicators accessible to most people.[16]

Some extend this reasoning to the issue of deadly force, arguing that the syndrome explains why these battered women reasonably believed deadly force to be necessary. According to this line of reasoning, the special capacity to perceive forthcoming violence absent overt indicators also enables these battered women to reasonably foresee that the violence will be of such severity as to justify the use of deadly force in self-defense. Thus, those who suffer the syndrome can reasonably believe that deadly defensive force is necessary in circumstances in which such a belief would not appear reasonable to others. This argument concludes that expert testimony regarding the syndrome can explain to the jury the manner in which the syndrome renders reasonable these beliefs.[17]

Some advocate expert testimony as relevant to the credibility of the defendants' testimony. Many cases involve such intense and prolonged patterns of abuse that many jurors might doubt the defendants' credibility. These jurors might conclude that the defendants must be exaggerating the abuse because no one would have remained in the relationship if abuse such as they describe had actually occurred.[18] Such doubts might then lead the jurors to generally discount the defendants' testimony. Courts and commentators contend that expert testimony regarding the battered woman syndrome and especially learned helplessness can correct this tendency to discount the defendants' testimony by enabling the jurors to understand that the defendants could have remained in

---

16 State v. Kelly 478 A.2d 364, 377–8 (N.J. 1984); People v. Torres, 488 N.Y.S.2d 358, 361–2 (Sup. 1985); Kinports, *supra* note 14, at 416.

17 *Kelly id.; Torres id.*

18 State v. Gallegos, 719 P.2d 1268, 1271–2 (N.M.App. 1986); State v. Norman, 378 S.E.2d 8, 9–11 (N.C. 1989); State v. Allery, 682 P.2d 312, 313 (Wash. 1984).

these relationships for extended periods despite severe and frequent abuse. These witnesses explain that defendants who suffer learned helplessness either fail to perceive available alternatives to the relationship or are unable to exercise these options. Thus, learned helplessness supports the credibility of these defendants by rendering plausible their testimony that they remained in battering relationships for extended periods despite enduring severe abuse.[19]

Some endorse testimony regarding the syndrome as relevant to the claim that battered women are unable to leave the relationship. Defendants might advance this argument for two purposes. The first is the variation of the credibility argument that depends on the contention that these defendants remained because they were unable to leave. Battered woman syndrome, particularly learned helplessness, explains the defendants' inability to leave their relationships earlier, and, thus, it renders credible the defendants' testimony that they did not leave despite the extended pattern of severe abuse.[20] Second, defendants might also offer this argument in order to address the necessity requirement in self-defense doctrine. Some jurors might conclude that the defendants' use of defensive force was not necessary because they could have avoided the danger by leaving the battering relationships. The defendants offer expert testimony regarding learned helplessness to explain why they were unable to leave the relationship, and, thus, that defensive force was the only remaining method of self-protection.[21]

4.3   Battered Woman Syndrome Research

Cases and commentators rely heavily on Walker's 1979 and 1984 books. The 1979 book contains a description of the battered woman syndrome as derived from Walker's clinical observation over an extended series of clinical cases. The syndrome formulated in this book provides the basis for the 1984 book, which reports a process of self-report data collection designed to validate and refine knowledge of the syndrome. Walker interprets these data as strong support for the syndrome as she describes it.[22] A more complete review of Walker's research and a series of related studies has been provided elsewhere; this section provides only a brief summary of that review.[23]

Walker's earlier hypotheses about the reactions of battered women to the experience of battering described these women as having low self-esteem,

---

19 State v. Kelly, 478 A.2d 364, 375 (N.J. 1984); Kinports, *supra* note 14, at 398.
20 State v. Kelly, 478 A.2d 364, 375 (N.J. 1984); Kinports, *supra* note 14, at 400.
21 State v. Hodges, 716 P.2d 563, 570 (Kan. 1986); State v. Kelly, 478 A.2d 364, 372, 377 (N.J. 1984); Kinports, *supra* note 14, at 416.
22 Battered Woman Syndrome, *supra* note 13.
23 Robert F. Schopp, Barbara J. Sturgis, & Megan Sullivan, *Battered Woman Syndrome, Expert Testimony, and the Distinction between Justification and Excuse,* 1994 Univ. Ill. L. Rev. 45, 53–64. Barbara J. Sturgis wrote the original draft of this section for that paper.

holding traditional attitudes about the role of women, being the keepers of the peace in the marriage, suffering from severe stress reactions, and having a history of childhood violence and sex-role stereotyping.[24] She also hypothesized that battered women suffer from learned helplessness. Learned helplessness is a concept derived from animal studies in which dogs were subjected to noncontingent aversive stimuli and later failed to take advantage of readily apparent opportunities to escape the aversive situation. Walker posited that the inability of battered women to control the violence in the battering relationship would produce learned helplessness, thus explaining why many women remain in the battering relationship when they might have left. Walker initially understood learned helplessness as including an external locus of control (the tendency to see one's life as controlled by forces outside oneself) and depression.[25] Walker developed the cycle theory of violence to further explain the battered woman's situation and to augment learned helplessness in explaining why battered women remain in battering relationships.

As Walker refined the theory, she correlated the battering relationship with a set of factors including traditional attitudes toward the role of women, external locus of control, low self-esteem, and depression intended to explain the behavior of battered women within the relationship. She reaffirmed the notion that both learned helplessness and the cycle of violence influence battered women's decisions to remain in battering relationships and reduce their motivation to escape.[26]

Between 1978 and 1981, Walker studied over four hundred women who were or had been in battering relationships.[27] The study included lengthy interviews as well as the administration of psychological scales to measure the various personality characteristics Walker identified as important in understanding battered women.

The data produced by this study did not provide strong support for her hypothesized personality characteristics of battered women. Contrary to hypotheses, the sample did not demonstrate low self-esteem, external locus of control, or traditional views of women's roles. The data provide evidence of significant depression, but depression is relatively common in the general population and especially among women. Depression is not uniquely indicative of battered woman syndrome. Although Walker claims support for her contention that battered women suffer learned helplessness, her data provide very little support for that claim. Walker's measures related to learned helplessness included depression, low self-esteem, external locus of control, and fearful rather than angry

---

24 Battered Woman, *supra* note 13, at 32–5.
25 *Id.* at 48–51. It is often difficult to determine the precise conception of learned helplessness employed by Walker as well as by other commentators and by courts.
26 Battered Woman Syndrome, *supra* note 13, at 75–85.
27 *Id.* at 1–4.

emotional responses. Contrary to hypotheses, the data regarding self-esteem and locus of control were not in the expected direction, and her analysis of current state, relationship, and child learned helplessness revealed minimal differences between those women who remained in the battering relationship and those who had left. Collectively, the data and theoretical foundations of learned helplessness support the proposition that battered women, and especially those who kill their batterers, do *not* suffer learned helplessness at least as well as they support the contention that they do. The data included some evidence for parts of the cycle of violence but provided no clear evidence of the entire cycle as a dominant pattern.[28]

Despite this pattern of data failing to confirm, and in some cases directly undermining the hypotheses, Walker concluded that the data support the cycle of violence and the battered woman syndrome, and courts and commentators have accepted expert testimony regarding the battered woman syndrome as well established.[29] At least one commentator discounts published criticisms of Walker's claims by contending that other sources provide independent support.[30] Other available research, however, provides no strong support for the proposition that the battered woman syndrome is an accurate description of a syndrome that regularly results from battering relationships.

A search revealed no studies investigating Walker's entire battered woman syndrome, including depression, low self-esteem, traditional attitudes toward the female role, external locus of control, and learned helplessness, but studies have addressed various aspects of the syndrome. A number of methodological problems make comparisons across studies difficult. These include varying samples (battered women in shelters versus battered college students), sample selection (usually volunteers), lack of control groups in many of the studies, and widely varying methods of measuring the variables in question (self-report, clinical interview, psychological testing). Even if one assumes that the studies are comparable and measure what they purport to, they do not support the battered woman syndrome as Walker describes it.[31]

Taken together, the data from Walker's study and from the later studies fail to support the hypothesis that battering relationships regularly produce the battered woman syndrome. The data support the contention that battered women suffer from depression and anxiety, and they provide lesser support for the contentions that battered women experience lowered self-esteem and have diffi-

---

28 Schopp, Sturgis, & Sullivan, *supra* note 23, at 53–64.
29 Battered Woman Syndrome, *supra* note 13, at 101, 147–8; State v. Kelly, 478 A.2d 364, 380 (N.J. 1984); Kinports, *supra* note 14, at 396–408. Legislatures have also endorsed the validity and relevance of expert testimony regarding the syndrome. *See, e.g.,* Cal. Evi. Code § 1107 (West Cum. Pocket Part 1993).
30 Kinports, *supra* note 14, at 407.
31 Schopp, Sturgis, & Sullivan, *supra* note 23, at 59–63.

culty with certain types of problem-solving tasks. It is quite possible, however, that depression can account for both the low self-esteem and difficulty with problem solving. The data provide no support for the contentions that battered women have traditional attitudes toward the female role in society or that they demonstrate external locus of control. Battered women were also seen as functioning in the normal range of assertiveness, although not in the battering relationship itself. None of the later studies evaluated Walker's cycle of violence. Taken collectively, the currently available data do not justify the claim that the battered woman syndrome as usually formulated characterizes those who have suffered battering relationships.

The data provide substantial support for the contention that battered women suffer significant depression and anxiety. This elevated level of distress may resemble the pattern of distress suffered by others who experience various types of trauma or ongoing stress.[32] The argument for expert testimony regarding the battered woman syndrome does not rest, however, on the claim that battered women suffer distress. Rather, it requires that they typically suffer a particular syndrome, specific to battered women, that carries special significance for self-defense. The presence of depression, anxiety, or a general distress syndrome does not substantiate this claim.

Perhaps most importantly from the perspective of the criminal courts, learned helplessness has been the aspect of battered woman syndrome most frequently cited as central to claims of self-defense by battered women, yet it draws very little support from the available data. The complete body of work provides neither any clear conception of learned helplessness nor any good reason to believe that it regularly occurs in battered women. Some factors that seem intuitively related to learned helplessness, such as decreased self-esteem and problem-solving skills, are supported by some sources but not by others. In addition, the studies consistently report elevated depression, which may account for these factors. The data consistently fail to support other intuitively plausible indicators of learned helplessness, including traditional gender roles and external locus of control. Collectively, the data reviewed support the proposition that battered women do not suffer learned helplessness at least as well as these data support the claim that they do. Finally, it would be more consistent with the theoretical and empirical foundations of learned helplessness to contend that battered women who kill their batterers differ from those who remain in the battering relationships without killing their batterers precisely because those who kill do *not* manifest learned helplessness.

This review does not preclude the possibilities that one or more battered

32 *See generally* Elaine Hilberman & Kit Munson, *Sixty Battered Women,* 2 Victimology: An Int'l J. 460 (1977–8); Elaine Hilberman, *Overview: The "Wife-Beater's Wife" Reconsidered,* 137 Am. J. Psychiatry 1336 (1980); Beth M. Houskamp & David W. Foy, *The Assessment of Post-traumatic Stress Disorder in Battered Women,* 6 J. Interpersonal Violence 367 (1991).

woman syndromes occur, that some particular battered women suffer such patterns of symptoms, or that future studies will provide strong supporting evidence for such a syndrome. For this reason, the following sections of this chapter assume for the sake of argument that such evidence is forthcoming, and they examine the significance for self-defense by battered women of a syndrome roughly similar to that usually formulated by the courts and commentators. The analysis in these sections demonstrates that the battered woman syndrome bears almost no relevance to these cases. Furthermore, clarification of important conceptual and normative issues regarding self-defense as a justification defense substantially advances the ability of the courts to address these cases satisfactorily.

4.4   The Battered Woman Syndrome and Conventional Self-defense Law

As self-defense provisions are currently framed in the majority of jurisdictions, they require roughly that defendants exercise proportionate force that they reasonably believe necessary to prevent the imminent or immediate use of unlawful force against them. Most of the cases and commentary regarding self-defense by battered women have addressed the relevance of the battered woman syndrome to the defendants' claims of reasonable belief in the necessity of force or to their credibility. These arguments raise a number of complex issues.

4.4.1   *Imminence or Immediacy*

Battered women who exercise force in nonconfrontation situations encounter a threshold difficulty in providing grounds for a reasonable belief that any force was necessary. Most jurisdictions allow self-defense only when necessary to prevent the imminent or immediate use of unlawful force.[33] Some courts and commentators contend that rules requiring an immediate attack create an unfair disadvantage for battered women or for women generally because the reasonableness of the force exercised by these defendants arises from their history with their batterers, but the requirement of an immediate, as opposed to imminent, attack does not allow consideration of these factors. For this reason they advocate provisions requiring imminence rather than immediacy.[34]

This putative distinction regarding relevance of past experience does not characterize the ordinary meanings of "immediate" and "imminence." In ordinary language, both terms refer to the latency between the present and a forthcoming event, and neither addresses the relevance of past events for any judg-

---

33 Criminal Law at § 5.7(d); Defenses at § 131(c).
34 State v. Hodges 716 P.2d 563, 570–1 (Kan. 1986); Maguigan, *supra* note 2, at 499–50.

ment of that latency. "Imminent" means "impending threateningly . . . ready to befall or overtake one; close at hand in its incidence . . . coming on shortly."[35] "Immediate" means "present or next adjacent . . . occurring, accomplished, or taking effect without delay or lapse of time."[36] Both terms describe a relationship between the present and some future event that either occurs instantaneously or follows very shortly. "Imminent" suggests an ominous tone and arguably allows slightly longer latency than "immediate," but both are silent as to the relevance of past events.

Legal authorities define and use these two terms in a manner consistent with ordinary language. *Black's Law Dictionary* defines "immediate" as "present, at once; without delay," while it defines "imminent" as "near at hand; mediate rather than immediate; impending; on the point of happening; threatening; menacing."[37] As with the ordinary language meanings, both terms generally refer to the relationship between the present and some future event, and "imminent" seems to allow somewhat more latency than "immediate." *Black's* specifically defines the meaning of "imminent danger" for purposes of homicide in self-defense in a manner that renders the two terms interchangeable. For that purpose, an "imminent danger" is an "immediate danger, such as must be instantly met."[38] Courts sometimes use "imminent" and "immediate" interchangeably[39] and when interpreting self-defense provisions using either term have accepted evidence of past history as relevant.[40] In short, although some courts and commentators have attributed significance to the selection of "imminent" or "immediate," neither ordinary nor legal usage supports this attribution when the two terms are accurately interpreted. Therefore, I use both terms interchangeably throughout the remainder of this discussion.

4.4.2   *Imminent or Immediately Necessary:*
The Justificatory Foundation

Although the choice between "imminent" and "immediate" carries no significance, courts and commentators sometimes overlook a related and more substantive distinction. *Black's* definition of an imminent danger as an "immediate danger, such as must be instantly met" suggests two different relationships. "Immediate danger" suggests the relationship discussed previously between the time defensive force is exercised and the time the harm defended against is

---

35 1 Oxford English Dictionary at 1380.

36 *Id.* at 1379.

37 Black's Law Dictionary 749, 750, *respectively* (St. Paul, Minn.: West Pub. Co., 6th ed. 1990).

38 *Id.* at 750.

39 State v. Norman, 378 S.E.2d 8, 13 (N.C. 1989); State v. Kelly 478 A.2d 364, 385n23 (N.J. 1984).

40 State v. Gallegos, 719 P.2d 1268, 1270 (N.M.App. 1986) ("immediate"); State v. Allery, 682 P.2d 312, 314–15 (Wash. 1984) ("imminent").

expected to occur; that is, the unlawful aggression must be present or impending when the defensive force is used. In contrast, "such as must be instantly met" addresses the relationship between the time the defensive force is exercised and the time at which it must be exercised in order to prevent the threatened harm. In many cases, these relationships are interchangeable for practical purposes because it is the immediacy of the expected harm that renders immediate the need to exercise defensive force. That is, X must shoot Y now rather than calling the police precisely because Y is about to stab X.

In unusual circumstances, however, these relationships may diverge in that it may be necessary to exercise force now in order to prevent harm that will occur in the more distant future. Consider, for example, the case of the hikers X and Y who engage in a ten-day race across the desert. The only source of water in the desert is a single water hole approximately halfway to the finish line. Each hiker must carry a five-to-six-day supply of water and replenish at the water hole in order to survive the race. During the first few days, X catches Y attempting to sabotage X by changing trail markers and attempting to steal X's compass and water. If successful, each of these efforts would have caused X to die in the desert.

As day five begins, both hikers are almost out of water and must replenish their supplies the next day at the water hole. As Y passes X on the trail on the morning of the fifth day, Y holds up a box of rat poison and says to X, "I'll get you this time; I'll beat you to the water hole, get my water, and poison the rest; You'll never get out of here alive." Both hikers walk all day, but due to a sprained ankle, X can barely keep up with Y. That evening, as X is forced to stop due to the sprained ankle and exhaustion, Y says, "I'll walk all night and get to the water hole by morning." As Y begins to walk away, X, who is unable to continue that night, says, "Wait," but Y walks away in the direction of the water hole. X shoots Y, convinced by Y's prior threats and sabotage that this is the only way to prevent Y from poisoning the water hole the next morning.

Y poses no immediate threat to X because Y will not poison the water until the next morning, and X will not suffer the fatal consequences of the act until a day or two later. Thus, even stipulating that X can prevent Y from killing X only by shooting Y, a statute limiting self-defense to circumstances threatening imminent harm would not include X's force within the scope of the defense. By requiring that the defensive force be "immediately necessary" rather than that the expected unlawful aggression be immediate or imminent, the MPC accommodates these cases by adopting a standard addressing the relation between the time the defensive force is exercised and the time at which it must be used in order to prevent the unlawful harm.[41]

Although the desert hiker case may seem somewhat fanciful, some battered women may encounter realistic circumstances in which this distinction

41 MPC at § 3.04(1); Criminal Law at § 5.7(d).

becomes critical. Assume for the sake of argument that some battered women can accurately predict forthcoming violence from their batterers who are not currently aggressing and that these women will be unable to defend themselves or secure assistance at the time of the future attack. Given these assumptions, if the battered woman is to prevent the forthcoming unlawful harm by the batterer, defensive force in the form of a "preemptive strike" may be immediately necessary during a period when battering is not imminent because the batterer is asleep, distracted, or too intoxicated to attack.

The central question involves the appropriate relationship between the necessity and imminence requirements. A standard allowing defensive force only when it is immediately necessary to prevent unlawful harm treats imminence of harm as a factor regarding necessity. That is, the defensive force is justified only if necessary to prevent an unlawful harm, and the imminence of that unlawful harm contributes to, but does not completely determine, the judgment of necessity. In unusual circumstances such as those confronted by the desert hiker or by some battered women, defensive force may be immediately necessary to prevent unlawful harm, although that harm is not yet imminent. In these cases, imminence of harm does not serve as a decisive factor in the determination of necessity. A standard allowing defensive force only when necessary to prevent an imminent harm, in contrast, treats imminence of harm as an independent requirement for justified force in that the force must be necessary and the unlawful harm must be immediately forthcoming. Such a standard does not allow defensive force necessary to prevent delayed unlawful aggression, even if the present situation represents the last opportunity to prevent such harm.[42]

Given the assumptions stated previously, some battered women defendants fall within the parameters of justified self-defense as measured by standards treating imminence of harm as a factor relevant to necessity but not under standards requiring necessity and imminent harm separately. Legislatures and courts must select one of these relationships between necessity and imminence of harm in adopting and interpreting legal rules. The justification for allowing the exercise of force in self-defense should inform this choice among standards.

Several principles and policies arguably support current self-defense provisions. Each theory offers some justification for allowing innocent victims the use of at least the degree of force necessary to prevent culpable aggressors from causing them a comparable degree of harm. Contemporary theories appeal to the social interests in minimizing harm, protecting the legal order, or favoring right over wrong. Some writers, for example, justify self-defense as minimizing social harm when the interests of assailants are appropriately discounted as compared to those of innocent parties. Others interpret self-defense as a legal device that allows individuals to protect their autonomy and the legal order by

---

42 Robinson argues that necessity entails immediacy, rendering any mention of imminence superfluous. Defenses at § 131(c)(1), (2). Unfortunately, statutes and common law rules do not ordinarily recognize this insight.

preventing illegal assaults when institutional enforcement is not available. By doing so, they correct circumstances in which right would otherwise have to yield to wrong.[43] Chapter 3 advances an account of self-defense supported by the significance of individual sovereignty and equality of standing for liberal principles of political morality.[44]

Due to the general social policies against the private use of force and causing unnecessary harm, each of these theories limits justified self-defense to those circumstances in which it is necessary to achieve the justifying goal or to protect the underlying principle. Thus, one can exercise defensive force to minimize harm or to protect the social order or individual sovereignty only when no nonviolent alternative will achieve that end. This necessity requirement is consistent with each proffered justification for self-defense, and, indeed, some writers interpret necessity as the core of self-defense doctrine.[45] Imminence of harm remains consistent with this theoretical foundation when it serves as a factor regarding judgments of necessity because in most circumstances the judgment that no nonviolent alternative will suffice is more likely to be accurate regarding an imminent harm than a remote one. Imminence of harm can undermine these justificatory theories, however, if it is accepted as an independent requirement of the defense.

Consider, for example, the desert hiker case discussed previously. A statute barring *X,* the victim of the initial aggression, from exercising immediately necessary force in self-defense because the harm was not yet imminent would protect the culpable *Y* at the expense of the innocent *X,* sacrificing an innocent life in order to protect the culpable party. This result would constitute a greater social harm rather than a lesser one when the interests of the culpable party are appropriately discounted. Similarly, *X* would acquiesce in a felony, allowing disruption of the social order, and right would give way to wrong because *Y*'s wrongful conduct would violate *X*'s legitimate claim. Finally, such a standard would protect *Y*'s concrete interests at the expense of *X*'s sovereignty and concrete interests, ratifying *Y*'s violation of *X*'s sovereignty and *Y*'s imputation of lesser standing to *X.* In short, imminence of harm can promote the underlying justifications of self-defense when it serves as a factor to be considered in making judgments of necessity, but it can undermine those justifications if it is accepted as an independent requirement in addition to necessity.

4.4.3   *Learned Helplessness as Disordered Thought and Special Capacity*

This analysis suggests that immediate necessity but not imminence of harm should be considered essential to self-defense claims, including those asserted

---

43 *See supra* § 3.1.
44 *See supra* §§ 3.4, 3.5.
45 Defenses at § 131(c); Rethinking at § 10.5.

by battered women. According to this interpretation, these defendants can justify the exercise of defensive force in nonconfrontation cases if they can demonstrate the ability to accurately perceive when that force becomes immediately necessary to prevent a future attack. Courts and commentators have advocated expert testimony regarding the battered woman syndrome for this purpose.[46]

The discussion of battered woman syndrome as relevant to this issue sometimes takes a rather perplexing turn in that the courts and commentators tend to emphasize the significance of learned helplessness, which they describe both as a distortion of perception and thought and as a special capacity that renders these women's beliefs reasonable by enabling them to accurately predict future attacks in the absence of overt cues recognizable to most people.[47] One court, for example, described those suffering battered woman syndrome as "unable to think clearly" and as suffering "emotional paralysis" and under the "delusion that things will improve."[48] This court also concluded, however, that evidence of the syndrome should be admitted because it would enable the jury to understand the defendant's "acute discriminatory powers" as relevant to her justificatory claim of self-defense.[49]

These sources appeal to the putative special predictive capacity to support the claim that defendants who exercise force in the apparent absence of explicit signs of imminent danger do so with a reasonable belief that the defensive force is immediately necessary. According to this reasoning, although an average juror might not perceive the danger in these situations as described in court, the defendants reasonably and accurately perceived the forthcoming danger and the immediate necessity of defensive violence by virtue of their special capacities.

The perplexing nature of the discussion arises from the apparent tension in describing those who suffer battered woman syndrome in a manner suggesting that this syndrome distorts their perceptions and judgment regarding the battering relationship yet simultaneously provides them with a special capacity to

---

46 People v. Aris, 264 Cal. Rptr. 167, 177 (Cal.App. 4th Dist. 1989) (quoting Lenore Walker as advocating this position); State v. Kelly, 478 A.2d 364, 378 (N.J. 1984) (describing the battered woman as particularly able to predict violence); People v. Torres, 488 N.Y.S.2d 358, 362 (Sup. 1985) (describing "acute discriminatory powers" regarding danger); Kinports, *supra* note 14, at 416, 423–6 (reasonable battered woman can perceive imminent danger when husband is sleeping).

47 State v. Hodges, 716 P.2d 563 (Kan. 1986) *compare* 567 (describing battered women as terror-stricken people whose mental state is distorted, as brainwashed and disturbed persons) *with* 569 (describing battered women as particularly able to accurately predict abuse); State v. Kelly, 478 A.2d 364 (N.J. 1984) *compare* 372 (describing battered woman syndrome as producing psychological paralysis and the belief that the batterer is omnipotent) *with* 378 (describing battered women as particularly able to predict abuse accurately); Kinports, *supra* note 14, at 416–22 (discussing the dispute regarding the notion that battered women suffer a syndrome that renders their beliefs more accurate and reasonable).

48 People v. Torres, 488 N.Y.S.2d 358, 361 (Sup. 1985).

49 *Id.* at 362.

predict events within that relationship with superior accuracy. The mere fact that people suffer certain impairments of perception, thought, or judgment does not preclude the possibility that they might also possess superior capacities for specified tasks. The account of the syndrome as including both impairment and special capacities seems particularly awkward, however, because both involve the accuracy of the battered woman's judgments about the batterer and the battering relationship. At least at first glance, the description of learned helplessness apparently undermines the reasonableness of any beliefs these defendants might have about their batterers or their relationships. In what manner does expert testimony about the battered woman's syndrome, with the impairment identified as learned helplessness, support the claim that these defendants possess a special capacity that grounds reasonable beliefs about forthcoming violence?

4.4.4   Necessary Force: Battered Woman Syndrome or the Pattern of Battering

Assume a particular battered woman does not suffer battered woman syndrome. She has experienced an extended battering relationship, but she has not developed the pattern of psychological characteristics such as depression, decreased self-esteem, and learned helplessness that constitute the syndrome assumed to have been established for the purpose of this section. This woman kills her batterer as he sleeps in a drunken stupor because she fears that he will attack her severely when he regains consciousness. She might plausibly argue that she reasonably believed she would be in severe danger when he awoke because she recognized a pattern of speech and conduct that preceded previous severe beatings. She might contend that the beatings have escalated over the past few months concurrent with his escalating alcohol consumption. She could further testify that she has learned to keep track of his drinking because the beatings have increased in intensity in proportion to the amount he drank, and that on the day in question he had drunk more than she had ever seen him drink in one day.

Alternately, she might provide a much less specific explanation. She might testify that she killed him as he slept because she felt very frightened when he threatened her before he passed out. She has learned to trust her fear, she testifies, because the intensity of the beatings often seemed to reflect the intensity of fear she felt when he threatened her. "I don't know how I can tell," she testifies, "but when I started to shake like that, I always knew it would turn out real bad."

This defendant's testimony presents a plausible claim of reasonable belief on the basis of her extended experience with the batterer.[50] Although the more precise explanation based on the amount he drank and the pattern of escalation provides a more detailed account of the origins of her belief, the second varia-

---

50 Here I address only the belief that an attack was coming, not the issue of legal alternatives to defensive force, which is discussed *infra* § 4.4.7.

tion based only on the intensity of her fear and her experience of severe abuse following more intense fear does not seem implausible. Many people who have lived with another for an extended period learn to recognize or predict the other's moods or conduct without being able to articulate an explanation.

This defendant has experienced an extended pattern of battering and puts forward a plausible claim of reasonable belief that an attack was forthcoming, but her evidence for this claim makes no reference to the battered woman syndrome or any component of that syndrome. Although her claim is plausible, it is not obviously persuasive, and any competent attorney would prefer to support it with additional evidence. It is not at all clear, however, that expert testimony regarding the battered woman syndrome would support the defendant's story. As described, this defendant does not suffer the syndrome. If she did, an expert could testify that she suffered depression, decreased self-esteem, and learned helplessness, but this testimony would not support the contention that she reasonably believed an attack forthcoming because these characteristics do not increase the reliability of her beliefs or the accuracy of her predictions.

Her testimony is plausible not because it is associated with a clinical syndrome but because it describes an ordinary pattern of inductive inference familiar to most people. She reasoned from her prior experience with this person in similar circumstances to an inference regarding his likely conduct the following morning. Although individual behavior is difficult to predict, the best indicators of future violence are past violent behavior by the same person in similar circumstances.[51]

Additional physical evidence or testimony confirming her account would render it more persuasive. Emergency room records might confirm her claim of escalating violence by documenting increasing severity of injuries, for example, or neighbors might testify that her husband had been drinking more heavily recently. Family or friends might be able to testify that they had observed suspicious injuries that seemed to be associated with increased distress. Each of these sources of evidence would confirm her account of the batterer's past conduct, supporting her inference regarding his expected behavior. Compelling evidence confirming her description of his past pattern of behavior in similar circumstances would render her belief regarding the forthcoming attack very reasonable because it would provide exactly the kind of information that ordinary people like the jurors usually rely on in drawing inferences about the likely behavior of other people. This kind of supporting evidence may not be available for defendants who have lived in isolation from friends, families, and medical care. Similarly, those who have successfully concealed the pattern of past abuse from others may not have access to such evidence. These defendants would find it difficult to establish their belief as reasonable because they would

51 John Monahan, *Predicting Violent Behavior* 88–92, 104–5 (Beverly Hills, Calif.: Sage Pub. Co., 1981).

have difficulty confirming the occurrence of the series of past events from which they drew their inference regarding the anticipated attack.

Testimony regarding the battered woman syndrome would not cure this problem, however, because it would describe the defendant's psychological characteristics rather than the series of events that serve to render her inference reasonable. To the extent that expert testimony emphasizes learned helplessness, it portrays the battered woman as unable to accurately perceive and evaluate the batterer, the relationship, and her options, actively undermining the contention that her beliefs regarding these issues were reasonable. That is, such testimony tends to portray her beliefs as the product of the type of psychological impairment known as learned helplessness rather than as a product of past experience, which the jury recognizes as providing good reasons for a belief.

In short, some battered women may well be able to predict forthcoming abuse with sufficient accuracy to support a reasonable belief, but these beliefs are the product of neither a special capacity nor the battered woman syndrome. They reflect an ordinary process of inductive inference from past behavior in similar circumstances. The appropriate supporting evidence involves confirmation of this past behavior, enabling the jury to draw the same reasonable inference. Thus, the critical evidence establishes the past pattern of battering rather than the syndrome. Although this evidence may not always be available, it is the type of evidence that supports the required inference and that lawyers, jurors, and courts are familiar with and likely to understand.

4.4.5   *Reasonable Belief in the Necessity of Deadly Force*

To establish self-defense the battered woman who kills her batterer in a non-confrontation situation must demonstrate not only that she reasonably believed an attack was forthcoming but also that she reasonably believed that deadly force was necessary and proportionate to the impending assault. Standard self-defense doctrine allows the exercise of deadly force only when such force is necessary in order to prevent another from using unlawful deadly force against the actor. Deadly force means force likely to cause death or serious bodily injury. An extended series of cases recognize considerations such as size, gender, and past history with the assailant as relevant to the reasonableness of the decision to exercise deadly force in self-defense. That is, the belief that deadly force was necessary must have been reasonable in light of the information available to the defendant at the time she acted.[52]

A defendant who has experienced an extended battering relationship involv-

---

52 Smith v. U.S., 161 U.S. 85, 88 (1896); State v. Hodges, 716 P.2d 563, 571 (Kan. 1986); Kress v. State, 144 S.W.2d 735, 738–9 (Tenn. 1940); State v. Painter, 620 P.2d 1001, 1004 (Wash.App. 1980); Maguigan, *supra* note 2, at 416–23.

ing serious bodily injury has reasonable grounds to believe that if an attack is forthcoming, it is likely to include the danger of serious injury.[53] Thus, by establishing her reasonable beliefs that an attack was forthcoming and that past attacks by this batterer have included conduct likely to inflict serious bodily injury, the defendant demonstrates the basis for a reasonable belief that deadly force is proportionate to the threat. If, in addition, the defendant's experience provides her with a basis to believe that due to factors such as size, gender, or physical disadvantage she can prevent the batterer from causing her serious bodily injury only by exercising deadly force, then she reasonably believes that deadly force is necessary.

Analogous reasoning applies in confrontation cases in which the defendant exercises deadly force that is apparently disproportionate to the attack. In these cases the defendant can demonstrate a reasonable basis for her belief that defensive force was necessary by presenting evidence that an attack occurred and alternatives were not available, but she may encounter difficulty supporting a reasonable belief that deadly force was necessary and justified if the attack in progress included only nondeadly force. If a battered woman has experienced a pattern of battering in which nondeadly force has escalated during the abuse, however, that history in conjunction with the occurrent nondeadly attack provides a basis for a reasonable belief that deadly force is forthcoming. She can support a reasonable belief in the necessity of exercising deadly defensive force, therefore, by presenting evidence of the occurrent nondeadly force, the past pattern of escalation, and the lack of safe alternatives.[54]

A critic might advocate admitting expert testimony regarding the battered woman syndrome in these cases on the following basis. Evidence of past battering sufficient to support the battered woman's exercise of deadly force in the circumstances would describe severe and repetitive abuse. Thus, it would elicit highly emotional reactions from many ordinary people, including jurors.[55] For this reason, some courts might preclude such evidence as relevant but inadmissible because highly prejudicial.[56] Expert testimony regarding the syndrome should be admitted, such a critic might contend, as the only available means of making the admittedly relevant evidence of past abuse available to the jury.

---

53 Kress v. State, 144 S.W.2d 735, 738–9 (Tenn. 1940) (recognizing the history of battering and the size and gender of the parties as relevant to the justification of the defendant's resorting to deadly force).

54 This reasoning accepts for the sake of argument the proportionality requirement as a legitimate constraint on self-defense. For an argument that it is at best a concession to error preference, *see supra* § 3.5.

55 *See, e.g.,* State v. Gallegos, 719 P.2d 1268, 1271–2 (N.M.App. 1986); State v. Norman, 378 S.E.2d 8, 9–11 (N.C. 1989). Both cases describe egregious patterns of abuse.

56 John Strong et al., McCormick on Evidence § 185 (St. Paul, Minn.: West Pub. Co., 4th ed. 1992).

The response to such a critic has three parts. First, a well-established exception to the general rule against character evidence allows evidence regarding past aggression by the victim in homicide cases when there is controversy regarding who initiated the aggression.[57] This exception, in conjunction with the relevance of the battered woman's past history with the batterer to her reasonable belief in necessity, supports the admissibility of such evidence. Second, I do not contend that all courts currently accept the argument presented in this chapter. As indicated previously, the purpose here is to demonstrate that the basic principles underlying widely accepted self-defense doctrine support the contention that courts *should* allow argument and evidence on the basis endorsed here.

Third, the relative weight of the probative value and prejudicial effect will vary from case to case. If the former outweighs the latter in a particular case, then this evidence of past abuse should be admitted for the reasons already stated. If the prejudicial effect outweighs the probative value in a particular case, then the evidence would not be admissible, but calling it part of a "battered woman syndrome" renders it no less prejudicial and no more probative. Thus, in each case, either the evidence of past abuse should be admitted under ordinary law or it should be precluded as overly prejudicial. Either conclusion depends on the relative weight of the probative and prejudicial effects of the evidence of past abuse without regard to the battered woman syndrome.

4.4.6   *Retreat as a Legal Alternative to Defensive Force*

The availability of safe legal alternatives to defensive force undermines the claim that the exercise of deadly defensive force was necessary. If victims of impending unlawful force can protect themselves through retreat or recourse to institutional resources such as police or the courts, then the private use of force is not necessary. In some circumstances, escape from the dangerous situation provides an alternative means of avoiding the threatened injury. This alternative rarely applies in confrontation cases because jurisdictions requiring retreat limit this duty to circumstances in which one can retreat in safety, and only in rare circumstances would one be able to retreat in safety during an attack.[58]

The opportunity to retreat can undermine the claim that defensive force is strictly necessary in nonconfrontation cases because the defendant with the opportunity to retreat before an attack begins may be able to avoid the threat of harm without exercising force. The account of self-defense advanced in Chapter 3 rejects a duty to retreat as inconsistent with the principles of liberal polit-

---

57 *Id.* at § 193.
58 MPC at § 3.04(2)(b)(ii); Criminal Law at § 5.7(f).

ical morality that provide the foundation for the defense. The majority of American jurisdictions concur with the theory in Chapter 3 on this matter in that they do not require that innocent individuals avoid using force in self-defense if doing so would require that they retreat from a place in which they have a right to stay. Of the minority of jurisdictions that enforce a general duty to retreat before exercising force or deadly force in self-defense, most recognize a dwelling-place exception allowing deadly force without retreat by those who are attacked in their homes.[59] Thus, the dispute regarding whether the battered woman syndrome renders the defendant unable to exercise the alternative of retreat is irrelevant to cases that occur in the home. Regardless of whether she could retreat, there is no legal reason why she *should* do so before using defensive force. Ordinary self-defense doctrine allows one to exercise defensive force, including deadly force, in one's own home when one has no safe alternative except retreat. The theory advanced in Chapter 3 explains and justifies this doctrine, rejects the cohabitant exception, and extends the doctrine to attacks occurring outside the home.[60]

4.4.7   Institutional Legal Alternatives

Available legal alternatives other than retreat may preclude the justified use of force in self-defense. Institutional assistance such as police intervention or restraining orders, for example, undermines the claim that defensive force is necessary provided that assistance is available and effective. Confrontation cases involving an attack in progress would rarely offer an opportunity to resort to these options, but the availability of legal alternatives may become a critical consideration in nonconfrontation cases. The defendant who exercises violence against a batterer who is not battering her at that time must explain why her exercise of force was necessary to prevent an anticipated attack. In order to support the claim that she reasonably believed that her exercise of force was necessary for self-defense, she must demonstrate that she reasonably believed that legal alternatives were either not available or not effective.

Data support this belief as both reasonable and accurate in at least some cases. The history of institutional failure to effectively intervene in ongoing battering relationships has been well documented elsewhere.[61] A comprehen-

---

59 *Id.* Although a few jurisdictions recognize an exception to this exception when the assailant is a cohabitant of the dwelling, most do not.

60 *See supra* § 3.5.

61 *See, e.g.,* Angela Browne, When Battered Women Kill (New York: Free Press, 1987); Stephen Brown, *Police Responses to Wife Beating: Neglect of a Crime of Violence,* J. Crim. Just. 277 (1984); Patricia Eber, *The Battered Wife's Dilemma: To Kill or Be Killed,* 32 Hastings L.J. 895 (1981); Amy Eppler, *Battered Women and the Equal Protection Clause: Will the Constitution Help Them When Police Won't?,* 95 Yale L.J. 788 (1986); Barbara Finesmith, *Police Responses*

sive review of the current availability and effectiveness of such alternatives has recently been reported as well.[62] Here, I only summarize that recent review.

Criminal prosecution and civil protective orders provide appropriate legal responses to battery. Effective intervention through either type of legal action requires that a series of legal actors implement the appropriate substantive law. Criminal prosecution is separate and distinct from a civil protective order, and in all states except New York, a victim of domestic assault may pursue the former while concurrently seeking the latter.[63] Physical assault or threat of assault constitutes a criminal offense in every state, regardless of whether a relationship exists between the victim and assailant. Many additional forms of domestic violence, including sexual assault, destruction or theft of property, kidnapping, and involuntary confinement, violate criminal statutes.

Civil protective orders may include *ex parte* temporary orders of protection, permanent orders, and orders to vacate. In forty-nine out of fifty states, a battered woman can apply for a protective or restraining order against her abuser.[64] A court may issue a temporary order of protection on an emergency basis within a few hours of request, usually after a hearing at which only the victim is present.[65] Many states also provide for orders to vacate whereby a judge requires an abusing spouse to temporarily vacate the home with the aim of allowing time for the resolution of underlying disputes.[66]

Although the criminal and civil branches of the legal system provide appropriate legal institutions to which battered women can and should appeal, the statutes, policies, and practices of these branches may vary significantly among and within jurisdictions. Thus, the quality and predictability of protection available varies substantially across battered women and their circumstances.[67] Defendants for whom such alternatives are not available can present a strong argument that defensive force is necessary despite the lack of an immediate attack. That is, if defendants have a basis in experience for anticipating a future attack, no duty to retreat, no access to legal alternatives, and good reason to believe that they will be unable to effectively protect themselves at the time of the attack, then they might reasonably believe that immediate defensive force

---

to Battered Women: A Critique and Proposals for Reform, 14 Seton Hall L. Rev. 74 (1983); Kinports, *supra* note 14.

62 Schopp, Sturgis, & Sullivan, *supra* note 23, at 76–87. Megan Sullivan wrote the original draft of that section of that paper.

63 National Institute of Justice, Civil Protection Orders Legislation, Current Court Practice and Enforcement (1990).

64 *Id.*

65 Lisa G. Lerman & Naomi R. Cahn, *Legal Issues in Violence toward Adults, in* Case Studies in Family Violence 73, 76–7 (Robert T. Ammerman & Michael Hersen eds., New York: Plenum Press, 1991).

66 National Institute of Justice, *supra* note 63.

67 *Id.* at 77–82 (the criminal branch) and 83–7 (the civil branch).

is necessary to protect themselves from the unlawful use of force by their batterers. This argument leaves open important questions regarding cases in which
the defendant was aware of available legal alternatives or in which her belief
regarding the lack of legal alternatives was unreasonable. These questions
require consideration of additional principles of criminal law, and, therefore, I
address them later in Section 4.5.4.

4.4.8   The Pattern of Battering as Support for Reasonable Belief

As the prior sections indicate, the defendant's claim that she reasonably
believed that the use of deadly force was necessary despite the absence of an
occurrent attack requires a broad body of evidence addressing the indicators of
forthcoming violence, the severity of past abuse, the relative size and strength
of the parties, the location of the violence, and the availability of legal assistance. Defendants' ability to secure and present this evidence may vary widely
according to the circumstances of the events, the legal assistance available, and
the willingness of others to testify. In order to demonstrate the reasonableness
of her belief that deadly force was necessary, the defendant must provide the
jury with evidence describing the events and information on which she based
the belief. By doing so, she enables the jury to draw the same inference that she
drew from these events.

Expert testimony regarding depression, decreased self-esteem, learned helplessness, or other psychological characteristics of the defendant does not
advance this enterprise. Such testimony may assist the jury in understanding
the defendant, but it does not inform them regarding the events and information
that would lead the jurors to the inference of necessity, enabling them to understand her corresponding inference as reasonable. The critical evidence establishing the defendant's reasonable belief in the necessity of deadly force must
demonstrate the pattern of battering and the lack of available legal alternatives
to defensive force rather than the presence of the battered woman syndrome.

4.4.9   Credibility and the Failure to Leave Previously

As described previously, defendants may offer the credibility argument for two
purposes. First, the defendant may offer testimony regarding the battered
woman syndrome generally in order to support her claim that she endured a
prolonged pattern of severe abuse without leaving the relationship. This general testimony supports her credibility by demonstrating that her conduct as she
reports it would not be unusual for a battered woman. Second, she may offer
testimony specifically addressing her learned helplessness to explain why she
was unable to leave the relationship earlier. Some defendants may offer testimony for either purpose separately, but a defendant might pursue both purposes

by offering expert testimony describing the syndrome generally and her own learned helplessness specifically as support for the claim that she was unable to leave, thus explaining why she did not do so despite the severe abuse.[68]

Defendants also offer social and economic explanations for their failure to leave. These might include, for example, their lack of financial resources or family support, the need to provide food and shelter for the children, or fear of retaliation from the batterer.[69] Insofar as these claims are supported by evidence, they may well improve the defendants' credibility in the eyes of the jury by providing plausible explanations for the defendants' failure to leave the battering relationships. These explanations may portray the earlier failure to leave as arguably reasonable insofar as these practical barriers might have appeared more difficult to overcome than the periodic abuse until that battering escalated to a degree of severity that triggered the defensive force. Alternately, circumstances that do not suffice to render the failure to leave reasonable may render it understandable in that jurors might conclude that the combination of periodic abuse and practical barriers to leaving would prevent many ordinary people from making the reasonable decision to leave.

Social or economic explanations that render the defendants' failure to leave either reasonable or unreasonable but understandable serve their purpose because the aim of the credibility argument is to render the defendants' accounts believable, rather than to portray their prior failure to leave as reasonable. Ordinary self-defense doctrine demands that one act on a reasonable belief that defensive force is necessary at the time it is exercised; it does not demand that one demonstrate an ideally reasonable life history. These practical explanations for the defendants' failure to leave earlier appeal to factual circumstances depriving defendants of the opportunity to leave or rendering the decision to leave very difficult to exercise, however, rather than appealing to the battered woman syndrome as a source of impaired ability to leave.

The variation of the argument appealing to the syndrome relies on learned helplessness as a psychological trait rendering the defendant unable to leave by preventing her from recognizing and taking advantage of available opportunities to alter her situation.[70] This section assumes for the sake of argument that there is evidence supporting the occurrence of some form of battered woman syndrome. If one also assumes that this syndrome is pathognomonic to battered women, then the fact that a particular woman suffers that syndrome supports

---

68　State v. Kelly, 478 A.2d 364, 375–7 (N.J. 1984); People v. Torres, 488 N.Y.S.2d 358, 362 (Sup. 1985); Kinports, *supra* note 14, at 398, 400, 416; Schulhofer, *supra* note 15, at 119.

69　State v. Kelly, 478 A.2d 364, 377 (N.J. 1984); People v. Torres, 488 N.Y.S.2d 358, 362 (Sup. 1985); State v. Allery, 682 P.2d 312, 315 (Wash. 1984); Kinports, *supra* note 14, at 405.

70　People v. Aris, 264 Cal. Rptr. 167, 178 (Cal.App. 4th Dist. 1989) (describing the proffered testimony of Lenore Walker); State v. Kelly 478 A.2d 364, 372, 377 (N.J. 1984); People v. Torres, 488 N.Y.S.2d 358, 361–2 (Sup. 1985); Kinports, *supra* note 14, at 398.

the claim that she has been battered.[71] Thus, a pathognomonic syndrome would support the defendant's credibility regarding her testimony about the battering relationship, and by extension it would support her general credibility or at least tend to correct the tendency to suspect that she exaggerated. For this reason, testimony regarding a well-grounded pathognomonic battered woman syndrome would be relevant to self-defense.

Alternately, the assumed syndrome may not be pathognomonic in that it may take a form that is also associated with etiologies other than battering. Walker's data, for example, support the contention that battered women experience elevated depression as compared to the general population. Depression is such a common disorder, however, that the presence of a depressive syndrome provides no support for the claim that the person suffering the syndrome had been battered.[72] Others claim that battered women suffer a pathological syndrome similar to that manifested by those who endure stress or trauma of various types. Such a syndrome provides little support for the defendant's credibility unless further evidence suggested that the probability of her having suffered other relevant forms of stress or trauma was low. In short, a well-supported pathognomonic battered woman syndrome would strengthen the defendant's credibility, and a nonpathognomonic syndrome might provide lesser support in proportion to the probability that this particular defendant's suffering that syndrome is attributable to battering rather than to some alternative etiology.

Regardless of the availability of a well-supported syndrome, evidence confirming a history of battering provides the best support for the defendant's credibility because it directly supports the aspect of her testimony that jurors may find dubious. Documents and witness testimony from various sources can support the claim of ongoing battering. The defendant's children, relatives, friends, neighbors, co-workers, medical personnel, or social workers might have witnessed either the battering or evidence of that abuse such as past injuries or chronic fear of the batterer. Medical records from emergency room visits might reveal a pattern consistent with battering, regardless of the explanation that was given for each event individually. In any particular case this type of evidence may not be available, but the same holds true for evidence regarding the claim that the defendant suffers battered woman

---

71 A symptom or syndrome is pathognomonic when it is "specifically distinctive or characteristic of a disease or pathologic condition; a sign or symptom on which a diagnosis can be made." Dorland's Illustrated Medical Dictionary 977 (Philadelphia: Saunders Press, 26th ed. 1981). Thus, if a syndrome were pathognomonic to women who had endured battering relationships, that a particular defendant suffered this syndrome would provide strong support for her claim that she had experienced a pattern of battering. In contrast, if a defendant suffers a common syndrome such as depression, which occurs in many people in a variety of circumstances, the mere presence of the depressive syndrome would not indicate any particular etiology.

72 American Psychiatric Association, Diagnostic and Statistical Manual of Mental Disorders 341, 347 (Washington, D.C.: American Psychiatric Association, 4th ed., 1994).

syndrome, even if one assumes that some syndrome has been generally established. To the extent that experts can testify regarding the general phenomena of battering relationships, as opposed to this particular defendant's relationship, testimony regarding the prevalence of such patterns of battering would support the defendant's testimony more directly than would testimony regarding a syndrome.

A defense attorney would appropriately use all available and relevant evidence, but it is important not to become preoccupied with the attempt to establish the presence of a syndrome at the expense of seeking and presenting traditional evidence from witnesses and documents. The traditional evidence has the advantages of directly supporting the defendants' credibility regarding the battering and of taking a form with which lawyers and courts are familiar, facilitating the process of seeking, presenting, and admitting the evidence. Finally, expert testimony regarding the battered woman syndrome carries potential risk for the defendant. Testimony regarding the syndrome, and particularly learned helplessness, portrays the defendant as one who suffers psychological impairment undermining the accuracy of her perceptions and judgment regarding the batterer and the relationship. As such it may actively undermine her credibility with the jury by portraying her relevant beliefs as the product of a pathological syndrome rather than as reasonable inferences from her experience. In short, testimony regarding a well-supported syndrome may be relevant to the defendant's credibility under certain limited conditions, but as with the claims of reasonable belief regarding the necessity of force or deadly force, traditional evidence demonstrating the pattern of battering rather than expert testimony regarding the syndrome is most directly relevant.

4.5　Self-defense by Battered Women as Justification and Excuse

4.5.1　Reasonable Belief

Section 4.4 identifies evidence describing the pattern of battering rather than expert testimony regarding the syndrome as the evidence most relevant to the self-defense claim advanced by battered women who kill their batterers in non-confrontation situations. Evidence confirming the pattern of events leading the defendant to infer the necessity of exercising deadly defensive force would provide jurors with the basis needed for them to draw the same inference, enabling them to understand the defendants' beliefs as reasonable. This section examines several controversial aspects of self-defense doctrine in order to integrate self-defense by battered women with the theory of self-defense advanced in Chapter 3 and the general category of justification defenses as analyzed in Chapter 2. Throughout this section, it is critical to recall that this book advances a prescriptive theory regarding the manner in which legislatures and courts ought to address these issues. I do not claim that all legislatures and courts currently do so.

Although the majority of jurisdictions require a reasonable belief in the necessity of exercising deadly force in self-defense, cases and commentators continue to debate the appropriate standard of reasonableness. Courts frequently frame this issue as a choice between subjective and objective standards.[73] This formulation can obfuscate rather than clarify the issue, however, because it is very difficult to ascertain the meaning of "subjective" and "objective." In some cases, two jurisdictions apparently adopt equivalent standards, yet one labels that test subjective while the other describes it as objective.[74]

Some cases require that the defendant's belief be reasonable from the defendant's point of view rather than from the perspective of the jury.[75] Unfortunately, it becomes rather difficult to explain exactly what it means to say that a belief is reasonable from a particular party's point of view. Ordinarily, standards requiring reasonable belief are labeled "objective" and contrasted to those labeled "subjective," which take into the account the individual's perspective in that they address actual mental states of that person.[76] Thus, the requirement that a belief be reasonable from the defendant's point of view seems to call for an objective assessment from the defendant's subjective perspective, whatever that might mean.

To be reasonable in ordinary language is to be "endowed with reason . . . sensible . . . marked by reasoning . . . agreeable to reason."[77] Thus, a belief is reasonable if it is formed and held according to reason or for sound reasons. Similarly, an arresting officer arrests a suspect on the basis of reasonable belief when he makes an arrest on the basis of "facts and circumstances within the arresting officer's knowledge, and of which he had reasonably trustworthy information."[78] A mistake relevant to criminal guilt is reasonable if it is based on reasonable grounds.[79] A person reasonably believes that a fact exists for the purpose of tort law if he believes it and "the circumstances which he knows, or should know, are such as to cause a reasonable man so to believe."[80] A reasonable man for this purpose possesses "normal acuteness of perception and soundness of judgment."[81] In short, a reasonable belief, in both ordinary lan-

---

73 State v. Hodges, 716 P.2d 563, 569 (Kan. 1986); State v. Leidholm, 334 N.W.2d 811, 816–18 (N.D. 1983); State v. Allery, 682 P.2d 312, 314–15 (Wash. 1984).
74 Maguigan, *supra* note 2, at 410 (comparing New York and Washington standards).
75 State v. Allery 682 P.2d 312, 314–15 (Wash. 1984); Maguigan, *supra* note 2, at 409.
76 Criminal Law at §3.7(a)(2).
77 II Oxford English Dictionary at 2432.
78 Blacks Law Dictionary, *supra* note 37, at 1265.
79 Rollin M. Perkins & Ronald N. Boyce, Criminal Law 1045–8 (Mineola, N.Y.: Foundation Press, 3d ed. 1982).
80 American Law Institute, Restatement of the Law Second, Torts § 11 (1965); Mitchell v. Harmony, 54 U.S. (13 How.) 115, 135 (1851).
81 Restatement of the Law Second, Torts, at § 11 comment (a).

guage and legal usage, is grounded in good reasons and reasoning. That is, a reasonable belief is formed and held on the basis of ordinarily reliable evidence as acquired by unimpaired perception and evaluated through normally sound reasoning and judgment.

The standard of reasonableness takes on particular significance in cases in which the defendant offers expert testimony regarding the battered woman syndrome. Psychologists, psychiatrists, or members of other clinical professions ordinarily present this testimony, emphasizing learned helplessness and other psychological characteristics of the defendant.[82] Such testimony appears to portray the defendant as suffering certain patterns of psychological impairment, suggesting to some courts and commentators that it is relevant to insanity or diminished capacity rather than to a justificatory defense requiring a reasonable belief.[83] Advocates of battered woman syndrome testimony in self-defense cases deny that the syndrome constitutes a mental illness, however, and offer the testimony to establish the reasonableness of the defendants' beliefs regarding the necessity of deadly force.[84] In order to understand the appropriate role for such testimony and its relevance to reasonable belief, one must clarify the meaning of "battered woman syndrome," "mental illness," and "reasonable belief" and examine the relationships among them.

4.5.2   Battered Woman Syndrome and Mental Illness

As usually described, the syndrome consists of a set of psychological characteristics including depression, decreased self-esteem, and learned helplessness. Although advocates deny that the syndrome constitutes a mental illness, courts and commentators discuss it as distortion of thought and perception, impaired ability to perceive and realistically appraise alternatives, and delusions regarding the batterer and the relationship.[85] This discussion of the syndrome as a pattern of impaired psychological process is consistent with its categorization as a syndrome.

A syndrome is a set of symptoms that tend to occur together in a recognizable pattern.[86] A symptom is a sign or manifestation of a pathological mental

---

82 State v. Hodges, 716 P.2d 563, 565–6 (Kan. 1986) (discussing proposed testimony of psychologist Dr. Ann Bristow); State v. Kelly, 478 A.2d 364, 372–3 (N.J. 1984) (discussing proposed testimony by Dr. Lois Veronen); *see supra* § 4.2.2 and accompanying text (discussing the nature of the testimony).

83 *See, e.g.,* State v. Necaise, 466 So.2d 660, 663–5 (La.App. 5th Cir. 1985); Rocco C. Cipparone Jr., Comment, *The Defense of Battered Women Who Kill,* 135 U. Pa. L. Rev. 427 (1987); Schneider, *supra* note 2, at 198–200.

84 State v. Hodges, 716 P.2d 563, 569 (Kan. 1986); State v. Kelly, 478 A.2d 364, 377–8 (N.J. 1984); Kinports, *supra* note 14, at 409–22; Schneider, *supra* note 2, at 199–215.

85 *See supra* §4.4.3.

86 American Psychiatric Association, *supra* note 72, at 771; Robert J. Campbell, Psychiatric Dictionary 615 (New York: Oxford Univ. Press, 5th ed. 1981); Dorland's Illustrated Medical Dictionary, *supra* note 71, at 1287; II Oxford English Dictionary at 3210.

or physical condition.[87] A clinically significant syndrome of psychological symptoms constitutes a mental or psychological disorder in contemporary clinical terminology.[88] "Disorder" differs from "disease" in that "disorder" refers to a functional disturbance or abnormality without implying any particular etiology. A disease, in contrast, is a structural or functional disorder of the body or part of the body.[89] Most recognized psychological disorders are syndromes rather than diseases in that identifying a pattern of psychological dysfunction does not in itself imply a specific underlying physical etiology.[90] In short, a psychological syndrome is a clinically significant pattern of impaired psychological functioning, and a psychological disorder is a recognized syndrome.

Ordinary and clinical usage defines "illness" in a manner more consistent with "disorder" than with "disease." People are ill when they suffer unsound or disordered health involving pain, discomfort, or inconvenience.[91] An illness consists of an impairment of function when measured against some predefined level of health or adequate functioning. Persons are ill when they suffer impairment of their capacity to function at an ordinary level. They suffer mental or psychological illness when they suffer functional impairments of mental or psychological processes.[92] Thus, a psychological disorder is a recognized psychological syndrome, which, in turn, is a recognized pattern of mental or psychological illness.

Legal authorities sometimes fail to clearly state any technical legal definition of "mental illness," assuming that this is a clinical term and relying on expert witnesses to determine whether an individual suffers such an illness.[93] Some statutes and court opinions advance legal conceptions of "mental illness" for specific purposes. Wisconsin's civil commitment statute, for example, defines mental illness for the purpose of commitment as "a substantial disorder of thought, mood, perception, orientation, or memory which grossly impairs judgment, behavior, capacity to recognize reality, or ability to meet the ordinary demands of life."[94] In *McDonald v. United States*, the court defined mental disease for the purpose of that jurisdiction's insanity test as "any abnormal

---

87 American Psychiatric Association, *supra* note 72, at 771; Campbell, *id.* at 615; Dorland's Illustrated Medical Dictionary, *supra* note 71, at 1285; II Oxford English Dictionary at 3208.

88 American Psychiatric Association, *supra* note 72, at xxi, 771.

89 Dorland's Illustrated Medical Dictionary, *supra* note 71, at 385; Michael S. Moore, Law and Psychiatry 186–9 (Cambridge: Cambridge Univ. Press, 1984); I Oxford English Dictionary at 748 (disease), 756 (disorder).

90 American Psychiatric Association, *supra* note 72, at xxi. This does not rule out the possibility, of course, that some physical disease might cause a particular psychological disorder.

91 I Oxford English Dictionary at 1373.

92 Moore, *supra* note 89, at 189–95. This brief analysis is sufficient for the purpose of this chapter; I do not pursue the extended philosophic debate regarding the concepts of illness and disease.

93 *Id.* at 228–30.

94 Wis. Stat. Ann. § 51.01(13)(b) (West 1987).

condition of the mind which substantially affects mental or emotional processes and substantially impairs behavior control."[95]

Both of these definitions are consistent with the ordinary conception of psychological disorder as functional impairment of psychological processes. Each describes certain types of functional impairment of psychological processes and identifies rough criteria of adequate functioning selected for a specific legal purpose. The Wisconsin commitment statute specifically lists the processes impaired and states criteria in terms of reality relatedness and ability to live independently in ordinary conditions because the statute is intended to limit involuntary commitment to those who are unable to live safely without confinement.[96] The *McDonald* standard addresses impairment ("abnormal condition of the mind") of mental or emotional processes, adopting behavior control as a criterion of adequacy because the court understood criminal responsibility as a matter of behavior control.[97]

Contrary to the assertions of some courts and commentators, the battered woman syndrome, understood as a set of psychological characteristics roughly similar to those usually subsumed under this syndrome, constitutes a psychological disorder and, thus, a mental illness. Depression is a widely recognized and quite common psychological disorder with a well-established clinical syndrome.[98] Learned helplessness as described by the courts and commentators consists of the woman's impaired ability to accurately perceive, evaluate, and adaptively act upon her own situation, the batterer, the relationship between the two, and her options. Some sources apparently understand learned helplessness as preventing battered women from recognizing more adaptive alternatives to continuing participation in ongoing battering relationships, while others seem to interpret it as a form of dysfunction that renders them unable to act on alternatives.[99] If one accepts the former interpretation, learned helplessness constitutes impairment of cognitive process, and if one accepts the latter, it represents some unexplained disruption of decision making or volitional ability. In either case, learned helplessness constitutes a form of psychological impairment. If battered women regularly manifest some recognizable pattern of impairment, we can legitimately refer to it as a battered woman syndrome, but in doing so, we identify it as a psychological disorder frequently suffered by battered women.

Some writers object to the characterization of the syndrome as a psycho-

---

95 McDonald v. United States, 312 F.2d 847, 851 (D.C. Cir. 1962).

96 Wis. Stat. Ann. §§ 51.001, 51.20(1) (West 1987).

97 McDonald v. United States, 312 F.2d 847, 851–2 (D.C. Cir. 1962). Legal authorities sometimes use various terms such as "mental illness," "mental disease," or "disorder of mind" interchangeably. I use the term "psychological disorder" to refer to any functional impairment of psychological processes.

98 American Psychiatric Association, *supra* note 72, at 320–7, 339–50.

99 *See supra* § 4.2.

logical disorder, contending that it is more appropriately understood as a normal response to an abnormally stressful situation.[100] As described in the literature, the syndrome occurs in response to a highly stressful abusive situation. Other well-established psychological disorders such as depressive and anxiety disorders occur in response to identifiable precipitants, yet they remain psychological disorders because the individual suffers a recognizable pattern of impaired psychological process.[101] Similarly, certain types of psychological impairment such as delusions or hallucinations are a normal response to certain toxic substances, yet they constitute impairment of psychological process and, thus, symptoms in a recognized psychopathological syndrome.[102] Indeed, fractured bones are a statistically normal and fully understandable response to abnormal physical stressors such as impact with a moving automobile, yet such fractures remain pathological.

The claim that the syndrome is a normal response to the situation might mean that it is either statistically normal, understandable, or free of functional impairment.[103] If future research substantiates a battered woman syndrome, the first two interpretations may well apply, but these do not undermine the categorization of the syndrome as psychological disorder. The syndrome may occur frequently and understandably to women in battering relationships, just as some of the psychological and physical disorders discussed previously occur frequently and understandably in response to various sources of stress. If it does, however, that relationship between the pattern of battering and the syndrome does not render the syndrome less a disorder; rather, it explains the situational source of the disorder. Only the claim that the syndrome is a normal response in the third sense is incompatible with its categorization as a psychological disorder. This claim, however, is also incompatible with the contention that it occurs at all. If a "Battered Woman *Syndrome*" roughly similar to that described in the literature occurs, it is a syndrome; that is, it is a recognizable pattern of psychological impairment that tends to occur in battered women. This syndrome consists of a recognizable pattern of disrupted psychological process, as does any well-established psychological disorder.

Although some cases apparently interpret the syndrome as a psychological disorder and thus infer that defendants who claim they suffer the syndrome must be raising the insanity defense, this does not follow.[104] The insanity defense does not apply to all who suffer psychological dysfunction; rather, it

---

100 *See, e.g.,* Kinports, *supra* note 14, at 417; Schneider, *supra* note 2, at 214–15.
101 American Psychiatric Association, *supra* note 72, at 424–32.
102 *Id.* at 109–11.
103 I Oxford English Dictionary at 1492 (normal as conforming to the usual condition or standard; i.e., statistically normal); III Oxford English Dictionary at 1246 (normal as health and not impaired).
104 Schneider, *supra* note 2, at 198–200.

exculpates those who suffer disorders giving rise to certain kinds of excusing conditions regarding their criminal conduct.[105] Although insanity standards vary across jurisdictions and commentators, psychopathology sufficient to establish the defense usually includes gross distortion of thought or perception such as hallucinations or delusions.[106] The battered woman syndrome as usually formulated does not include such pathology.

In summary, if future research substantiates a battered woman syndrome roughly similar to that usually formulated by courts and commentators, that syndrome constitutes a psychological disorder and, therefore, a type of mental illness in both ordinary and legal usage. The vague and confused discussion of the syndrome in court opinions often arises from the attempt to accept and understand the pattern of psychological impairment described while simultaneously denying that it constitutes mental illness. Although the putative syndrome is a psychological disorder if it occurs, it does not follow either that a defendant who suffers the syndrome must rely on the insanity defense rather than self-defense or that the syndrome constitutes the type of disorder that can ground the insanity defense.

4.5.3   Reasonable Belief: Justification and Excuse

Courts and commentators find it difficult to explain the relationship of the syndrome to self-defense because the syndrome consists of a pattern of psychological impairment, rendering it more relevant to excuse than to justification. Self-defense constitutes a justification rather than an excuse because the rationale for the defense rests on the acceptability of the conduct under the circumstances rather than on any claim of disability or lack of responsibility on the part of the actor. The defense reflects the justificatory circumstances consisting of the unlawful attack on the defendant by the party the defendant injured and the necessity of the defensive force as the only available means of preventing unlawful harm to the defendant by the assailant.[107]

Understood in this manner, the foundation of the defense rests on the circumstances in which the defendant exercised defensive force, rendering the defendant's mental states apparently irrelevant. Yet, the majority of jurisdictions formulate the defense in terms of a reasonable belief regarding necessity rather than in terms of actual necessity. This formulation reflects two intuitively plausible concerns. A statute allowing the defense on the basis of actual necessity regardless of the defendant's beliefs regarding that necessity would allow exculpation of those who maliciously injured others while unaware of the jus-

---

105 Robert F. Schopp, Automatism, Insanity, and the Psychology of Criminal Responsibility § 2.1.1 (Cambridge: Cambridge Univ. Press, 1991).
106 *Id.* at §§ 6.4, 6.5.
107 *See supra* §§ 3.4, 3.5, 4.1.

tificatory circumstances, and it would deny exculpation to those who honestly but mistakenly thought they were acting from necessity. Yet, some consider both of these results unjust because the unknowingly justified defendant does not seem intuitively to deserve exculpation while the mistaken defendant does.[108]

Statutes formulated in terms of reasonable belief regarding necessity apparently address both of these concerns in a more satisfactory manner. Malicious but unknowingly justified defendants fail to qualify for exculpation because they lack reasonable beliefs that the justificatory circumstances apply, while honestly mistaken defendants qualify as long as their mistakes were reasonable. Finally, these statutes inculpate defendants who exercise force as a result of unreasonable mistakes, and these defendants arguably deserve to be held liable for exerting force without taking reasonable care in evaluating the circumstances and formulating their beliefs.

Despite these apparent advantages, statutes requiring reasonable belief for justified self-defense remain seriously flawed in general and specifically regarding cases involving battered women. One can form unreasonable beliefs for at least three different types of reasons, some of which generate important discrepancies regarding culpability and justified liability under these statutes. First, some defendants might form unreasonable beliefs because they fail to exercise appropriate care in evaluating a situation before acting. A racist defendant, for example, who sees an individual of another race approaching with a baseball bat might honestly but mistakenly believe that he is in danger. If this defendant shoots the approaching person without exercising the care necessary to notice that he is only one block from a ballfield and that many people on the street are carrying balls, bats, and gloves, we might reasonably conclude that he ought to be held liable for acting on a negligently held unreasonable belief. This defendant's culpability would lie in his exercising potentially lethal force without exercising a corresponding degree of care in assessing the situation. In cases of this type, a standard requiring reasonable belief for self-defense might seem appropriate to many observers. The MPC approach might address some of these cases more precisely in holding defendants liable for negligent offenses, but the reasonable belief standard might address other cases involving nondeadly force more satisfactorily in the absence of a statute establishing liability for negligent assault.

Second, one can form an unreasonable belief regarding necessity due to circumstances that limit or distort the information available to the actor. Suppose, for example, that while walking home from work, a plumber is confronted in the dark by a person who appears to be a robber armed with a pistol. When the person says "Your money or your life," the plumber strikes the apparent robber

---

108 *See supra* § 2.4.

with the wrench the plumber is carrying home from work. It later becomes clear that the apparent robber was a retarded person playing a game with a toy gun. Standard self-defense law accommodates these cases, however, by specifying that the defendant's belief must be reasonable in the circumstances. The defendant's belief must be reasonable to one who sees what she sees and knows what she knows.[109] Thus, the plumber's belief may be unreasonable in light of all relevant information, yet reasonable in the circumstances the plumber confronted because these circumstances provided the plumber with access to only a subset of the relevant information.

Third, a defendant might form an unreasonable belief in the necessity of exercising defensive force due to impaired capacity. Suppose two retarded adolescents get into an argument in the school doorway when they both try to pass through a door in opposite directions at the same time. The one attempting to enter the building yells "I'll get you" and picks up a rock in order to hit the other with it. The second could simply swing the door closed and call the teacher, but due to fear and limited intelligence, he never thinks of that possibility. Instead, he hits the first in the head with the baseball bat he was carrying out to the school yard, inflicting serious injury. This defendant's belief was not reasonable in the circumstances because any reasonable person exercising ordinary care and competence in the circumstances would have recognized the alternative of closing the door and calling the teacher. In contrast to the racist defendant in the first case, this defendant failed to derive a reasonable belief due to lack of competence rather than inadequate care.

Some readers may conclude that this retarded defendant ought to be held to the standard of an ordinary person and, thus, endorse conviction of this defendant in this case. These readers would find satisfactory self-defense provisions requiring reasonable beliefs. Those who find this conclusion intuitively unjust might consider several possible strategies. First, they might endorse the MPC's approach, requiring only a belief in the necessity of exercising deadly force rather than a reasonable belief. This approach would also exculpate the racist defendant in the first case, however, and many readers may think that these defendants differ in a manner that warrants different treatment.[110]

Second, some might argue that the defendant's limited intelligence should be considered among the circumstances relevant to the reasonableness of his belief. A reasonable belief, then, would be a belief one would reasonably expect of a person with such limited intellectual endowment. Such an approach would hold this defendant to the standard of the reasonable retarded person. It is difficult to explicate this notion in any useful manner because limited men-

---

109 *See supra* § 4.4.5.
110 This assumes that both defendants cause injury but not death and that the jurisdiction has no negligent assault statute.

tal capacity directly undermines the capacity to reason with ordinary speed and accuracy, apparently leaving us with the notion of "reasonable person with impaired reasoning." Such an interpretation renders the reasonable person standard incoherent in light of the ordinary and legal meaning of "reasonable" as grounded in good reasons and good reasoning. Furthermore, once we incorporate psychological aberration into the standard of reasonableness, consistency would seem to require a separate standard for the "reasonable psychotic." If defendants can demonstrate long-term patterns of unreasonable beliefs, attitudes, and behavior, should they be measured by the standard of the "reasonable unreasonable person?"

Although the suggestions that one might formulate standards for the "reasonable retarded person" or the "reasonable psychotic" seem implausible, courts and commentators have proposed standards for the "reasonable battered woman."[111] One could understand this standard as applying to the reasonable woman who has been battered or to the reasonable woman with battered woman syndrome. Courts and commentators can be interpreted in either fashion, and they sometimes do not differentiate between these two interpretations. The first variation is merely a statement of standard self-defense doctrine as applied to a defendant who has been battered. Standard doctrine measures reasonableness in light of all that the defendant knows including her history with the person against whom she exercises the defensive force. A reasonable woman who has been battered by the batterer includes this past history in the information she considers in forming her reasonable belief. As a restatement of standard doctrine, this interpretation fails to serve its intended purpose because those who suggest it apparently understand it as a proposal to revise and improve that doctrine.[112] Furthermore, understood in this manner, the proposal calls primarily for ordinary factual evidence supporting the defendant's claims regarding the past pattern of abuse rather than expert testimony addressing the syndrome.

The second variation has been proposed as one that more appropriately allows for the defendant's battered woman syndrome, including especially her experience of learned helplessness.[113] This proposal ordinarily accompanies the claims that this syndrome is not a mental illness and that testimony regarding it is relevant to the defendant's reasonable beliefs.[114] As argued previously, however, the syndrome as usually formulated is a psychological disorder if it occurs at all. It is difficult, therefore, to contend that one ought to apply a special standard to the reasonable person with battered woman syndrome but ought not apply a special standard for the reasonable psychotic or the reasonable retarded person. This approach requires a rationale for indexing reason-

---

111 Maguigan, *supra* note 2, at 442–3.
112 Kinports, *supra* note 14, at 409–22; *id.* at 442–5.
113 Kinports, *supra* note 14, at 396–422.
114 State v. Kelly 478 A.2d 364, 377–8 (N.J. 1984); *id.* at 417–22.

ableness to one particular psychological disorder but not to others, and it calls for some coherent notion of "reasonableness" that can vary according to the presence of psychological disorder. Psychosis, retardation, and the presumed syndrome differ in the manner and degree in which they distort psychological process but share in common the property that they involve distortion of psychological process.

Recall the retarded defendant in the school door who seems to raise serious concerns about the reasonable belief standard, and consider the possibility that he might have an insanity defense available as a third strategy for exculpating such defendants. Due to his intellectual impairment, he believed that his use of force was necessary and, therefore, that it was justified. That is, because of the functional impairment of his psychological processes, he did not know that his conduct was wrong. The most common standards for the insanity defense include provisions excusing those whose psychological disorders prevent them from knowing their conduct is wrong.[115] Thus, one could plausibly argue for inclusion of such a defendant under these provisions.

This approach to the retarded defendant who mistakenly believes that defensive force is necessary exculpates the defendant, but it does not endorse his conduct as justified. It excuses the defendant for committing unjustified conduct because he was not culpable for the mistaken belief on which he acted, and, thus, he was not culpable for his conduct. A statutory system that observed the distinction between justification and excuse by justifying on the basis of actual necessity and maintaining a separate excuse for those who engage in unjustified conduct because they nonculpably but mistakenly believe their conduct to be justified would accommodate this defendant under that excuse, bypassing the need to appeal to the insanity defense. This excuse would not apply to the negligently mistaken bigot in the first hypothetical because his failure to exercise due care before inflicting serious harm renders him culpable for his mistake. It would, however, exculpate the plumber who exercised what he reasonably and nonculpably but inaccurately believed to be necessary defensive force in response to deceptive circumstances.

An independent excuse for those who mistakenly but nonculpably believe defensive force is necessary appropriately addresses the culpability of the defendant rather than the acceptability of the conduct or the reasonableness of beliefs in circumstances in which the force was not appropriate because not necessary. The criterion of culpability allows appropriate disposition of all three cases, inculpating the negligent bigot but exculpating the plumber and the retarded defendant. Standards that compress justification and excuse into a single provision requiring reasonable belief in justificatory conditions accommodate only one subset of nonculpable but unjustified defendants. These standards

---

115 Schopp, *supra* note 105, at § 2.1.

exculpate those who, like the plumber, are misled by deceptive circumstances into forming beliefs that are false but reasonable in the circumstances. They do not, however, appropriately exculpate those defendants, like the retarded boy in the school door, who form unreasonable beliefs through no fault of their own due to impaired capacities.

One must clearly distinguish reasonable, understandable, and nonculpable beliefs in order to address these cases and issues in a satisfactory manner. As discussed previously, reasonable beliefs are formed and held on the basis of ordinarily reliable evidence as acquired through unimpaired perception and evaluated through normally sound judgment. Although the reasonableness of a belief is determined by the soundness of the evidence and psychological processes that produce and maintain it, it might be understandable that a person would hold an unreasonable belief. That is, others might understand why a person holds an unreasonable belief because they can advance an explanation for that person's holding that belief. These explanations might appeal, for example, to the bigoted defendant's prejudice and lack of due care and to the retarded defendant's impaired reasoning ability in order to explain how they derived their false and unreasonable beliefs in the necessity of exercising defensive force. These explanations render such defendants' beliefs understandable to others but not reasonable because they explain those beliefs by appeal to the defendants' unreliable belief-forming processes.

Unreasonable but understandable beliefs can be either culpable or nonculpable. The bigot's belief, for example, is understandable but culpable because the explanation that renders it understandable appeals to his negligent failure to exercise due care by seeking and considering easily available evidence that would have called his belief into question. The retarded defendant's belief, in contrast, is understandable but not culpable because the explanation that renders it understandable appeals to his impaired capacity to reason clearly or quickly. Thus, understandability is a property of the relationship between a belief and the ability of other parties to explain it, while reasonableness is a property of the relationship between a belief and the belief-holder's foundation in evidence and belief-forming processes for that belief.

Judgments of culpability for a mistaken belief represent attributions of responsibility for that mistake to the belief-holder as a competent moral agent. Attributions of culpability for a belief require both that the individual possessed the capacities of a competent agent and that she had the opportunity to exercise them regarding this belief.[116] That a belief is understandable, therefore, does not entail any conclusion regarding either its reasonableness or the belief-holder's culpability because each of these latter properties addresses different relationships from those addressed by understandability. A fully satisfactory

---

116 *Id.* at §§ 4.2, 4.4, 6.5, 7.4.

system of criminal defenses must provide the conceptual structure needed to evaluate reasonableness, understandability, and culpability independently.

4.5.4   Culpability and Battered Women as Justified or Excused

A statutory scheme justifying self-defense on the basis of actual necessity, regardless of beliefs, and maintaining a separate excuse for those who exercise force due to nonculpable mistakes regarding necessity conforms to the structure of justification defenses established in Section 2.4, reflects the conceptual distinctions among reasonableness, culpability, and understandability, and addresses a particularly problematic subset of self-defense cases involving battered women. Battered women who kill their batterers in nonconfrontation situations must demonstrate not only that further abuse was forthcoming but also that their own use of defensive force was necessary to prevent it. Although self-defense does not require that one retreat from one's own home before exercising such force, it does require that one make use of available legal protection. Nonconfrontation cases, especially those in which the defendant approaches the batterer, raise serious questions about the defendant's failure to exercise legal alternatives.[117]

Some defendants may not have such alternatives available. If the battered woman called police but they failed to respond or they responded but failed to make an arrest, for example, she can cogently argue that effective legal alternatives were not available. Furthermore, a defendant who had unsuccessfully sought legal protection in the past can reasonably argue that her experience demonstrates that such alternatives are not available.[118]

Defendants who have not personally sought legal assistance might demonstrate the necessity of defensive force through expert testimony regarding the lack of effective legal protection in their jurisdictions. Although many jurisdictions have recently initiated new statutes, policies, and practices in order to provide more effective legal alternatives to defensive force for battered women, the practical effect of these changes varies widely, and no one suggests that all battered women have access to effective legal protection across jurisdictions.

Defendants who can enter evidence to demonstrate that their jurisdictions

---

117 *See, e.g.,* People v. Aris, 264 Cal. Rptr. 167, 171 (Cal.App. 4th Dist. 1989); People v. Norman, 378 S.E.2d 8, 9–11 (N.C. 1989); State v. Allery, 682 P.2d 312, 313–14 (Wash. 1984).

118 The issue may be more complex if the defendant has not received assistance because she refused to cooperate with legal officials. Suppose, for example that this defendant has previously elicited assistance from officials but then changed her story or refused to cooperate in the prosecution of the batterer. These circumstances raise the additional question regarding defendants' responsibility for causing the conditions of their own defenses. *See* Paul Robinson, *Causing the Conditions of One's Own Defense: A Study of the Limits of Theory in Criminal Law Doctrine,* 71 Va. L. Rev. 1 (1985).

have not yet established reliable patterns of effective legal intervention in battering relationships can use this evidence to support the claim of necessity required for justified self-defense. That is, by showing that the past pattern of battering supports their claims that serious bodily injury was forthcoming and that they would be unable to protect themselves at the time of the attack, and by showing that effective legal protection was not available in their jurisdiction, they can support their contentions that their own exercise of force was necessary to prevent the unlawful use of force against them.

A penal code clearly differentiating justification based on actual necessity from excuse based on nonculpable mistake regarding necessity would accept as justified the defensive force exercised by these defendants who lack legal alternatives. This justification defense would reflect the circumstances necessitating their defensive force and would require no inquiry into the defendants' beliefs or into the reasonableness, understandability, or culpability of those beliefs. Some battered women might kill their batterers out of a desire for revenge in circumstances in which they believed they had effective legal alternatives, although in fact they did not. These unknowingly justified defendants would qualify for a justification defense based upon actual necessity in the circumstances. They would remain vulnerable, however, to attempt liability because their conduct would have constituted illegal homicide had the circumstances been as they believed them to be.[119]

Some battered women might kill their batterers while motivated by both their awareness of actual necessity and their desire for revenge. Suppose, for example, Jones accurately believes that her batterer will beat her severely, as he has previously, when he awakens from his drunken stupor. Jones attempts to call the police but discovers that the January blizzard that prevents her from leaving her isolated farmhouse has also blown down the telephone lines, preventing her from securing legal assistance. Jones responds to this discovery with malevolent glee, realizing that these circumstances create actual necessity because the forthcoming beating is virtually certain, she will be unable to defend herself at that time, and legal assistance is not available. She plunges a kitchen knife into her batterer's chest, delighted by the opportunity to exploit the justificatory circumstances.

Some readers might respond intuitively that Jones does not deserve a defense due to her malevolent delight in killing the batterer. These readers might contend that Jones killed the batterer because she wanted to, rather than because she had to.

Justification defenses exculpate actors because their conduct was acceptable under the circumstances, however, not because they manifest admirable atti-

---

119 *See supra* § 2.4.3.

tudes.[120] Suppose Smith is carrying his softball bat home from a softball game. As he turns a corner, he encounters Spike in the act of swinging a tire iron at Mother Beneficence in order to steal the alms she has collected for the poor. As the attack is already in progress, Smith has only two choices: he can hit Spike with the bat, protecting Mother Beneficence, or he can refrain, allowing Spike to severely injure Mother Beneficence. Suppose also that as Smith perceives the situation, he feels no concern for Mother Beneficence, but he recognizes Spike as someone he has always hated and experiences a sensation of delight when he realizes that he now has an opportunity to attack Spike as he has always wanted to.

Although Smith's intervention with the bat is motivated by his hatred for Spike, it seems clear that Smith acts as he ought to. Some readers might evaluate Smith's character more positively if he were to intervene from a sense of duty or from concern for Mother Beneficence, but few would argue that he ought to allow Spike's attack to continue rather than act from impure motives. Smith's act seems clearly the more justified of the only two available options. When forced to choose between intervening in a manner that injures the culpable Spike or refraining and allowing comparable injury to the innocent Mother Beneficence, Smith justifiably chooses the act that directs the unavoidable injury toward the party whose culpable attack creates the need for someone to absorb such injury. Although Smith acts with malice, Smith performs the right act, and, therefore, Smith's act is justified.

Jones, like Smith, engages in acceptable conduct under the circumstances. Smith and Jones both encounter circumstances in which they must act in a manner that directs forthcoming injury either toward the culpable party who embodies the danger or toward an innocent victim. The malicious satisfaction that each experiences might affect one's evaluation of these actors' characters, but it does not alter the conditions that justify their acts. The mere fact that the same person fills the roles of innocent victim and intervener in the Jones story creates no morally relevant reason that renders the intervention less justified.

Most battered women who kill their batterers probably experience serious distress at having done so. Some may not, however, and some may experience relief, satisfaction, or exhilaration. As a justification defense, self-defense applies to conduct justified by the circumstances, rather than to defendants who seem contrite. Distinct justification defenses addressing justificatory circumstances and excuses addressing culpability facilitate satisfactory analysis and disposition of such cases by directing attention toward the presence or lack of justificatory circumstances rather than toward the actor's motives or beliefs.

A clear distinction between justification defenses grounded in justificatory circumstances and excuses recognizing the defendants' lack of culpability

---

120 *See supra* § 2.4.1.

facilitates differential analysis of at least three additional types of cases involving self-defense claims by battered women. First, evidence presented to the court may demonstrate that legal protection was available and that this defendant resorted to violence despite being aware of these alternatives. Second, evidence may establish that such alternatives were available but that the defendant exercised force because she was unaware of these opportunities. Third, the court may lack reliable information about the availability of legal protection because the jurisdiction lacks a reliable pattern of performance in this area.

Consider each type of case in sequence. The first set of cases involves defendants who resorted to violence despite their awareness of effective legal alternatives. Self-defense arguments probably would not succeed for these defendants, but there is no reason to think they should. These cases would involve the knowing use of unnecessary force, and homicide statutes would appropriately apply, although provocation may reduce the appropriate degree of homicide.[121]

The second set of defendants resorted to violence because they mistakenly believed that they lacked legal alternatives and, thus, that defensive force was necessary for self-protection. If the penal code compresses justification and excuse into a single provision by granting a justification defense to those who reasonably believed their force was necessary, the court must inquire into the reasonableness of these defendants' beliefs. Although it may not be decisive, the evidence before the court indicating that alternatives were available weighs against the defendants in this inquiry. This evidence may be misleading in that the court's opportunity to gather and weigh this evidence differs significantly from that of the defendants who must decide and act under great stress, but the stronger the evidence demonstrating the availability of legal alternatives, the stronger the inference that the defendant's contrary belief was not reasonable.

An appeal to the battered woman syndrome cannot render these defendants' beliefs reasonable. As a syndrome it constitutes a pattern of psychological dysfunction that cannot provide the foundation in reliable evidence and belief-forming processes needed to establish a belief as reasonable. If further research supports the syndrome as a clinical syndrome, and if clinical evidence supports the contention that a particular defendant suffers that syndrome, this evidence may well explain why she believed her action necessary. Such an explanation might assist the jury in understanding, for example, that due to learned helplessness, the defendant perceived the batterer as omnipotent and failed to recognize the availability of legal assistance. By appealing to learned helplessness, this explanation renders the belief understandable rather than reasonable, however, and understandability entails neither reasonableness nor any conclusion regarding culpability. One cannot resolve these cases by modifying the notion

---

121 MPC at § 210.3(1)(a); Criminal Law at § 7.10.

of reasonableness for the reasons discussed previously.[122] Rather, one must differentiate defenses reflecting justificatory circumstances from those excusing the actor as lacking culpability.

A separate excuse for those who exercise force due to a nonculpable mistake regarding justification emphasizes the defendant's culpability for her mistake rather than the reasonableness of her belief constituting the mistake. From this perspective, the central question is not whether she had good reason for her belief but rather whether she is appropriately held culpable for it. The retarded defendant in the school door discussed earlier lacked good reason for his mistaken belief that force was necessary, but he was not culpable for his mistake because it was the product of defective capacities.

Assuming for the sake of argument that a battered woman syndrome occurs, then learned helplessness may constitute an impairment analogous to that of the retarded defendant in that it undermines the individual's ability to accurately assess the relevant information and draw appropriate conclusions. As usually described, learned helplessness differs from retardation in that it is a relatively narrow impairment, affecting only the battered woman's ability to accurately perceive and evaluate the batterer, the relationship, and her options regarding that relationship. This could be sufficient in some cases, however, to generate a nonculpable mistake regarding her ability to secure legal protection. Under this rationale, a defendant suffering the hypothetical syndrome might qualify for excuse because the syndrome produces an unreasonable but nonculpable mistaken belief that she lacks any alternatives to violence.

Alternately, assume for the sake of argument that additional research fails to support the claim that the battered woman syndrome occurs. This failure would not undermine the well-documented occurrence of battering. In the absence of a syndrome, the battered woman remains an individual who suffers periodic assaults. Given the prior assumptions regarding the forthcoming abuse and her inability to protect herself at that time, she might exercise force in a nonconfrontation situation out of fear of the anticipated abuse. If legal alternatives were available but her abuse-driven fear led her to believe that her defensive force was necessary, the jury must determine in each case whether the severity of the abuse and her resulting fear was sufficient to render her mistake nonculpable. Thus, a statutory system separating justification defenses from excuses for nonculpable mistakes regarding justification would provide these defendants with plausible arguments for exculpation.

A clear distinction between justification and excuse for nonculpable mistakes regarding justification explicates the intuition represented by the proposals for a subjective standard of reasonableness or for a "reasonable battered woman" standard. The plumber who strikes the retarded "assailant" with the

---

122 *See supra* § 4.5.1.

toy gun reacts reasonably to the circumstances with which he is confronted. Although the relevant reasons that actually apply do not provide external justification for the plumber's use of force, the reasons to which he has access provide internal justification. The plumber responds in a reasonable manner to the reasons that provide internal justification, and, thus, he behaves responsibly.[123] Because he behaves responsibly, he is not culpable for his actions. Thus, he is appropriately excused for his nonculpable mistake.

The retarded boy in the school door and the battered woman who fails to exercise available legal alternatives due to the hypothetical syndrome or abuse-driven fear also lack culpability for their mistaken beliefs that contribute to their unjustified use of force. The plumber's misleading circumstances, the retarded boy's impaired capacities, and the battered woman's syndrome or abuse-driven fear all constitute factors relevant to the appropriate exculpation of these defendants because they defeat ascriptions of culpability.

Although the plumber's misleading circumstances provide internal justification, the retarded boy's impaired capacities render his mistake nonculpable without providing internal justification. Rather, his impaired capacities prevented him from reasoning effectively about the reasons to which he had access. In this regard, the battered woman's syndrome or abuse-driven fear is more similar to the retarded boy's impairment than it is to the circumstances that provide the plumber with internal justification. That is, in contrast to the plumber who is internally justified by the reasons to which he has access, the retarded boy and this battered woman are neither internally nor externally justified in their beliefs regarding justification. They may not be culpable, however, for their externally and internally unjustified beliefs. Thus, courts should engage in subjective inquiries regarding these defendants, but these inquiries are relevant to culpability and excuse rather than to reasonableness for justification.

Finally, consider the third set of cases in which the court lacks clear information regarding the availability of legal assistance in this jurisdiction at the time the defendant exercised force. If the court cannot ascertain this information at trial, it almost certainly would not have been available to the defendant when she exercised force. If the penal code compresses justification and reasonable mistake regarding justification into a single defense by allowing the justification for those who reasonably believed their conduct was necessary, it seems plausible to say that one cannot reasonably believe that legal alternatives are not available in the absence of information. That is, if one has no reliable information regarding alternatives, one does not have good reason to conclude that they are unavailable and, therefore, that lethal action is justified. One can only conclude that one does not know whether it is justified. Thus, one who

---

123 *See supra* §§ 2.4.2, 2.4.3 regarding external and internal justification.

lacks information providing good reason to believe that alternatives are un-available cannot reasonably believe that defensive force is necessary.

By addressing justification defenses and nonculpable mistakes regarding justification separately, the criminal law can accommodate these cases appropriately through an analysis parallel to that which has already been discussed. Although these defendants lacked reliable information regarding legal alternatives, it remains true that in each case either such alternatives were available or they were not. If they were not, the defensive force was justified by actual necessity. If the alternatives were available but the defendant's syndrome or abuse-driven fear led her to believe that they were not, the jury would have to determine for each defendant whether the severity of the syndrome or the abuse was sufficient to render that defendant's mistake nonculpable rather than reckless or negligent. The former conclusion would generate exculpation under the excuse for nonculpable mistake regarding justification, and the latter would result in liability for negligent or reckless homicide.

This practical result is less than fully satisfactory for two reasons, but these concerns arise from the realistic problems involving factual uncertainty rather than from inadequacies in the law. First, the jury would face difficult determinations of fact in the absence of satisfactory evidence or clear criteria of adequacy. They would have to make judgments, for example, of the probability that assistance was available, of the potential danger to the defendant in an unsuccessful call for assistance, and of the severity of each defendant's impairment or abuse-driven fear. Although these determinations are troubling, so are many similar judgments juries must make in other types of cases.[124] Second, some cases would result in exculpation in circumstances that would render it impossible for anyone including the jury to differentiate justification from excuse. Although this result would blur the expressive significance of the decision, it reflects the unavoidable responsibility of courts to make decisions in conditions of uncertainty.

Finally, although it is true of each case that either legal alternatives were available or they were not, this formulation masks an important property of the situation as it is encountered by the defendant and by the court. Neither the defendant nor the court can clearly ascertain which condition applies in these cases. Thus, the defendant confronted, and the court must evaluate, a situation calling for some estimate of the probability of assistance and of the risk presented by each specific set of circumstances. The immediate availability of effective legal protection becomes a critical factor precisely because some pattern of abuse and threats renders defensive force immediately necessary unless effective legal alternatives preclude the necessity of self-defense. Those threats

---

124 The criminal law can address error preference regarding some of these issues through procedural devices such as the burden of proof.

and abuse constitute the violation of the victim's sovereignty that justifies defensive force absent effective legal protection.

Recall from Chapter 3 that the aggressor's violation of the victim's sovereignty justifies the victim in protecting herself at the cost of the aggressor's concrete interests at the levels of harm and of risk. Assuming, therefore, that the prior abuse, recent threats, and current circumstances would justify defensive force if legal protection were not available, the victim has no obligation to protect the aggressor's concrete interests at the expense of risk to her sovereignty. The theory advanced in Chapter 3 would justify the victim in resorting to force if the circumstances created by the aggressor included significant risk that legal alternatives would not be available and effective.[125]

In short, a penal code that maintains a rigorous distinction between justification and excuse by separating self-defense justified by actual necessity from excused mistakes regarding justification can accommodate many of the problematic cases. Those who fail to qualify under this interpretation are those who have the weakest claims to exculpation because they knowingly refuse to take advantage of available legal alternatives. Furthermore, this approach relies primarily on evidence regarding a series of events and circumstances, including the pattern of battering and the performance of law enforcement, rather than on the tenuous support for the syndrome. Finally, it is consistent with the conceptual and normative foundations of self-defense, and it clarifies the relevance of the battering evidence for the appropriate defenses.[126]

Compressing these defenses into a single provision and interpreting "reasonable belief" as innocent, blameless, or nonculpable belief fails to address the issues in a satisfactory manner. This approach blurs the conceptual distinction between justification and excuse, undermining the theoretical clarity of the criminal law. Although both justification and excuse exculpate, conflating the two in a single defense can also have practical significance. First, it can have practical effects on the rights and duties of third parties who may become involved.[127] Second, it distorts the expressive function of the criminal law because it becomes impossible to determine whether a particular decision

---

125 *See supra* § 3.4.
126 Although the excuse for nonculpable mistake regarding justification appropriately addresses some cases involving battered women, the experience of battering is neither necessary nor sufficient for the excuse. The analysis presented throughout this chapter demonstrates that battering is not sufficient because some battered women who kill their batterers qualify for justification rather than excuse, and some qualify for neither. Battering is not necessary for the excuse because the core of the exculpatory condition consists of the distorted information, impaired capacities, or other significant conditions that render the defendant nonculpable for the mistake. Notice that a defendant who makes such nonculpable mistakes regarding justification due to significant psychological dysfunction might also be subject to the insanity defense or to civil commitment.
127 *See supra* § 2.5.

expresses approval of the defendant's use of force or merely absolves her of responsibility.

Third, the failure to clearly differentiate justification and excuse can undermine legitimate exculpatory defenses for defendants such as those previously discussed who exercised deadly force due to an unreasonable but nonculpable belief that they lacked legal alternatives. Finally, conflating the two types of defenses promotes the current state of confusion regarding the putative relevance of expert testimony regarding the battered woman syndrome to claims of self-defense. It is at least plausible to suspect that juries might be more likely to arrive at legally and morally defensible verdicts when presented with distinct claims of justification and excuse accompanied by instructions and evidence clearly identified with each. We should consider the possibility that some cases in which expert testimony was admitted resulted in intuitively unsatisfactory decisions because of that testimony rather than despite it.

4.6   Conclusion

The controversy regarding battered women who kill their batterers in the absence of occurrent attacks or threats demonstrates the critical importance to the criminal law of empirical rigor, careful attention to the jurisprudential foundations of legal doctrine, and the integration of the two. Although expert testimony regarding the battered woman syndrome has been widely endorsed by courts, commentators, and statutes, this syndrome lacks empirical support as a clinical syndrome. Furthermore, it bears almost no relevance to rigorously formulated and interpreted self-defense doctrine, either in its current form or as developed in Chapters 2 and 3. If future research were to provide adequate empirical support for such a syndrome, it could have limited relevance for the purposes of supporting the defendant's credibility or advancing an excuse for nonculpable mistake regarding justification.

When justification and excuse are distinguished, other central concepts of self-defense doctrine are clarified, and expert testimony regarding the syndrome is differentiated from ordinary factual evidence and expert testimony regarding the pattern of battering, many of the problematic issues and cases can be addressed more satisfactorily. A statutory scheme reflecting the structure of justification defenses and related excuses as analyzed in Chapter 2 and the moral foundations of self-defense advanced in Chapter 3 would accommodate many of the most troubling circumstances in which battered women kill their batterers in nonconfrontational situations. Some of these defendants would qualify for a justification defense based on necessity, while others would be excused due to nonculpable mistakes regarding justification. Finally, some would fail to qualify for either type of defense. Thus, this approach has the additional virtue of avoiding a new stereotype by treating each defendant in the manner appropriate to the circumstances in which she acted.

Evidence regarding the pattern of battering rather than the syndrome addresses the critical issues most directly. Many cases remain difficult to decide satisfactorily, but these cases reflect the widespread practical impediments to accurately reconstructing and evaluating past events as well as the ordinary requirement that courts decide under conditions of uncertainty. These difficulties are not unique to the substantive legal doctrine of self-defense generally or to cases of defensive force exercised by battered women specifically.

5

Duress and Systemically
Complete Mitigation

Chapters 2, 3, and 4 advance accounts of the general category of justification defenses, of the role of self-defense in a liberal society, and of the particularly difficult subset of self-defense cases involving battered women who kill their batterers in nonconfrontation situations. Each chapter, however, fails to provide a completely satisfactory account because a residual of difficult cases remains unresolved. These cases share at least some properties with those that qualify for the duress defense. Although Section 2.5 addresses the prison escape cases as candidates for justification, and as raising the possibility of mutually justified violent conflict, certain factors render them arguable candidates for excuse. Prisoners who face impending violence experience coercive threats that would elicit strong fear in most people. If they are unable to secure reliable official protection in the prison, then many observers might reasonably think that these defendants "had no choice," "could not help it," or "could not control themselves." These interpretations seem particularly apt when applied to individuals who run impulsively in panic rather than as part of a well-planned escape.

The analysis advanced in Section 2.5.3 denies justification to the innocent C for shooting the innocent B when C realizes that B is about to redirect the floodwaters, killing C in order to save a thousand innocent townspeople. That discussion also recognizes that C would be heroic, however, if he should accept his fate in the face of such frightening prospects. The stranded sailors G and H in Section 2.5.3, who struggle for the only available plank, arguably engage in unjustified homicidal conduct toward each other. Many observers who would deny G and H a legal justification defense might question the decision to punish them because their circumstances left them no reasonable alternatives. Some might intuitively say that they, like the endangered prisoners, could not help themselves.

Similarly, the theory of self-defense endorsed in Chapter 3 refuses justification in certain cases in which the defendant exercises defensive force under circumstances that intuitively seem to justify neither the use of force nor punishment of the defendant for exercising that force. These cases arise, for example, when A threatens V with severe harm in circumstances in which V can prevent that harm only by killing innocent parties. Suppose, for example, that A has taken two innocent hostages as shields and is about to kill V. V can prevent A from killing her only by taking action that will result in the deaths of A and both innocent hostages. On the analysis in Section 3.4, V is justified in killing A but not in killing the two innocent hostages.

Consider also a battered woman who accurately believes that the police in her jurisdiction will probably provide the protection she needs but who kills her batterer while he sleeps because she is frightened that he will kill her if she calls the police and they do not respond as she expects. Given the assumption that she was correct in her belief that they probably would respond adequately, her use of force was not necessary, and she did not mistakenly believe that it was. Rather, she correctly believed that it was not, but she was afraid to risk the possibility that her belief was wrong. Thus, she qualifies neither for justification due to actual necessity nor for excuse due to mistake regarding necessity.[1] Yet, some people will find it unreasonable to hold her liable for acting out of fear or to hold V liable for defending herself by causing the death of A and both hostages.

Cases such as these seem to support the *se defendendo* excuse in some circumstances. This excuse applies when a severe and imminent threat elicits an involuntary reaction in self-protection. The victim responds reflexively to an imminent threat to life in a manner that leads many people to say that the victim had "no real choice." Thus, V is excused from liability although the action was not justified.[2] The *se defendendo* defense raises perplexing issues, however, because excuses usually apply to defendants who suffer some disability that differentiates those defendants from the population in general and gives rise to an excusing condition that justifies exculpation.[3] The insanity defense, for example, exculpates defendants who suffer a serious psychological disorder (disability) that differentiates them from most people and prevents them from understanding that their conduct is wrongful (excusing condition). In the hypotheticals described above, however, the defendants suffer no disability differentiating them from most people.

These cases do not present the appropriate conditions for classic duress claims because the actors do not engage in their illegal conduct in response to

---

1 She would qualify under justified self-defense if one stipulates that her fear was in response to the batterer's threat and that there was realistic risk that legal help was not forthcoming and if one accepts the argument regarding the priority of sovereignty regarding both harm and risk in §§ 3.4 and 4.5.4.

2 *See supra* § 3.1.1.

3 Defenses at § 161.

orders from another party who exercises or threatens to exercise coercive force unless they comply.[4] The actors in these cases encounter circumstances similar to those encountered by defendants with standard duress claims, however, in that compliance with the law would result in severe and undeserved harm, or at least the risk of such harm. Most people would probably experience extreme fear in these circumstances, and few people could confidently say that they would resist that fear in order to comply with the law.

5.1   The Theoretical Interpretation

Although duress is well established as a criminal defense, the theoretical explication of the defense remains controversial. Certain aspects of the defense lend themselves to classification as a justification, while other aspects seem more appropriate to an excuse. Some commentators have classified the defense as a justification, but most interpret it as an excuse.[5]

Those who classify duress as an excuse sometimes contend that this defense applies to defendants who are not culpable for their offenses because their conduct is not voluntary. Some commentators contend that those who are subject to severe coercive pressure to commit a crime have no real choice or are unable to control themselves; their wills are overborne by the force or threats of force.[6] These claims remain extremely difficult to explicate. The conduct in question fulfills the voluntary act requirement, and the actors suffer no disorder such as paralysis or convulsion that severs the usual association between individual behavior and psychological process such as deliberation and decision. Defendants raise the duress defense regarding conduct performed in an organized, goal-directed, and often efficient manner.[7]

For this reason, Herbert Fingarette rejects the interpretation of duress as a claim of involuntariness, advancing an alternative interpretation of duress as a species of victimization. According to Fingarette, *X* victimizes *Y,* giving rise to a duress defense for *Y,* when *X* wrongfully intervenes in the situation in order to manipulate *Y* into performing the crime by making it appear to be the reasonable thing to do. *Y* should be excused from the burden ordinarily associated with the crime because *Y* is the victim who acts reasonably under the circumstances.[8] Fingarette's account of duress as victimization provides an interesting analysis of the relationship between the defendant and the victimizer who

4 *Id.* at § 177(e)(5).

5 Criminal Law at § 5.3; Joshua Dressler, *Exegesis of the Law of Duress: Justifying the Excuse and Searching for Its Proper Limits,* 62 S. Calif. L. Rev. 1331, 1349–67 (1989).

6 Defenses at § 177(a); Rethinking at 831.

7 Herbert Fingarette, *Victimization: A Legalist Analysis of Coercion, Deception, Undue Influence, and Excusable Prison Escape,* 42 Wash. & Lee L. Rev. 65, 71–82 (1985).

8 *Id.* at 66, 82–6, 105–14. This account would also apply to cases in which *X* tricks *Y* into committing a crime.

exerts the coercive force. This relationship arguably lies at the center of the historical defense. In addition, it illuminates the relationship between duress and other variations of victimization that carry legal significance.[9]

Although victimization places duress in an interesting framework within which one can study its relationships to other legal issues, it does not provide an adequate formulation of duress as a criminal justification or excuse. Fingarette sometimes presents the victimized defendant as acting reasonably in the circumstances, but in other passages he describes the defendant as one who acts in a manner that appears reasonable to the defendant.[10] This distinction is analogous to that raised earlier between external and internal justification and, therefore, between justification and excuse.[11] If the victimizer's intervention actually renders the defendant's conduct reasonable by systemic standards, why does duress excuse rather than justify the conduct as the lesser evil? Alternately, if it renders the conduct reasonable only in terms of the defendant's personal interests and standards, why would it have any effect on the status of the criminal conduct from the perspective of the criminal law? Finally, if the victimization causes the offensive conduct to appear reasonable only to the defendant, how does duress differ from the excuse provided for mistake regarding justification?

Perhaps most importantly, the victimization interpretation fails to accommodate an important subset of plausible duress cases in which the defendant realizes that the criminal conduct is not reasonable. Suppose K runs a day-care center where he takes care of several preschool children, including his own. Mobsters enter the center, place a gun at the head of K's child and threaten to kill the child unless K identifies the children of a rival mobster on whom they intend to take revenge by killing his children. By identifying the mobster's two children, K trades two innocent lives for one. K's act would not satisfy the requirements of a lesser-evils justification, but K would have a plausible argument for the duress defense. This argument would remain plausible, and perhaps even become more persuasive, however, if K admitted that he acted believing that his conduct was not reasonable, but "I was just too scared to say no." Perhaps the most intuitively credible duress defendants are those who suffer guilt and remorse for their action, admitting that they knew they were doing wrong when they performed the criminal conduct but claiming that they were so frightened that they did it anyway.

Dressler advances an interpretation of duress as an excuse that captures difficult duress cases such as K's and addresses the feature that cases 5.2, 5.3, and 5.4 have in common with duress.[12] Dressler contends that duress is the excuse

---

9 *Id.* at 86–104.
10 *Compare id.* at 66, 86, 104, 108, 117 *with* 105, 110–13.
11 *See supra* § 2.4.2.
12 *See supra* § 1.1.7 identifying cases 5.2, 5.3, 5.4.

provided by the criminal justice system for those who commit crimes because they encounter conditions demanding more courage than society can fairly demand of its citizens. In Dressler's view, defendants who raise the duress defense each claim "I am only human," and society exculpates them because they committed their crimes in response to threats that persons of "nonsaintly" moral strength cannot be expected to withstand.[13] This formulation captures the plea advanced by *K* regarding his identification of the mobster's children. "I knew I should not give up two innocents to save one," *K* explains, "but I am only human; I was too frightened of what would happen to my child if I refused them, as I knew I should." Similarly the escaping prisoners in case 5.2, the innocent farmer *C* in case 5.4, and the stranded sailors *G* and *H* in case 5.3 all faced circumstances that arguably demanded more of them than a society can reasonably expect. *V,* who defends her life at the expense of the two innocent hostages, and the battered woman who kills her batterer because she is too frightened to take the chance that she might be wrong also reflect this pattern.

These cases are exceptional due to the extremely difficult choices these defendants faced. Our intuitive judgment that we ought not punish them reflects neither justification nor disability-based excuse but rather the recognition that few people, including ourselves, would have performed differently in these circumstances.

Although Dressler's formulation of duress captures the intuitive significance of the circumstances that give rise to many claims of duress, it remains difficult to reconcile with an integrated system of excuses. Robinson contends that excuses conform to a basic structure consisting of a disability giving rise to an excusing condition. The disability is some abnormal condition of the individual that differentiates that person from the population in general and causes the excusing condition. The excusing condition, such as impairment of the actors' abilities to voluntarily control their conduct or to understand the nature of their conduct, renders them not blameworthy for their illegal behavior.[14]

Defendants who qualify for excuses do not merit the fourth type of condemnation expressed by criminal punishment. Individuals who suffer disabilities such as severe psychopathology or mental subnormality, which give rise to excusing conditions, lack the capacities of rational agency, at least regarding their conduct that violated the fully articulated conventional public morality. Those who lack the capacities of rational agency do not violate the dictates of the criminal law as accountable agents, and hence the courts cannot appropriately subject them to the fourth type of condemnation that inheres in criminal punishment.[15]

---

13 Dressler, *supra* note 5, at 1334, 1363–7.
14 Defenses at §§ 26, 161.
15 *See supra* § 2.3.3.

Certain excuses exculpate defendants who do not suffer disabilities giving rise to excusing conditions. Nonculpable mistakes regarding justification, for example, exculpate those who act on those mistakes under the excuse discussed previously as putative justification. Although these defendants lack disabilities, situational factors undermine attributions of culpability for these mistakes. These defendants possess the capacities of rational agency, but their illegal conduct is not appropriately attributed to them in their status as accountable agents because their nonculpable mistakes prevented them from bringing their capacities of accountable agency to bear on their decision to engage in that conduct. Their action-plans, which represent them as accountable agents, did not include the conduct which fulfills the objective offense elements.[16] These defendants do not merit the fourth type of condemnation because they did not violate the criminal law in their status as accountable agents, although they generally possess the relevant capacities.

Duress defendants, in contrast to those who claim disability or mistake-based excuses, possess the capacities of accountable agents, and they have the knowledge that provides the opportunity to exercise those capacities. They act on action-plans that include the acts exemplifying the objective offense elements as intended components. Although excuses usually exculpate defendants who suffer some disability that differentiates them from most people, the "person of reasonable firmness" clause in the duress provision of the MPC appeals to the similarity between the defendant's behavior and that which would have been expected from most reasonable people.[17] This focus on situational factors and criteria generalizable across persons ordinarily applies more appropriately to justifications than to excuses.

As usually formulated, duress apparently combines properties of justification and of excuse, yet it qualifies as neither. Many crimes committed under conditions that raise plausible duress claims do not qualify for justification because the defendants engage in conduct that society does not condone and intends to discourage rather than encourage. The day-care operator *K,* the innocent farmer *C* (in case 5.4), and *V* who protects herself at the expense of two innocent hostages, for example, each promote the greater harm by sacrificing two or more innocent lives in order to save one. Yet none of these actors suffers a disability or excusing condition that would ground an excuse other than duress.

Robinson identifies the state of coercion and the resultant inability to control behavior as the disability and excusing condition, respectively.[18] As discussed previously, however, many duress defendants violate the law through organized, efficient, goal-directed conduct, demonstrating no indication of

---

16 *See supra* § 2.4.2.
17 MPC at § 2.09; Defenses at § 177(a).
18 Defenses at § 177(c).

impaired ability to control their actions.[19] Disabilities are abnormal conditions of actors, but a "state of coercion" does not constitute a condition of an individual. Coercion is "the application of force to control the action of a voluntary agent," and to coerce is "[t]o constrain or restrain (a voluntary or moral agent) by the application of superior force."[20] Thus, a state of coercion is not a condition of an actor but rather a relationship between an actor and a source of power, usually another person or group. As such, it may carry exculpatory force, but it does not constitute a disability as Robinson defines it, nor is it a defective capacity similar to those that ground insanity or mental subnormality excuses.

These arguments do not deny the intuitive moral force of the coercive circumstances that raise strong claims of duress, but they raise serious question about the rationale and parameters of the defense and about the accuracy of classifying duress as an excuse as that category is usually understood. Defendants who raise this defense demonstrate neither standard excusing conditions nor disabilities that differentiate them from the general population. Duress does not undermine the fourth type of condemnation expressed by criminal punishment because these defendants possess the capacities of accountable agents, and they have the knowledge required to apply those capacities to the decision at hand. The "person of reasonable firmness" provision appeals to the similarity between these actors and most others rather than to any condition that differentiates them. The intuitive judgment that these people do not deserve punishment arises not from circumstances or disabilities that would ordinarily support justification or excuse, but rather from the recognition that only saints or heroes would have resisted the coercive circumstances they encountered. An adequate theory of duress should reflect the difference between this intuitive judgment and the corresponding intuitions underlying justification and excuse.

5.2 Systemically Complete Mitigation

The criminal law ordinarily addresses wrongful conduct committed by responsible agents under difficult circumstances through mitigation in sentencing. By mitigating the degree of punishment, the law recognizes the defendant as less blameworthy for any of several reasons including unusually difficult circumstances.[21] If defendants raise the duress defense as a claim of mitigation, rather than excuse, they contend that they deserve less punishment than most people who commit similar offenses because they are less blameworthy.

---

19 Robinson describes the excusing condition as comparable to the volitional component of some insanity standards. *Id. See* Robert F. Schopp, Automatism, Insanity and the Psychology of Criminal Responsibility 165–76 (Cambridge: Cambridge Univ. Press, 1991) (analyzing these standards as vacuous).

20 I Oxford English Dictionary at 457.

21 MPC at § 7.01(2); H. L. A. Hart, Punishment and Responsibility 14–16 (Oxford: Oxford Univ. Press, 1968).

The criminal law constitutes a substantial component in the conventional public morality adopted by a society as the framework required for cooperative social interaction. The role of mitigation in this framework differs significantly from that of excuse. Defendants who assert excuses contend that they did not act in the capacity of systemically accountable agents because they lacked either the capacities of rational agency or the knowledge required to effectively apply those capacities to the behavior in question. Those who assert mitigating conditions, in contrast, acknowledge their standing as accountable agents but contend that certain recognized conditions render them less blameworthy than those who commit similar offenses under ordinary circumstances. When compliance with the law requires exceptional discipline or fortitude, they contend, the blameworthiness and appropriate punishment of those who fail to comply decreases just as the praise deserved by those who comply increases.

Mitigation ordinarily reduces the severity of punishment, however, rendering it apparently inadequate for those defendants who commit offenses in circumstances so severe as to completely undermine blameworthiness by conventional standards. Some readers might intuitively reject any attribution of blameworthiness to K (the day-care operator), C (in the flood case), G and H (contesting the plank), V (who kills A and two innocent shields), or the battered woman who kills her sleeping batterer because she is too frightened to rely on her accurate belief that legal assistance is available. These defendants and others act in circumstances that may seem intuitively to render any punishment excessive.

To the extent that the criminal law represents the conventional public morality we need for cooperative interaction, then one who is not blameworthy by the standards of the criminal law is not necessarily one who merits no blame at all by the most stringent standards of critical morality, but rather one who displays the degree of moral discipline and fortitude that citizens must generally exercise in order to maintain the cooperative social process. Just as the criminal law does not forbid every type of wrongful conduct that critical morality would prohibit, it does not require the degree of moral discipline and fortitude that an ideal critical morality would demand. Rather, the criminal law proscribes those violations of the conventional public morality that undermine effective social cooperation, and it requires the level of discipline and fortitude that citizens must generally exercise in order to maintain social cooperation in the public jurisdiction.

Individuals who encounter extraordinarily coercive circumstances might commit unjustified and unexcused offenses despite exercising the degree of discipline and fortitude required by the conventional public morality. The difficult cases just discussed all involve defendants who commit offenses in circumstances that do not establish justification defenses under the theory defended in Chapters 2 through 4. Neither do they qualify for excuse because they acted as accountable agents by the standards of the conventional public morality. Yet, the degree of fortitude required for compliance with the law in circumstances such as these individuals encountered may well exceed that which the conventional public morality generally requires in order to maintain cooperative interaction in the public jurisdiction. Rarely must citizens sacrifice their own lives or those of loved ones in order to maintain a cooperative society.

On this view, the criminal law defines and enforces the degree of individual discipline and fortitude required by the conventional public morality in order to maintain cooperative social interaction by punishing those who fall below this level while committing unjustified and unexcused offenses. Offenders who fail to exercise the required discipline and fortitude are blameworthy by the standard of the conventional public morality and subject to punishment. Circumstances that demand unusual discipline and fortitude mitigate blameworthiness, reducing the appropriate punishment in criminal justice systems that punish in proportion to blameworthiness. Extraordinary circumstances may elevate the level of discipline and fortitude required for compliance beyond that which the conventional public morality demands. People who confront such extraordinary circumstances might exercise more discipline and fortitude than a society can reasonably demand, yet fail to successfully resist the coercive pressure. *K, C, G, H, V,* the frightened battered woman, and others who commit offenses in response to such extreme circumstances are not blameworthy by the standards of the conventional public morality because they have not fallen below the level of discipline and fortitude required by those standards.

These offenders are neither justified nor excused, yet they are not appropriately subject to punishment in a system that punishes in proportion to blameworthiness because they are not blameworthy by systemic standards. As usually understood, legal punishment involves harsh treatment of an offender, for an offense, administered by an authority in such a manner as to express moral condemnation. The harsh treatment usually takes a form, such as incarceration, that expresses condemnation in that society, and the severity of the punishment is usually intended to reflect the degree of condemnation deserved by the offender.[22] Individuals who commit offenses under extremely demanding circumstances merit conviction by the standards of the criminal justice system because they have fulfilled the offense elements without justification or excuse. They do not deserve punishment in a retributive system that punishes in proportion to blameworthiness, however, because they are not blameworthy by the standards of the conventional public morality, which does not require heroic discipline and fortitude.

When extraordinary circumstances render the defendant inappropriate for blame by the standards of the system but do not provide any justification or

---

22 Joel Feinberg, Doing and Deserving 95–118 (Princeton: Princeton Univ. Press, 1970); Hart, *supra* note 21, at 4–5.

excuse, then mitigation completely precludes the harsh treatment that expresses condemnation within the system, but it does not preclude conviction. Defendants who commit crimes under these conditions merit *systemically complete mitigation* leading to conviction without the harsh treatment that constitutes part of legal punishment. Conviction without harsh treatment would serve an important expressive purpose by vindicating the law that proscribes acts of these types, as defined at the level of generality available in the penal code, and by vindicating the standing of innocent victims by acknowledging that they were wronged. These *purely vindicating convictions* would also recognize, however, that the defendant acted under conditions such that they were not blameworthy by the standards of the conventional public morality represented by the criminal law.[23]

Some individuals might commit unjustified offenses under conditions that render them accountable but not blameworthy for at least two distinct reasons. First, they might not qualify as blameworthy under the standards of some comprehensive doctrine. As an institution of the conventional public morality, however, the criminal law cannot accommodate such criteria. The conventional public morality of a liberal society addresses only those aspects of morality that fall within the legitimate scope of the public jurisdiction because they affect the process of cooperative social interaction among citizens who endorse a variety of comprehensive doctrines.[24] The criminal justice system must confine itself to criteria of blameworthiness that fall within the scope of the public jurisdiction and that are amenable to formulation in terms of sufficient generality to serve as rules or principles of law. The attribution of blameworthiness within the criminal law is necessarily incomplete from the perspective of critical morality, because any attempt to derive a critically complete standard of blameworthiness would extend beyond the boundaries of the public jurisdiction in order to address those aspects of blameworthiness that arise in the nonpublic domain. In doing so, the criminal law would effectively institutionalize at least part of some comprehensive doctrine, transgressing the basic liberal boundary between the public and nonpublic domains.

Second, some defendants might lack blameworthiness by the standards of the conventional public morality because extreme circumstances require discipline or fortitude beyond the level required for cooperative social interaction. Although these cases fall within the legitimate scope of the criminal law, the legal provisions addressing offense elements, excuses, and mitigation do not

---

23 Although this discussion specifically advocates the interpretation of duress as systemically complete mitigation leading to purely vindicating conviction, duress does not exhaust the appropriate scope of this approach. The innocent farmer *C*, the stranded sailors *G* and *H*, *V* who kills the innocent shields, and the frightened battered woman do not qualify for duress as usually formulated, but they provide plausible candidates for systematically complete mitigation.
24 *See supra* § 3.3.

accommodate them. Thus, courts, juries, and theorists must either advocate punishment that intuitively seems undeserved or rely on vague assertions that these defendants had no real choice, could not help themselves, or had their wills overborne. Systemically complete mitigation leading to purely vindicating convictions would provide an institutional alternative that would explicitly recognize the unique exculpatory force of extraordinarily coercive circumstances in a conventional public morality.

Purely vindicating convictions differ significantly from suspended sentences. Courts sometimes sentence defendants to a conventional term of years but suspend that sentence pending successful completion of a period of probation. Courts ordinarily suspend sentence in favor of probation for a variety of reasons including the following: the defendant is not considered dangerous, the defendant has a job and a family to support, the defendant is a promising candidate for rehabilitation, or the facilities for incarceration are overcrowded.[25] In contrast to a purely vindicating conviction, a suspended sentence marks the defendant as blameworthy to the degree represented by the severity of that suspended sentence. Probation serves as a social instrument applied by the court for purposes of social policy and is revocable by the court upon violation of conditions precisely because the suspended sentence has been identified as the harsh treatment deserved by the blameworthy defendant. According to usual practice, courts apply probation and suspended sentences as a matter of mercy, efficiency, or social policy.[26] In contrast, the purely vindicating convictions advocated here reflect considerations of justice grounded in blameworthiness and desert according to the standard of the conventional public morality.

In some cases, courts may suspend sentences because the defendant is not blameworthy and does not deserve harsh treatment for an offense committed in response to provocation or fear. A criminal justice system that recognized purely vindicating convictions would provide courts with a distinct verdict that would enable them to treat these defendants differently than those who are blameworthy but receive suspended sentences for policy reasons. This alternative would authorize the court to convict and release without suspended sentence, avoiding the inconsistency of setting a sentence that ostensibly measures blameworthiness and suspending that sentence because the defendant is not blameworthy.

5.3   Two Potential Criticisms

Potential critics might raise two objections to the proposed purely vindicating convictions. First, they might claim that this practice is inconsistent in that it

---

25 MPC at §§ 6.02, 7.01.
26 Arthur W. Campbell, The Law of Sentencing §§ 5.1, 5.3 (Deerfield, Ill.: Clark Boardman Callaghan, 1991) (discussing social policies underlying probation and conditions of probation).

implicitly asserts both that these defendants are appropriate subjects of condemnation and that they are not. Purely vindicating convictions vindicate precisely because they represent social condemnation of the defendant's conduct, they might contend, yet we withhold the harsh treatment on the premise that these defendants are not sufficiently blameworthy to merit the condemnation represented by punishment. Second, some critics might deny that exculpation under excuse differs from mitigation to purely vindicating conviction. In either case, the verdict rejects the claim that the act is justified but exempts the actor from punishment.

Neither of these two potential criticisms accurately applies to the proposed purely vindicating conviction. This proposal avoids contradiction because the apparent inconsistency actually reflects the complexity of the institution of punishment. Any particular case of legal punishment involves the application of a complex social institution of punishment to a particular person for a particular offense. In order to establish rules of relatively broad generality, the institution must define offense elements as well as conditions of culpability and excuse in terms of relatively broad properties that do not capture every morally significant factor.

Purely vindicating convictions reflect the separate functions of justification, excuse, and mitigation within the conventional public morality represented by the criminal law, and they provide a legal device through which officials can express the social judgement relevant to this conventional morality in a more precise manner. Vindicating convictions ratify the systemic prohibition of acts of the type performed by the defendants as defined at the level of generality available to the system, and they recognize these defendants as accountable agents who have committed offenses as defined by the code. These convictions also vindicate the standing of innocent victims by explicitly denouncing the criminal conduct. They withhold harsh treatment, however, in recognition of the specific factors that rendered conformity in these cases so difficult as to demand discipline and fortitude beyond that required by the conventional public morality.

In short, purely vindicating convictions reaffirm systemic condemnation of acts of the type performed by the defendant but refrain from condemning this defendant as blameworthy for this particular act due to the extremely demanding circumstances. As such, they provide a special legal device for addressing defendants who commit offenses under conditions that warrant the first and fourth types of condemnation inherent in criminal punishment, but who do not merit the fifth type of condemnation as morally blameworthy by systemic standards. These convictions provide us with an official procedure for publicly communicating to the defendant, "You are a responsible person, and acts of the type you performed are prohibited, but we realize that under those conditions most citizens might have done the same thing and that the conventional public morality does not require heroism."

Although purely vindicating conviction and excuse both exempt the actor from harsh treatment without approving of the act as permissible, they are not interchangeable. Excuses exempt defendants who manifest excusing conditions due to disabilities that undermine their status as systemically accountable agents who are appropriately subject to punishment. Excuses usually cite some impairment of the actors' capacities that deprived them of the functional abilities that we expect people to exercise in order to conform to the law, or they cite some source of ignorance or mistake that deprived the actor of the information needed to effectively exercise their capacities.

Purely vindicating conviction, in contrast, provides a method for explicitly recognizing those situations in which individuals fail to conform to the law due to extraordinary circumstances that neither justify their acts nor undermine their status as accountable agents. Such circumstances undermine the justification of punishment for a distinctly different reason from those that support justification or excuse. That is, compliance with law in these conditions would require discipline and fortitude well beyond that ordinarily demanded by the conventional public morality establishing the framework for social interaction. Categorizing these cases as excuses distorts them by directing attention away from the highly significant circumstances and toward nonexistent disabilities.

Some potential critics might argue that defendants such as K (the day-care operator) or C (the victim of the redirected flood) suffer disabilities in that they lack the capacities needed to conform in these circumstances. This claim distorts the relevant notions of responsibility and disability. The disability that grounds an excuse must differentiate excusable defendants from the general population and give rise to an accepted excusing condition.[27] Ordinarily, these disabilities deprive the offender of the capacities identified by Hart as capacity-responsibility.[28] On this understanding, "capacity-responsibility" refers to competence for a particular role; that is, the role of a citizen with the ability to participate as an accountable agent in the conventional public morality represented by the criminal law. Individuals possess the relevant capacities to greater or lesser degrees, and to say of persons that they are responsible in this sense is to say that they possess these capacities at least to the degree that we ordinarily require of persons before we hold them accountable under the law. Actors suffer disabilities relevant to these capacities when their level of ability falls below this norm defined by the minimally accountable citizen. Thus, the assertion that an actor who possesses the capacities of ordinary citizens suffers a disability because he fails to successfully conform in unusually difficult circumstances distorts this usual conception of capacity-responsibility by misrepresenting extraordinarily demanding circumstances as defective capacities.

In addition to distorting the relevant concepts, categorizing duress as an

---

27 Defenses at § 161(a).
28 Hart, *supra* note 21, at 227–30.

excuse distorts the expression of condemnation inherent in conviction and punishment, denigrating certain defendants and misleading concerned citizens. Justifications and excuses preclude conviction and punishment by rendering inappropriate the fourth type of condemnation ordinarily expressed by legal punishment.[29] Justifications do so by creating exceptions to the prohibitory norms. Thus, actors who engage in justified violations of offense definitions do not violate the fully articulated conventional public morality. Excused actors violate the public morality, but they do not do so in their capacity as accountable agents by systemic standards. Those who do not merit this fourth type of condemnation do not merit conviction and punishment, which inherently expresses this type of condemnation.

Defendants who qualify only for duress, in contrast, violate the fully articulated conventional morality as accountable agents. Extraordinary circumstances undermine attribution of blameworthiness relevant to the fifth type of condemnation, which is ordinarily expressed by punishment. These cases and systemically complete mitigation reveal the inadequacy of the previous explication of the condemnation inherent in punishment. According to that analysis, the only type of condemnation inherent in all institutions of punishment is the condemnation of act-types, which occurs at the institutional level through the articulation of offense definitions. The fourth type of condemnation also inheres in conviction and punishment by any criminal justice system that is retributive in the minimal sense that it limits punishment to those who fulfill criteria of accountability. This analysis did not include the fifth type of condemnation among those inherent in punishment.[30]

The formulation of duress as systemically complete mitigation suggests a more complete analysis of the fifth type of condemnation. Judges and jurors make determinations regarding both conviction and sentencing, and they have access to systemic criteria of blameworthiness reflecting the conventional public morality as well as to personal criteria rooted in their comprehensive doctrines. Conviction does not imply blameworthiness by either personal or systemic criteria. It does not imply that the defendant is blameworthy by the personal standards of triers of fact because each trier's personal moral standards may differ from the legal criteria for reasons arising from that person's comprehensive doctrine and from the institutional requirements of law. Thus, triers of fact who take seriously an institutional responsibility to set aside their personal standards in order to subject the participants only to the conventional public morality embodied in judicial instructions will sometimes bring verdicts that do not reflect their personal moral standards of blameworthiness.

Conviction does not imply blameworthiness by systemic criteria because conviction in a retributive system entails only the first and fourth types of con-

29 *See supra* § 2.3.3.
30 *See supra* § 2.3.1.

demnation. Although the fourth type of condemnation, and thus conviction, requires that the defendant violated the offense definition in his capacity as an accountable agent, systemic criteria of accountability do not exhaust the set of factors relevant to blameworthiness. The criminal justice system addresses other considerations relevant to blameworthiness as mitigating and aggravating factors regarding sentencing rather than as complete defenses.

Punishment does not imply blameworthiness by personal standards for the same reasons that prevent conviction from doing so. Punishment implies blameworthiness by systemic standards, however, in retributive institutions that distribute punishment in proportion to blameworthiness because such a system cannot administer the harsh treatment that constitutes part of punishment to a defendant who is not blameworthy by systemic standards. That is, any punishment must imply some blameworthiness by systemic standards in a retributive institution that punishes in proportion to blameworthiness. Thus, punishment by a criminal justice system that is retributive in this sense implies blameworthiness by the systemic criteria, but circumstances that demand discipline and fortitude beyond the level required by these criteria undermine the attribution of blameworthiness. Purely vindicating convictions provide courts in these retributive systems with a device for addressing those cases in which the defendants violate fully articulated norms as accountable agents but do not merit condemnation as blameworthy by systemic criteria. In this manner, these convictions enable the court to articulate more precisely the judgment of the conventional public morality represented by the criminal justice system.

Some readers might accept the argument for systemically complete mitigation but contend that it should be categorized as a separate type of defense leading to acquittal rather than to purely vindicating convictions. Although such an interpretation would preserve the basic analysis of justification and duress advanced in this book, I prefer the fully vindicating conviction for the following reasons. As presently developed, our criminal justice system addresses circumstances that increase or decrease blameworthiness for a particular crime through aggravation in sentencing. Current defenses that address defendant culpability, broadly construed, exculpate defendants either because they have not violated the fully articulated conventional public morality by committing a legal offense, or because they have not done so as responsible agents. Failure-of-proof defenses address those who have not committed legal offenses. Justifications exculpate those who have not violated fully articulated conventional morality. Excuses exculpate those who do not violate the norms as responsible agents.[31] The approach advanced in this chapter promotes conceptual consistency with this framework by classifying systemically complete mitigation as a sentencing issue rather than as a defense that precludes conviction.

31 *See supra* § 2.4.2.

The purely vindicating conviction retains the explicit condemnation of this type of conduct at the systemic level, possibly enhancing the ability of many people, especially innocent victims, to accept the outcome. The vindicating conviction also affirms the broader structure by explicitly confirming the defendant's status as an accountable agent by systemic standards. Finally, the vindicating conviction recognizes the separate expressive functions of conviction and punishment in retributive institutions. That is, conviction condemns this person's performing a particular type of conduct as an accountable agent, and punishment expresses the degree of blameworthiness attributable to that agent. Some might suggest, of course, that the entire current framework ought to be revised, but that issue extends well beyond the scope of this book.[32]

The classification of duress and similar cases within the broader framework of the criminal law carries significance beyond the quest for conceptual consistency. The currently dominant classification of duress as an excuse denigrates the identified defendants by misrepresenting them as lacking the capacities of accountable agents. Perhaps most importantly from the perspective of the expressive function of the criminal law, excusing these actors encourages the rest of us to engage in an insidious form of self-deception in which we direct our attention toward the putative defects suffered by these particular individuals rather than confronting the uncomfortable likelihood that they acted as they did not because they differ from us but rather because they are very much like us.

5.4 Conclusion

Those who act within the scope of justification defenses do not merit the condemnation inherent in criminal conviction. Legal conviction and punishment ordinarily expresses condemnation of five types at two levels, but only the first type of condemnation, expressed at the institutional level by the proscription of certain act-types as criminal offenses, inheres in any institution of legal punishment. Conviction in a retributive system of specific defendants for specific offenses also expresses condemnation of the actors for violating the fully articulated conventional public morality as accountable agents by systemic standards.

Justification defenses exempt certain defendants who do not merit this type of condemnation because their actions do not violate the fully articulated conventional public morality. Excuses, in contrast, exculpate those who violate this conventional morality but not in the capacity of accountable agents. Some excused defendants lack the capacities required to qualify them as accountable

---

32 *See, e.g.,* Karl Menninger, The Crime of Punishment (New York: Viking Press, 1968); Barbara Wootton, Crime and the Criminal Law (London: Stevens, 1963).

agents, while others lack the knowledge that would provide the opportunity to apply these capacities to the decision to perform the proscribed conduct.

Duress has traditionally been very difficult to classify as either a justification or an excuse, and so it should remain because it is neither. Duress represents a subset of a broader set of cases that should be subject to systemically complete mitigation resulting in purely vindicating convictions. In a retributive system that punishes in proportion to systemic criteria of blameworthiness, this approach would accommodate defendants who do not merit blame by systemic standards and thus do not merit the fifth type of condemnation, which is inherent in punishment by these retributive systems. Although conviction in a retributive system entails only the first and fourth types of condemnation, punishment also entails condemnation as blameworthy by systemic criteria in proportion to the severity of the punishment. Thus, accountable agents who commit unjustified offenses under extraordinarily coercive circumstances merit the condemnation inherent in conviction but not the condemnation inherent in punishment.

6

The Limits of Justification
Necessity and Nullification

Consider three types of atypical criminal defendants. The first trespasses at a nuclear weapons plant (or a segregated bus station or women's health clinic) in order to publicly protest some law or public policy represented by that facility or by the activity that occurs there. The second operates an underground railroad in violation of the Fugitive Slave Act (or smuggles South American residents into the United States or breaks into a women's health clinic in order to disable equipment and prevent scheduled abortions). The third causes the death of a loved one by disconnecting that person from life-sustaining medical machinery in order to fulfill a promise to that person or to spare that person the pain or indignity of such an existence.

All three types of defendants violate valid law from a sense of conscience. All understand the nature and consequences of their acts, and none suffers any disability that might ground a legal excuse. No ordinary defense clearly applies, yet punishment may raise intuitive discomfort. Many readers might ask, "Are these the types of people and conduct we had in mind when we built the prisons?"

Such defendants sometimes seek judicial instructions regarding either the necessity defense or jury nullification.[1] Appellate courts almost universally reject these requests, although trial courts occasionally instruct regarding the necessity defense, and these instructions sometimes generate acquittals.[2] Commentators debate each separately without clear resolution or clarification of the

---

1 Matthew Lippman, *The Necessity Defense and Political Protest,* 26 Crim. L. Bull. 317 (1990); Alan Scheflin & Jon Van Dyke, *Jury Nullification: The Contours of a Controversy,* 43 Law & Contemp. Probs. 51 (1980).

2 Arlene D. Boxerman, Comment, *The Use of the Necessity Defense by Abortion Clinic Protesters,* 81 J. Crim. L. & Criminology 677, 690n90 (1990); Lippman, *id.* at 38–43; Scheflin & Van Dyke, *id.* at 63–8; Laura J. Schulkind, Note, *Applying the Necessity Defense to Civil Disobedience Cases,* 64 N.Y.U. L. Rev. 79, 81n13 (1989).

relationship between the necessity defense and jury nullification or of the relationships between each and crimes of conscience.[3]

This chapter examines the appropriate roles for the necessity defense and jury nullification as jury responses to crimes of conscience. It clarifies the role and parameters of each and examines the relationship between the two. Thus, it delineates the boundaries of the general category of justification defenses by distinguishing the function of necessity as a residual justification defense from that of nullification. Finally, the analysis considers the significance of these doctrines in understanding the juror's responsibilities as a subject of and a temporary official in the conventional public morality represented by the criminal justice system and as an individual moral agent.

Although some commentators have concentrated on the historical roles of necessity and nullification, this chapter directly addresses analytic and normative rather than historical questions. Analytically, what constitutes necessity and jury nullification, and what is the relationship between the two in context of the broader structure of offense definitions and justification defenses? Normatively, do the principles of political morality underlying the criminal justice system justify distinct functions for necessity and nullification as legitimate components of that system?

Section 6.1 briefly explicates three types of crimes of conscience discussed in this chapter. I do not provide a complete analysis or defense of crimes of conscience because the chapter directly addresses jury responses to this conduct, rather than the crimes themselves. Section 6.2 explores the ongoing debate regarding jury nullification in order to clarify the central issues and evaluate the recent arguments. Section 6.3 advances and defends an interpretation of the legitimate roles of necessity and of nullification in a liberal society. Section 6.4 explores the ramification of this interpretation for the responsibilities of persons as citizens of a conventional public morality and as independent moral agents. Section 6.5 concludes the chapter.

6.1   Crimes of Conscience

According to one widely endorsed conception, civil disobedience involves violation of the law performed in public, motivated by conscience, and intended as an act of communication that appeals to the conscience of the majority.[4] Those

---

3 Regarding the necessity defense, *see* Steven M. Bauer & Peter J. Eckerstrom, Note, *The State Made Me Do It: The Applicability of the Necessity Defense to Civil Disobedience,* 39 Stan. L. Rev. 1173, 1186–7 (1987); Boxerman, *id.;* Lippman, *supra* note 1; Schulkind, *id.* Regarding nullification, *see* Scheflin & Van Dyke, *supra* note 1; Alan W. Scheflin & Jon M. Van Dyke, *Merciful Juries: The Resilience of Jury Nullification,* 48 Wash. & Lee L. Rev. 165 (1991); Gary J. Simson, *Jury Nullification in the American System: A Skeptical View,* 54 Tex. L. Rev. 488 (1976).

4 John Rawls, A Theory of Justice § 55 (Cambridge, Mass.: Harvard Univ. Press, 1971).

who engage in this conduct do so as a dramatic appeal to the conscience of the community in order to encourage the majority to demand change in the law or policy at issue. Some writers would limit the category of civil disobedience to nonviolent offenses and require that the offenders accept the prescribed legal punishment, while others would contest these limitations.[5] Clear cases of civil disobedience include crimes of trespass at various facilities including segregated bus stations, nuclear facilities, or women's health clinics, provided that these acts are intended as public acts of communication designed to elicit the majority's support in challenging the law or policy protested.

Conscientious resistance involves conduct contrary to law and motivated by conscience, but it differs from civil disobedience in that it does not take the form of an act of communication appealing to the majority's sense of justice. Individuals might perform crimes of conscientious resistance in order to challenge law or policy, to prevent its evil effects, or at least to refuse to ratify or acquiesce in that law or policy.[6] Crimes of conscience that constitute conscientious resistance rather than civil disobedience include, for example, secretly smuggling immigrants across the border for the purpose of securing their safety rather than as an attempt to publicly challenge immigration policy or occupying women's health centers for the purpose of physically preventing scheduled abortions from taking place rather than as an appeal for legal change.[7] A particular act or series of acts might qualify as both civil disobedience and conscientious resistance if that behavior is intended both to appeal to public opinion in order to elicit public pressure for change in the law or policy challenged and to ameliorate the effects of that law or policy.

Crimes of personal moral obligation involve conscientious violations of law, but they do not constitute civil disobedience or conscientious resistance because they do not take the form of acts of communication, and they are not intended to change, resist, or perfect law. The individuals who commit these crimes pursue personal rather than institutional goals. Individuals perform crimes of personal moral obligation when they commit criminal offenses in order to fulfill some extralegal source of obligation that they understand as overriding any obligation they have to obey the law in question. A husband might conclude, for example, that an obligation of loyalty to his wife requires that he fulfill her request that he disconnect the medical life support equipment

5 Hugo Adam Bedau, Civil Disobedience in Focus (London: Routledge, 1991); Paul Harris, Civil Disobedience (Lanham, Md.: Univ. Press of America, 1989); Rawls, *id.* at § 55 (requiring nonviolence). I will not attempt to address these disputes here because this chapter addresses juror responses to crimes of conscience rather than the crimes themselves.

6 Rawls, *supra* note 4, at § 56; Henry David Thoreau, *Civil Disobedience,* in Bedau, *id.* at 28. Thoreau also engaged in conscientious resistance through participation in the underground railroad. Henry S. Salt, Life of Henry David Thoreau 72–3 (Champaign, Ill.: Univ. of Illinois Press, 1993).

7 U.S. v. Aguilar, 883 F.2d 662 (9th Cir. 1989); Com v. Wall, 539 A.2d 1325 (Pa. Super. 1988).

from which she is unable to free herself, and he might conclude that this relationship-based obligation is so strong as to outweigh any obligation he might have to conform to law in general or to the homicide statute specifically.

Crimes of civil disobedience, conscientious resistance, and personal moral obligation share the following characteristics. Those who commit all three types of crimes conscientiously believe that important moral considerations justify their conduct. All such crimes fulfill the offense elements of some offense definition, and no specific defense clearly applies.[8] Either the act, the person, or both may seem intuitively not to be "criminal" in the usual sense. Criminal punishment of these people for these acts may elicit discomfort; "are these the types of people and conduct we had in mind when we built the prisons?"

6.2 Jury Nullification

6.2.1 The Central Explicit Debate

Although commentators sometimes endorse either the necessity defense or jury nullification as jury responses to crimes of conscience, they do not provide a comparative analysis of the two. A clear understanding of nullification and its relationship to necessity informs the boundaries of the necessity defense specifically and of the general category of justification defenses. Courts and commentators generally do not dispute the jury's power to engage in nullification by acquitting despite legal guilt. The power arises from the criminal justice system's reliance on general verdicts, the refusal to allow inquiry into the grounds for the jury verdict, and the double jeopardy prohibition on retrying an acquitted defendant.[9] The jury does not possess the same unconstrained power to convict despite legal innocence because the judge can set aside a jury verdict of guilty, and the defendant can appeal a conviction.[10]

Commentators generally discuss nullification as a jury verdict that departs from the law as applied to the evidence, but they sometimes differ in the precise manner in which they characterize nullification. Some, for example, describe juries as having the ultimate power to decide facts and law in criminal cases.[11] Others describe nullification as a process through which jurors take a judicial or legislative role.[12] The commentators agree, however, that nullification does not

---

8 The necessity defense remains an arguable possibility, but it is not ordinarily accepted.
9 Understanding at 10; Scheflin & Van Dyke, *supra* note 1, at 55, 111; Phillip B. Scott, *Jury Nullification: An Historical Perspective on a Modern Debate,* 91 W. Va. L. Rev. 389, 391 (1989); Simson, *supra* note 3, at 524.
10 Fed. R. Crim. P. 29 (judgment of acquittal); Wayne R. LaFave & Jerold Israel, Criminal Procedure § 27.1 (St. Paul, Minn.: West Pub. Co., 2d ed. 1992) (discussing appeals).
11 Scheflin & Van Dyke, *supra* note 1, at 79–85.
12 Simson, *supra* note 3, at 506–7.

involve the power to invalidate a statute, overturn it as unconstitutional, or create new law or precedential force. Thus, any particular jury's power to "decide law" extends only to the case before it.[13]

The central explicit debate involves the manner in which judges should instruct juries regarding their power to nullify. Opponents of explicit nullification instructions defend the status quo, according to which the judge instructs the jurors regarding applicable law and directs them to resolve the case by deciding the factual issues and applying the law as instructed by the judge to those facts. Standard instructions do not inform jurors of their power to depart from the law as instructed. Rather, these instructions frame the jurors' responsibility in a manner that explicitly or implicitly communicates to jurors that they must apply the law as instructed.[14] Advocates of nullification instructions criticize these standard instructions as deceptive. They contend that the judge should instruct the jurors regarding the relevant law and should direct them to grant substantial weight to that law. The judge should also inform them, however, that they may acquit despite legal guilt if mercy or justice requires acquittal as a matter of conscience.[15] The arguments for or against nullification instructions appeal explicitly or implicitly to normative arguments supporting or repudiating the recognition of nullification as falling within the jury's authority.

6.2.2   The Arguments

The disputants debate historical, consequentialist, and deontic issues regarding jury nullification and corresponding instructions.[16] These arguments have been

---

13 Scheflin & Van Dyke, *supra* note 1, at 55–6, 72, 80–1, 87; Scott, *supra* note 9, at 392.

14 CALJIC 0.50 (5th ed.) (July 1995 Pocket Part) ("You must accept and follow the law as I state it"); 4 OJI § 4.03.03 (1995) ("It is your sworn duty . . . to apply the law as it is given to you"); Josephine R. Potuto, Stephen A. Saltsburg, & Harvey S. Perlman, Federal Criminal Jury Instructions § 3.55 (Charlottesville, Va.: Michie, 2d ed. with 1993 sup.) ("I will give you the law . . . you must decide whether (the) (a) defendant is guilty or not guilty by applying the evidence to the law").

15 Scheflin & Van Dyke, *supra* note 1, at 54–5. Jurors should be instructed that "although they are a public body bound to give respectful attention to the laws, they have the final authority to decide whether or not to apply a given law to the acts of the defendant . . . that they represent their communities and that it is appropriate to bring to their deliberations the feelings of the community and their own feelings based on conscience. . . . [D]espite their respect for the law, nothing would bar them from acquitting the defendant if they feel that the law, as applied to the fact situation before them, would produce an inequitable or unjust result." *See generally* Scheflin & Van Dyke, *supra* note 1.

16 As I use the terms in this book, purely consequentialist theories identify the right action as that which will produce good outcomes, where good outcomes are those that maximize production of the value endorsed by the theory as the fundamental good. Deontic theories deny this direct relationship between the good and the right, contending that the right action is determined at least partially by generally formulated duties and principles that carry positive moral weight independent of the consequences. William K. Frankena, Ethics 14–16 (Englewood Cliffs, N.J.:

discussed at length elsewhere.[17] In this section, I discuss them briefly, clarify the notion of jury nullification at issue, and identify the argument that merits careful consideration for the purpose of this book. Section 6.2.3 discusses that argument in more detail.

Some commentators debate the historical role of nullification and the significance of that historical role for a Constitutional right to a trial by jury. Advocates of nullification instructions contend that current instructions undermine the historical role of the jury and, thus, violate the defendant's right to a jury trial, which historically includes the jury's power to decide the facts and the law.[18] Opponents contend that the jury's historical power to decide the law and facts addressed the responsibility to apply the law to the facts rather than authority to make independent determinations of law.[19] They argue that important considerations supporting authority to nullify during the colonial period do not currently apply because contemporary judges, in contrast to colonial judges, are substantially more knowledgeable about the law than are the jurors, and because contemporary American law is democratically established rather than imposed by a foreign power.[20] This chapter does not pursue the historical disputes because they are not central to the analytic and normative issues addressed in this book.

The consequentialist debate involves the relative effectiveness of nullification instructions and of current instructions in attaining just outcomes. Advocates of nullification instructions contend that such instructions would promote equal justice rather than anarchy because appropriate instructions would enable juries to understand the power and its appropriate role, leading them to exercise it seriously, carefully, and consistently when justice demands departure from the written law. They contend that the current approach distorts the jury function and undermines equality of justice because some defendants will have access to jurors who are aware of their power to nullify while others will not. This difference among juries is arbitrary in that it depends on jurors' fortuitous awareness of their power to depart from the judges' instructions and on their willingness to reject the judges' apparent authority rather than on any morally relevant factor, such as justice or desert.[21]

Prentice Hall, 2d ed. 1973) (Frankena uses the term "teleological" rather than "consequentialist").

17 Robert F. Schopp, *Verdicts of Conscience: Nullification and Necessity as Jury Responses to Crimes of Conscience*, S. Calif. L. Rev. 2039, 2044–65 (1996).

18 Scheflin & Van Dyke, *supra* note 1, at 56–79; Chaya Weinberg-Brodt, *Jury Nullification and Jury-Control Procedures*, 65 N.Y.U. L. Rev. 825 (1990).

19 Scott, *supra* note 9, at 406, 414–16; Simson, *supra* note 3, at 491–6.

20 Scott, *supra* note 9, at 416–19; Simson, *supra* note 3, at 496–505.

21 U.S. v. Dougherty, 473 F.2d 1113, 1136 (D.C. Cir. 1972); George C. Christie, *Lawful Departures from Legal Rules: "Jury Nullification" and Legitimated Disobedience*, 62 Calif. L. Rev. 1289, 1303 (1974); Scheflin & Van Dyke, *supra* note 1, at 102–8.

Opponents of nullification instructions contend that current practices promote the rule of law and equality under law. By constraining the jury to the legal rules rather than judgments of conscience, the status quo assures that each defendant's conduct will be evaluated under legal rules that were in force at the time the conduct occurred, and barring legislative change in the law, that the same legal standard will apply to all persons accused of engaging in similar conduct. Nullification instructions might encourage jurors to depart from the law frequently, casually, or on the basis of bias, resulting in disparate verdicts for defendants who engaged in similar conduct in similar circumstances.[22]

Those who support the current approach contend that it discourages nullification but does not prevent jurors from nullifying when extreme circumstances demand rectification. By refusing to instruct jurors regarding their power of nullification but providing no mechanism to reverse or sanction juries that nullify, the criminal justice system maintains a generally consistent rule-based system, yet it allows nullification in circumstances so clear that jurors converge on the need to do so on their own. Thus, the status quo allows nullification but limits it to cases in which the prospect of clear and serious injustice motivates jurors to override judicial instructions.[23] Finally, the current mandatory instructions support jurors who encounter cases in which justice demands an unpopular decision. Jurors can resist popular opinion more effectively when their institutional role requires that they apply the law as instructed.[24]

As with many consequentialist disputes, the central controversies between the participants in this debate are primarily empirical rather than normative. The writers do not advance competing conceptions of just outcomes, nor do they disagree about the relative merits of anarchy and equal justice. Rather, they disagree about jurors' current knowledge regarding the power of nullification absent instructions and about the likely effect of explicit instructions as a method for promoting the mutually endorsed values and outcomes. Thus, this aspect of the debate regarding these consequentialist arguments involves competing empirical hypotheses regarding the frequency, circumstances, and effects of nullification in response to various types of instructions. These hypotheses are difficult to verify.

Commentators sometimes infer nullification from popular accounts of recent trials, from systematic observations within a jurisdiction, or from controlled studies with mock juries.[25] These inferences remain tentative because it

---

22 Mortimer R. Kadish & Sanford H. Kadish, Discretion to Disobey 64–5 (Stanford: Stanford Univ. Press, 1973); Simson, *supra* note 3, at 512–15, 518–19.
23 Kadish & Kadish, *id.* at 65; Simson, *supra* note 3, at 523–5.
24 Christie, *supra* note 21, at 1304; Scheflin & Van Dyke, *supra* note 1, at 108–11.
25 The inferences from recent trials include: James P. Levine, *The Role of Jury Nullification Instructions in the Quest for Peace,* 18 Legal F. 473, 480–1 (1994); Candace McCoy, *If Hard Cases Make Bad Law, Easy Juries Make Bad Facts: A Response to Professor Levine,* 18 Legal F. 497, 501 (1994). The systematic observations include Harry Kalven Jr. & Hans Zeisel, The

is very difficult to distinguish nullification from departures due to misunderstanding of instructions or evaluations of the evidence that differ from those of the judges or researchers.[26] Some commentators contend that most nullification may take the form of indirect or subconscious nullification, which occurs when misgivings about the law or about the justice of anticipated outcomes affect the interpretation and evaluation of ambiguous evidence regarding factual issues.[27] Jury verdicts that deviate from strict compliance with law due to misunderstanding of judicial instructions or to misinterpretation of evidence raise important empirical and normative issues, but the appropriate analysis might differ from that which applies to nullification as a deliberate verdict of conscience. For the sake of clarity, throughout the remainder of this analysis, I use "jury deviation" to refer to the broad category of cases in which jury verdicts deviate from those most consistent with the judicial instructions as applied to the evidence. I reserve "jury nullification" for that subset of jury deviation in which jurors deliberately deviate as a matter of conscience.

Although the nullification instructions provided to mock jurors in the controlled studies specifically addressed the jury's power to acquit, the juries who received these instructions demonstrated tendencies toward increased acquittals in certain cases and toward increased convictions in other cases.[28] The evidence gathered regarding deliberations indicated that juries receiving nullification instructions were less narrowly focused on the evidence, directing more attention toward issues such as the defendant's character and their own related experience. The precise content of this nonevidentiary material varied with the type of case presented as did the tendency toward acquittals or convictions.[29]

This set of data suggests that nullification instructions may increase the danger of "malignant" jury deviation. That is, instructions that render jury deliberation and decision relatively susceptible to nonevidentiary influences may decrease the probability of just outcomes by increasing the potential effect of contaminating influences such as bias or animosity. Such malignant deviation

---

American Jury 494–5 (Boston: Little, Brown, 1971); James P. Levine, *The Legislative Role of Juries,* 1984 Am. B. Found. Res. J. 605, 633; Martha A. Myers, *Rule Departures and Making Law: Juries and Their Verdicts,* 13 Law & Soc'y Rev. 781 (1979). The controlled studies include Irwin A. Horowitz, *The Effect of Jury Nullification Instruction on Verdicts and Jury Functioning in Criminal Trials,* 9 Law & Hum. Behav. 25 (1985); Irwin A. Horowitz, *The Impact of Judicial Instructions, Arguments, and Challenges on Jury Decision Making,* 12 Law & Hum. Behav. 439 (1988); Jeffrey Kerwin & David R. Shaffer, *The Effects of Jury Dogmatism on Reactions to Jury Nullification Instructions to Jury Nullification Instructions,* 17 Personality & Soc. Psychol. Bull. 140 (1991).

26 Paul H. Robinson, *Are Criminal Codes Irrelevant?* 68 S. Calif. L. Rev. 159, 172–6 (1994).
27 Valerie P. Hans & Neil Vidmar, Judging the Jury 154 (New York: Plenum Press, 1988); Kalven & Zeisel, *supra* note 25, at 495; Levine 1984, *supra* note 25, at 633.
28 *Jury Nullification Instruction, supra* note 25; *Impact of Judicial Instructions, supra* note 25.
29 *Id.;* Kerwin & Shaffer, *supra* note 25.

might occur as a conscious decision to depart from the law out of malice, bias, or personal preference. Alternately, it might take the form sometimes referred to as indirect or subconscious nullification in which bias or expectation distorts the interpretation of evidence. It may take either exculpatory or inculpatory forms in that a juror may exercise bias that favors or disfavors a defendant.

The legal system provides some protection against malignant deviation in that judges can overturn jury convictions that lack a foundation in evidence and defendants can appeal to higher courts.[30] These limitations on the jury's power to deviate may afford minimal protection, however, for several reasons. First, they apply only to convictions, providing no recourse for malignant exculpatory deviation. Second, although judges have the authority to set aside jury convictions unsupported by evidence, they are unlikely to do so in cases in which the evidence was sufficient to preclude dismissal prior to sending the case to the jury for deliberation.[31] Similarly, the appellate courts' deferential standard of review regarding determinations of fact renders reversal on the basis of insufficient evidence unlikely in cases in which the evidence was sufficient to get to the jury.[32]

The review of available empirical evidence provides no clear resolution to the central disputes of the consequentialist debate.[33] The database is relatively small, and the studies reflect methodological limitations that warrant caution in extrapolating to firm conclusions about criminal trials. The available data suggest that nullification instructions and arguments addressing nullification by attorneys during trials would alter both verdicts and deliberations by rendering them less rule-bound. The degree to which these changes would promote or undermine just outcomes remains clouded. The possibility that different nullification instructions could increase just outcomes by promoting corrective nullification while discouraging malignant deviations remains open.[34]

In summary, jury deviation occurs when a jury's verdict deviates from that which is most consistent with the judicial instructions as applied to the evidence. Jury deviation might take the form of a deliberate decision, or it might occur accidentally due to misunderstanding of instructions or evidence or to unintended bias in interpretation. It might be exculpatory or inculpatory in effect, and it might be conscientious or malicious in motive. Finally, it might

---

30 *See supra,* sources listed in note 10.
31 Fed. R. Crim. P. 29. The same standard applies to judgment of acquittal before or after submission to the jury.
32 Steven Alan Childress & Martha S. Davis, Federal Standards of Review § 9.01 (New York: Wiley, 2d ed. 1992).
33 Schopp, *supra* note 17, at 2049–55.
34 Some evidence indicates, for example, that corrective instructions can reduce the legally undesirable effects of hindsight bias. David B. Wexler & Robert F Schopp, *How and When to Correct for Juror Hindsight Bias in Mental Health Law Malpractice Litigation: Some Preliminary Observations,* 7 Behav. Sci. & L. 485, 487–9 (1989).

serve a corrective function by promoting just outcomes, or it might constitute a malignant influence that renders outcomes less just.

As usually advocated, jury nullification constitutes an exercise of conscience, and as such, it must be deliberate. Although an act of conscience may be misguided, it must involve an attempt to do what one believes one ought to do rather than an act of malice. Thus, it is analytic in the concept of jury nullification as an act of conscience that deviation qualifies as nullification only if it is deliberate rather than accidental and conscientious rather than malicious.[35]

Although commentators call for nullification instructions specifying exculpatory nullification intended to promote just outcomes, neither just outcomes nor exculpatory verdicts are analytic in the concept of deliberate, conscientious deviation from law. Whether conscientious nullification or nullification instructions produce on balance exculpatory or inculpatory verdicts and corrective or malignant outcomes remain open questions. Clear evidence regarding the answers to these questions might provide important premises in a comprehensive argument addressing the legitimate roles of various instructions. Such an argument must also consider the deontic issues.

Advocates of nullification instructions advance at least two separate deontic arguments that do not depend primarily on empirical claims. First, they claim that the principle of democratic self-government requires nullification instructions. The current approach prevents the jury, as the representatives of the people in the criminal process, from making a final decision regarding the laws under which the people shall be judged.[36] Second, they argue that the current approach undermines the moral force of the criminal law because it deceives jurors regarding their power of nullification.[37] The deontic variation of this argument contends that regardless of the possible effects of these deceptive instructions, they undermine the moral authority of the system by violating important moral principles requiring honesty and respect for the participants in the process.

The first deontic argument fails because jury nullification and democratic self-government do not represent or protect common principles. Democratic self-government legitimizes government authority and coercion by vesting the decision-making power in the hands of the people who are subject to that authority and to coercive force. It discourages abuse of power by making officials answerable to the people, and it curbs the tendency to pass oppressive laws by placing the lawmaking power in the hands of the people who will be subject to the laws. Finally, it provides equality of citizenship by recognizing equal standing in the democratic process.

35 Martin Benjamin, *Conscience,* in I Encyclopedia of Bioethics 469 (Warren T. Reich ed., New York: Macmillan, rev. ed. 1995).
36 Scheflin & Van Dyke, *supra* note 1, at 93–4, 111.
37 *Id.* at 105–6; Scheflin & Van Dyke, *supra* note 3, at 179–83.

When juries engage in nullification, in contrast, jurors who are neither democratically elected nor accountable for their decision to nullify reject laws established through a democratic process in order to apply unenacted standards to which they are not themselves subject to individuals who had no opportunity to vote in any process by which these standards were selected. Thus, nullification represents an explicit rejection of democratic self-government.[38] The possibility remains, however, that other important principles support the practice. The contention that deception undermines the integrity and, thus, the moral force of the criminal law provides a potentially powerful argument against any deceptive practice in the process of criminal adjudication. The next section examines this argument in greater detail.

6.2.3 *Deception and the Moral Force of the Criminal Law*

Although the criminal law prescribes punishment for those who commit offenses in order to deter such conduct, deterrence constitutes only one function of the criminal law. Legal punishment for infractions of the core rules of the criminal law expresses moral condemnation, marking such conduct as unacceptable by the conventional public morality of the society.[39] Deception in the administration of criminal justice undermines the criminal law's standing as the embodiment of the conventional public morality in at least two ways. First, those who discover this deception may lose respect for the system, undermining its role as a source of guidance for voluntary compliance by the majority. That is, citizens who become aware of the deception may no longer accept the criminal justice system as an embodiment of a public morality they endorse, and, therefore, they will no longer grant any moral authority to its prohibitions or to its expressions of condemnation. These people would view the criminal justice system as merely the "gunman writ large."[40] Such an institution loses its capacity to guide behavior by articulating moral standards for voluntarily compliance, becoming merely a source of coercion for those who fear arrest and punishment.

Second, the deception itself, independent of anyone's discovery of it, renders the system a morally defective institution because it violates an important principle of the morality it represents according to most plausible theories of political morality. Deception in the administration of criminal justice violates an important principle of any public morality that values honesty, but it is a particularly serious infraction in a liberal democracy. Liberal democracies establish systems of social cooperation that recognize distinct spheres of public and

---

38 Schopp, *supra* note 17, at 2055–8.
39 *See supra* §§ 2.3, 3.3.2.
40 H. L. A. Hart, The Concept of Law 80 (Oxford: Oxford Univ. Press, 1961).

nonpublic jurisdiction and that respect individual self-determination at both levels.[41] Deception in the administration of the institutions of the public domain undermines the individual's ability to participate meaningfully in the political process that establishes and operates the public jurisdiction, and it infringes on the individual's ability to order a nonpublic life in a manner that prevents intrusion.

The argument from deception, as advanced by advocates of nullification instructions, takes a somewhat puzzling form. Advocates frame the argument in terms of deception regarding the power to nullify. They contend that current instructions deceive jurors regarding this power by informing them that it is their responsibility to apply the law as provided by the judge.[42] They propose alternative instructions that inform jurors of their power to acquit despite legal guilt in order to avoid an inequitable or unjust result, and they contend that honesty and the integrity of the process requires such instructions.[43]

Yet, these instructions also deceive jurors regarding their power to deviate from judicial instructions. Honest instructions regarding the jurors' power would inform them that "nothing bars you from acquitting the defendant to avoid an unjust or inequitable result, as an exercise of bias or hate, or for any reason you damn well please, including no reason at all; furthermore, you can largely ignore the beyond reasonable doubt standard and convict anyone against whom the state has entered significant evidence." The jury's *power* to acquit is open-ended, and its *power* to convict despite evidence that raises reasonable doubt is broad due to the deferential standard of review.

The instructions proposed by advocates inform jurors of that subset of their powers that advocates believe the jurors *ought* to exercise, rather than of the complete scope of their power. These instructions implicitly appeal to some justificatory theory in order to select the limited range of reasons for nullifying that justify the exercise of the power. In order to support nullification instructions that specifically endorse some limited range of the complete power, such as nullification based on appeal to conscience, justice, or mercy, one needs normative argument justifying the grounds selected as falling within the authority of the jury.

The plausible form of the argument from deception contends that current instructions are defective, not because they fail to inform jurors of all possible options, but rather because they deceive jurors by concealing from them options that fall within the scope of their legitimate authority. Thus, those who advocate nullification instructions on the basis of the argument from deception must establish not only that deception undermines the moral force of the crim-

41 *See supra* § 3.3.
42 Scheflin & Van Dyke, *supra* note 1, at 80 102–6; Scheflin & Van Dyke, *supra* note 3.
43 Scheflin & Van Dyke, *supra* note 1, at 54–5; Scheflin & Van Dyke, *supra* note 3.

inal law, but also that the current instructions deceive jurors regarding the scope of their legitimate authority.

Standard instructions inform jurors that they must apply the law as they receive it from the judge.[44] The current power to nullify renders these instructions deceptive if one understands them as informing jurors that they will not be allowed to depart from the law as stated by the judge or that they will be penalized for doing so. If, however, one understands these instructions as informing jurors regarding their responsibility to apply the law rather than any putative inability to depart from it, then the mere power to nullify is not sufficient to render them deceptive.[45] Thus, the claim that current instructions deceive the jury regarding their legitimate authority requires logically prior argument demonstrating not only that juries have the power to nullify but also that the discretion to exercise this power falls within the scope of their authority. Courts and commentators sometimes frame this issue as a question regarding whether the jury has not only the power to nullify but also the right.[46]

If X has a right to do act A, then all Y against whom X holds this right have a duty not to interfere with X's doing A.[47] Standard jury instructions lead jurors to believe that they must apply the law as they receive it from the judge, and research indicates that this belief renders them less likely to nullify. Thus, the instructions apparently interfere with nullification, at least in the sense that they prevent jurors from nullifying as often as they would with instructions explicitly acknowledging this power.[48] Arguably, then, if jurors have a right to nullify, standard instructions burden the exercise of that right by directing them in such a manner as to render them less likely to exercise it. By parallel reasoning, if defendants have a right to have their cases decided by jurors who are aware of their right to nullify, standard instructions burden this right. If nullification constitutes a right as well as a power, therefore, standard instructions undermine the moral force of the criminal law by informing the jury about their responsibilities in a manner that interferes with their ability to exercise this right.

The force of this argument requires some logically prior argument to establish that the jury's power to nullify also represents a right to do so. According

---

44 *See supra* note 14.

45 Some jury instructions frame the juror's role in terms of "it is your duty" rather than or in addition to "you must." *See, e.g.,* 4 OJI § 4.03.03 (1995); NJI2d. Crim. § 9.1(2) (1992). It remains an open empirical question whether jurors understand such instructions differently than they understand those framed as "you must."

46 Scott, *supra* note 9, at 391–2, 424; Simson, *supra* note 3, at 523–5.

47 Wesley Newcomb Hohfeld, Fundamental Legal Conceptions 36–8 (Walter Wheeler Cook ed., Westport, Conn.: Greenwood Press, 1964) (1919).

48 I Oxford English Dictionary at 1462. To interfere is "to come into collision or opposition, so as to affect the course of; . . . to interpose, take part, so as to affect some action." Interference implies opposition, but not necessarily violence.

to one view, the power without a legal remedy available to address exercise of that power establishes the right.[49] It is not clear whether those who support this view claim that the power without the remedy constitutes the right or that it gives rise to the right, but they contend that the jury's power to nullify absent any remedy for the exercise of that power establishes the right to do so. They do not identify any special property of the power of nullification that produces the corresponding right. It appears, therefore, that this claim rests on the more general assertion that legal powers without remedies either constitute or give rise to rights to exercise those powers.

This argument supports the putative right to nullify by appeal to the logical relationships between rights and powers without remedies. I have argued elsewhere that legal powers without remedies do not logically entail legal rights.[50] More importantly, however, any attempt to resolve this issue through purely analytic inquiry into the conceptual relationship between powers and rights frames the analysis inappropriately. The debate between those who endorse explicit nullification instructions and those who oppose such instructions cannot be resolved through purely analytic argument because it is a normative dispute regarding the authority that the criminal justice system *ought* to vest in the jury.[51]

If one could show that this particular legal power entails the corresponding legal right, that demonstration would not resolve the normative question regarding the justification of nullification according to persuasive principles of political morality underlying the criminal justice system. From the normative perspective, the demonstration that this particular power entails the right would be equally consistent with the conclusions that we ought to explicitly recognize the right through instructions or that we ought to extinguish the power. A justification supporting the authority to nullify within a particular criminal justice system must appeal to principles that are consistent with those supporting the broader set of legal institutions within which that system is embedded.

If the applicable principles of political morality justify vesting the authority to nullify in the jury, current instructions undermine those principles and deceive jurors regarding their responsibilities under those principles. If these principles do not justify such authority, current instructions neither deceive the jurors regarding their responsibilities nor undermine the moral authority of the

---

49 Sparf and Hansen v. U.S., 156 U.S. 51, 172–4 (1985) (Gray, Shiras, JJ. dissenting); Kent Greenawalt, Conflicts of Law and Morality 361 (New York: Oxford Univ. Press, 1987). Greenawalt quotes but does not support Chancellor James Kent.
50 Schopp, *supra* note 17, at 2062–5.
51 Hohfeld, *supra* note 47, at 43. Hohfeld makes a similar point regarding privileges not entailing rights and contending that whether there should be such a right is a separate question of justice and policy.

system. Thus, the argument from deception and the integrity of the criminal law requires logically prior normative argument to support the contention that the moral principles that justify the criminal justice system also justify vesting the jury with the authority to nullify.

In summary, the consequentialist dispute regarding the likely effects of nullification instructions in promoting equal justice or anarchy remains an open empirical inquiry. In order to resolve it, the disputants need both further empirical evidence and some mutually acceptable criteria of justice and of anarchy. The analytic argument that the power without a remedy entails the right and the deontic argument from democratic self-rule fail to provide the kind of support that could justify the authority to nullify and mandate nullification instructions. The deontic argument from deception and the integrity of the criminal justice system remains an open normative issue requiring an account of the manner in which the principles of political morality supporting the criminal law would justify vesting the authority to nullify in the jury as part of an integrated set of political institutions.

6.3 Necessity and Nullification in a Liberal Society

6.3.1 Deception and the Integrity of a Liberal Criminal Justice System

Jury instructions that deceive jurors regarding their responsibilities strike at the core of the principles of political morality that justify the larger system of legal institutions in a liberal society. Deceptive instructions misrepresent the parameters of the conventional public morality in which citizens can recognize common moral ground, regardless of differences in their comprehensive doctrines. Such deception distorts a central legitimate jury function, and it violates the standing of the jurors and of the participants. It interferes with the legitimate jury function by impairing the jury's ability to hold the government to the conventional public morality; that is, it undermines the jury's ability to fulfill its duty to assure that government wields coercive power against the individual only as it is authorized by the law representing the conventional public morality. It violates the jurors' standing as responsible citizens of the public institutions by interfering with their ability to fulfill their responsibility as full participants in the conventional public morality. Finally, it violates the standing of the defendant and of the victim by subjecting them to a distorted version of the public morality rather than to the system of law that represents the conventional morality in the liberal society, and in the development of which they had the opportunity to participate as members of the electorate.[52]

---

52 *See supra* § 3.3.

Common jury instructions inform a jury that they must apply the law as the judge describes it or that it is their duty to do so. These specific instructions are consistent with the liberal political morality in that they instruct the jury to apply the conventional public morality to the defendant's conduct that falls within the public domain. Absent additional instructions regarding the necessity defense or nullification, these instructions violate the liberal political morality if but only if the principles of that political morality justify vesting authority in the jury to invoke the necessity defense or nullification as legitimate responses within the public domain to defendants who have committed crimes of conscience. Thus, in order to establish that current jury instructions violate the conventional public morality of a liberal society by deceiving the jurors regarding their responsibilities, one must demonstrate that the principles of this public morality justify the necessity defense or nullification as intrasystemic responses to these offenses. This requires, in turn, that one establish the legitimate functions of each and the relationship between the two.

6.3.2   Necessity and Nullification: The Conceptual Puzzle

Theoretical interpretations of necessity and nullification sometimes render it difficult to clearly distinguish the functions of each, particularly as applied to crimes of conscience. Consider, first, the necessity defense. As discussed in Section 3.3, the criminal law contains a series of specific offense definitions and justification defenses designed to instantiate the prohibitory norms and justificatory principles of the political morality represented by that legal system. Ideally, the criminal law's offense definitions and justification defenses would provide a complete set of conduct rules representing a fully articulated conventional public morality. That is, the offense definitions would address all conduct violating the underlying prohibitory norms in such a manner as to accurately represent the relative severity of offenses, and the justification defenses would accommodate all possible circumstances generating exceptions to the prohibitory norms by appeal to the other principles contained in the conventional public morality.

Realistically, no set of criminal offense definitions and justification defenses will completely represent the underlying conventional morality and all possible relevant circumstances. The necessity defense serves as a residual justification defense that addresses cases in which the defendant's conduct fulfills the elements of an offense definition, yet it does not merit condemnation by the criminal justice system because the prohibitory norm underlying the offense definition is overridden by other principles in the conventional public morality in a manner that has not been articulated in the form of a specific legal defense. Thus, the defense serves as a residual corrective device in the sense that it provides a defense with which the courts can adjust the legal verdict in order to render it consistent with the conventional public morality represented by the law in the absence of an applicable specific legal defense.[53]

Mortimer and Sanford Kadish, for example, interpret necessity as a defense accommodating legitimate disobedience by citizens. According to this theory, citizens raise the necessity defense when they claim that their violations of specific rules were justified in the circumstances by the goals and ends of the system in which those rules are embedded. The courts review these claims and the conduct in question in order to confirm or reject the defendants' contentions that the goals and ends of the system justified their conduct in the circumstances.[54] Other commentators articulate compatible interpretations of the necessity defense as a corrective device in the criminal law. Some articulate this function in terms of violating the letter of the law in order to serve the spirit of the law.[55] Although the language varies somewhat across accounts, these commentators converge on a common interpretation of the necessity defense as an unspecified justification defense designed to serve as a corrective device. It applies in circumstances in which offense definitions and the lack of an applicable specific legal defense would generate a conviction for engaging in conduct that was more consistent than any available alternative behavior with the principles and purposes of the conventional public morality represented by the criminal law.

As previously discussed, jury nullification consists of deliberate, conscientious, jury deviation. Those who endorse nullification instructions would inform jurors that nothing bars them from departing from the law in order to acquit a defendant if they determine that applying the law to the facts would produce an inequitable or unjust result. Kadish and Kadish discuss jury nullification as one type of legitimated interposition by an official. As such, it is a departure from the rules of the system that is justified as consistent with the goals and ends of that system and independent of review by others.[56] Other commentators characterize nullification as a perfecting or ameliorative device.[57]

According to these interpretations of necessity and nullification, both involve departures from specific legal rules in order to promote the goals and ends of the broader legal system of which the rule is a part. Necessity might appeal to the goals and ends of the system in a narrower sense in that the defense has some

---

53 Greenawalt, *supra* note 49, at 286–310; Understanding at § 22.01.
54 Kadish & Kadish, *supra* note 22, at 120–7.
55 James L. Cavallaro Jr., *The Demise of the Political Necessity Defense: Indirect Civil Disobedience and United States v. Schoon,* 81 Calif. L. Rev. 351 (1993); Greenawalt, *supra* note 49, at 286–310; Rethinking at § 10.2; Understanding at § 22.01.
56 Kadish & Kadish, *supra* note 22, at 45–72.
57 George P. Fletcher, A Crime of Self-defense 154–6 (Chicago: Univ. Chicago Press, 1988) (perfecting); Greenawalt, *supra* note 49, at 359–67 (amelioration).

legal structure and does not apply when the legislature has preempted the issue. Nullification, in contrast, appeals to the principles underlying the criminal process in more abstract terms such as justice or fairness. Both are intrasystemic, however, insofar as they are interpreted as correcting or perfecting the system by accommodating deviation from some specific clause of that system in circumstances in which deviation promotes the ends or values of the system more effectively than would conformity with that clause.

Kadish and Kadish address the two differently in that they address necessity as a claim raised by a citizen whose judgment is subject to review by officials, but they discuss nullification as deviation by an official who is not subject to review or sanction. Some commentators endorse each as a jury response to some crimes of conscience, however, and each constitutes an alternative to conviction that jurors might invoke in some cases. When both are considered as jury responses to citizen conduct as endorsed by the commentators, both involve acquittal of a defendant despite behavior that fulfills offense elements in the absence of any specific defense. When interpreted as corrective devices in the legal system, both are intrasystemic insofar as they appeal to the purposes and values of the system for support. On the corrective interpretation, nullification grounded in the claim that the defendant's conduct was justified by the broader purposes and values of the system seems to collapse into the necessity defense. Yet, necessity is an explicitly recognized component of the system, while nullification lacks explicit authorization in statutory language and jury instructions.

The following sections differentiate necessity and nullification by virtue of the relationship in which each stands to the principles of the conventional public morality underlying the criminal law in a liberal society. This interpretation clarifies the role and significance of each, the difference between the two, and the boundaries of the general category of justification defenses in a criminal justice system representing liberal principles of political morality.

6.3.3   Necessity

The necessity defense provides a residual justification defense that functions as a corrective device by allowing exculpation through appeal to justificatory principles contained in the conventional morality embodied in the law. Statutes and cases recognize the defense in circumstances in which the defendant engaged in some ordinarily illegal conduct reasonably believed to be a lesser evil than some imminent, legally recognized harm and necessary in order to avoid that greater evil.[58] The defendant bears the burden of production regarding the requirements of the defense, and the court determines whether the

---

58 Defenses at § 124; Understanding at § 22.

defendant has met that burden by providing evidence regarding each element such that a reasonable jury could return a verdict based on the defense.[59] Courts have consistently denied the defense in cases of political protest on various grounds including the following: the evil avoided was remote and speculative rather than imminent; the illegal conduct was not reasonably calculated to abate the anticipated harm; legal alternatives were available in the form of political or judicial action; the legislature preempted the issue in setting the law or policy in question; or the "evil" avoided could not constitute a legally recognized evil because it consisted of the exercise of a legally recognized right.[60]

Some commentators contend that these decisions invade the province of the jury.[61] Some requirements of the defense clearly fall within the purview of the jury. Did the defendants reasonably believe, for example, that the events they identified as the harm to be avoided were imminent and that their illegal actions were likely to abate the danger? Regarding these requirements, courts appropriately determine whether the defendants have met the burden of production. If the defendants have met that burden, the trier of fact determines whether they have met the burden of persuasion. Some commentators contend that the courts have interpreted and decided these issues erroneously, but the distribution of responsibility is relatively clear.

The appropriate distribution of responsibility regarding the determination whether the events identified by the defendants as the evils to be avoided can qualify as legally recognized greater evils for the purpose of the necessity defense remains contentious. If one interprets this question as one that addresses the conscience of the community in the sense of widely held personal moral beliefs within the community, it appears to raise an issue of fact about the degree to which the defendants' evaluations of the relative magnitude of the evils in question would be endorsed by a consensus of community residents. This interpretation suggests that the court should submit the comparison of the evils performed and avoided to the jury and admit empirical evidence regarding the opinions and attitudes of community residents relevant to that balance of evils. Thus, a survey of public opinion regarding this particular case or the general issues involved should qualify as relevant evidence.

If one understands the necessity defense as a residual corrective device appealing to the principles of the conventional public morality embodied in the law, however, the evaluation of two events as the greater or lesser evil raises an issue of legal interpretation. This approach explains the well-established doctrine of legislative preemption and suggests that the balancing of evils falls within the jurisdiction of the court.[62] According to this analysis of the defense,

---

59 Defenses at § 4.
60 *Id.* at § 124(d)(1); Lippman, *supra* note 1, at 328–43; Understanding at § 22.03.
61 Cavallaro, *supra* note 55; Lippman, *supra* note 1, at 343–56.
62 N.Y. Penal Law § 35.05 (McKinney 1987); MPC at § 3.02(1)(c); Defenses at § 124(d)(1) (law or policy as conclusive evidence of the community view).

courts must decide as a matter of law whether the events identified by the defendants as evils to be avoided can qualify as legally recognized evils, and if so, whether these events would constitute greater evils than the illegal conduct the defendants are charged with performing.

Courts have frequently adopted the latter interpretation and relied on legislative preemption in cases of political protest.[63] Having construed the matter as one of legal interpretation, courts appropriately adopt a deferential attitude toward legislators and higher courts. Although theorists debate the precise nature and range of judicial authority in reviewing legislation, the general responsibility of the court to interpret and apply the law as passed by the legislature within the bounds set by the Constitution is relatively widely accepted. Thus, the review of a current law or policy for compliance with the Constitution provides the systemically approved method by which courts test legislative decisions by appeal to the principles of political morality represented by the legal system. If a court were to accept the necessity defense in a case of political protest on the basis of its own determination that a Constitutional statute or policy constitutes a greater evil by systemic standards than a violation of a Constitutional offense definition, it would violate the standards of that system regarding the scope of its authority regarding legislative decisions.

The point here is not, of course, that legislative or executive decisions within Constitutional limits invariably converge with the best interpretation of the substantive principles of the conventional public morality represented by the law. Rather, it is that the conventional morality includes the procedural principles that define the legitimate roles and authority of each branch, and, thus, a court that independently evaluated a Constitutionally valid law or policy for consistency with its interpretation of the conventional public morality or that subjected such a law or policy to review by the jury would in doing so violate its responsibilities under those principles. Thus, insofar as the necessity defense qualifies as an intrasystemic corrective device that appeals to the conventional public morality represented by the law, the court appropriately applies it in light of the procedural principles that require it to interpret and apply, rather than independently evaluate, Constitutional law and policy.

According to this interpretation of a court's responsibility regarding the determination of greater evils for the necessity defense, the court must evaluate the relative magnitude of the evils at issue according to the principles of public morality represented by the law. Some cases raise no concern about the legitimate scope of the court's authority. Suppose, for example, that a bicyclist on a remote country road discovers an automobile that has run off the road into a tree. The driver suffered a heart attack, causing the accident, and now has additional injuries caused by the crash. If the bicyclist breaks into the only

---

63 Criminal Law at § 5.4, 1996 Pocket Part at 68n11; Defenses at § 124(d)(1).

nearby farmhouse in order to telephone for an ambulance because that is the only way to secure immediate assistance for the driver, the court must determine whether the principles represented by the law support the bicyclist's contention that breaking and entering constituted a lesser evil than allowing the driver to die. Presumably, most courts would conclude that the criminal law's structure of offenses and defenses, including those addressing homicide, assault, self-defense, defense of others and property, and illegal entry represent underlying principles that value the protection of innocent life more highly than prevention of relatively minor violations of property rights.

Other cases, particularly those involving civil disobedience or conscientious resistance to some law or policy, raise questions regarding the limits of the courts' authority to review law. Defendants who claim the necessity defense regarding crimes committed for the purpose of preventing women from securing legal abortions, for example, ask courts to find that the exercise of a legally protected right constitutes an evil to be avoided. Some defendants who claim the necessity defense regarding crimes committed in protest of nuclear energy policy ask courts to find that the pursuit of the policy at issue is likely to produce effects that constitute harms to be avoided. These cases raise two distinct types of questions with different ramifications for the courts.[64]

Consider first the case in which the exercise of the legal right constitutes the putative harm to be avoided. If the relevant statutes permit the abortions in question and higher courts have concluded that these statutes and procedures are Constitutional, the lower court lacks authority under the conventional public morality represented by the law to consider the exercise of rights recognized by these statutes as evils to be avoided through criminal conduct. This conclusion does not reflect the premise that the legislature and higher courts must be correct in their assessment of substantive values embodied in the conventional public morality. Rather, it reflects the procedural principles of the lawmaking and enforcing process that establish the boundaries of authority in public institutions instantiating that public morality. It would be perfectly consistent for a trial court judge to conclude that the legislature and the Supreme Court were wrong in their interpretations of the substantive principles of the public morality but that the procedural principles defining the limits of the trial court's authority precluded it from correcting or acting contrary to this error.[65]

The second case might occur in either of two variations. First, the protestors who claim the necessity defense might simply disagree with the legislative assessment of risks and benefits regarding the nuclear energy policy. The legislature might have considered evidence that the risk of a meltdown was one in

---

64 Recall that this discussion addresses only the existence and relative magnitudes of legally recognized evils. It does not address other relevant questions such as imminence or reasonable belief that the offense charged would prevent the evils.

65 Furman v. Georgia, 408 U.S. 238, 405–14 (1972) (Blackmun, J. dissenting); Otey v. Stenberg, No. 4: CV94-3191, slip op. at 22 (D. Neb. filed Aug. 22, 1994). Justice Blackmun's dissent in

one million, for example, and concluded that the expected benefits were worth the risks. The protestors might simply disagree, concluding that these benefits are not worth the risk, and, thus, that the balance of risks over benefits produced by the policy constitutes an evil to be avoided. This variation confronts the trial court with circumstances very similar to those just discussed in that the protestors who claim the necessity defense ask the court to assume a responsibility allocated to the legislature by the procedural principles of the conventional public morality.

Suppose, in contrast, that the protestors blockade the gate to the nuclear energy facility in order to prevent the delivery of fuel that would allow activation of the reactor that they claim differs from that considered by the legislature such that it poses a one in one thousand probability of a meltdown rather than the one in one million considered by the legislature. Considering only the issue of relative magnitude of harm, these protestors do not ask the court to override the legislative assessment of the relative magnitude of evils. Rather, they ask the court to balance the harm of a trespass against this level of risk because the legislature had never considered this question. That is, they ask the court to make a determination according to the substantive principles of the conventional public morality in circumstances that do not raise issues of authority under the procedural principles. In this manner, this second variation of the nuclear protest case resembles the bicyclist case more closely than it resembles either the abortion case or the first variation of the nuclear protest case.

This approach to the necessity defense is consistent with liberal principles of political morality in that the court subjects the participants to a determination of the lesser evil according to the principles of public morality embodied in the law as established through the democratic institutions of the public jurisdiction. Although either the legislature or the court may make an erroneous determination in a particular case, the allocation of authority conforms to the procedural principles of the conventional public morality, and the resulting jury instructions involve no deception of the jurors regarding their responsibilities as jurors within the conventional public morality.

Some might object, however, that the necessity defense should justify conduct that qualifies as the lesser evil by the community conscience in the sense of widely held personal beliefs rather than according to the conventional morality represented by the law. According to this view, the jury represents the community and should apply the community conscience in deciding whether the conduct constituting the offense qualifies as a lesser evil than that which it was performed to avoid.[66]

Furman denies the court's authority to override the legislature, although he clearly considers the legislation misguided. Judge Urbom's opinion in *Otey* eloquently expresses the anguish of a judge who considers it his obligation in the public sphere to enforce law that he considers wrong.

66 Cavallaro, *supra* note 55; Lippman, *supra* note 1, at 350–6.

Jurors might represent the conscience of the community in at least two different senses. First, six to twelve jurors selected from the community and exercising their own consciences might serve as a sample of the community conscience. Second, the jurors might understand their responsibility as requiring that they exercise the moral standards that they perceive as representing a consensus of the community. The first alternative may not, however, provide a highly satisfactory approach for the purpose of representing the community conscience. Although juries are selected from the community, they often include only a nonrepresentative subset of the entire population as measured by demographic factors, and no positive effort is made to secure a sample that represents the range of moral views in the community.[67] Furthermore, the process of voir dire narrows the sample by providing each lawyer an opportunity to remove at least some of those who appear to hold inconvenient views. In light of these factors, it is not at all clear that juries applying the consciences of their members represent the community conscience as accurately as does the legislature that passed the law to which the jury would provide an exception through the necessity defense.

According to the second alternative, juries should understand their role as including the responsibility to identify and represent the moral standards that are most representative of the community. If jurors are to exercise community standards, in what way should they derive these standards? Is there reason to believe that jurors who accept the responsibility to apply the community standard are likely to correctly identify it? It seems reasonable to expect that a jury working collectively to a common conclusion regarding the community standard is more likely than an individual working in isolation to accurately identify that standard. One should rely on this hypothesis with some caution, however, for the reasons discussed previously regarding the limited representativeness of the jury. To the extent that the members of a jury are drawn from a nonrepresentative subset of the community, they seem more likely to converge on the standard of that subset than on one that represents a broad community consensus.

One must also ask whether it is reasonable to expect a community to arrive at a consensus that differs significantly from the current criminal law. The criminal law as written may represent the best evidence of the community consensus regarding basic principles of public morality in a democratic society. In circumstances in which the law fails to accurately represent a consensus, that failure may often signal the lack of any clear consensus to represent. The claim here is not that the criminal law infallibly portrays the informal community conscience. It is rather that those cases in which the criminal law fails to reflect such a consensus may well be those that involve issues that remain contentious

---

67 Saul M. Kassin & Lawrence M. Wrightsman, The American Jury on Trial 24 (New York: Hemisphere Pub., 1988); LaFave & Israel, *supra* note 10, at § 22.2.

in the community and, thus, those regarding which no jury can identify a community consensus because none has yet developed.[68]

Although the criminal law may represent a close approximation of the community morality, one might argue that it does so at the level of relatively broad generalization necessary to establish rules. On the interpretation of the necessity defense as a residual corrective device, that defense serves to perfect the law in the sense that it allows the jury to adjust the generalizations of the law to unusual circumstances. This argument merely restates the initial problem, however, in that one must determine whether the generalized rules are to be adjusted by appeal to the principles of the conventional public morality embodied in the law or by appeal to the informal conscience. If the appropriate appeal is the former, the responsibility for the adjustment falls within the jurisdiction of the courts. Alternately, if one endorses the latter approach, one encounters the concerns raised above regarding the likelihood of any particular jury converging upon an understanding of the community conscience more accurate than that represented by the law itself.

In short, the approach to the necessity defense that calls upon the jury to represent the informal conscience of the community may encounter the following dilemma. If the community has arrived at a broad consensus, the criminal law may well represent the best indicator of that community standard, and, thus, the community conscience supports application of the conventional public morality represented by the law. This, in turn, requires an interpretation of the lesser evils according to the law, a function best performed by the court. If the community has not arrived at a broad consensus regarding the issue, then the jury cannot represent it.

This notion of necessity as an application of the informal community conscience rather than of the conventional public morality represented by the law encounters two additional difficulties. First, as a component of a legal structure justified by liberal principles of political morality, it violates one of those principles by subjecting the participants in the case to the unenacted moral standards of some unspecified set of persons, rather than to enacted standards of public morality regarding which the parties had notice and the opportunity to participate in developing. Thus, an institution of the public jurisdiction would retrospectively define the public morality for these participants, subjecting them to standards that had not been enacted at the time of their conduct and that do not bind other members of the community, including those jurors who apply them to these participants.

The conventional public morality of the liberal society includes both the substantive content of the law and the institutionalized democratic lawmaking

---

68 It is not at all clear that cases of apparent nullification cited by commentators represent circumstances regarding which a clear community consensus had formed. *See, e.g.,* Levine 1994, *supra* note 25, at 480–1; McCoy, *supra* note 25, at 501–2.

process. This process respects the standing of the citizen in that it establishes the content of the public morality through a political process in which competent citizens can collectively decide which limits on liberty they will accept. It promotes self-determination by providing notice to citizens regarding the types of behavior that will elicit legal intervention, either to prevent them from engaging in such behavior, or to protect them from others who do so. Finally, it institutionalizes equality of citizenship insofar as it provides for equal participation and equal liability. Thus, a necessity defense that applied the informal community conscience would violate the standing of the participants as equal citizens under law by subjecting them to standards that were not established as part of the conventional public morality through the political process that constitutes part of that morality.

Juries are not democratic institutions in that jurors are not elected representatives of the electorate or of the participants in the case. Furthermore, juries that function according to the view advanced here are not responsive to the public in that they neither answer to the public nor rely on the informal community conscience. At first glance, juries that function in this manner may seem inconsistent with democratic government. According to liberal principles of political morality, however, this nonresponsiveness represents an asset of the jury system. A jury that confines itself to the conventional public morality represented by the law, rather than responding to the informal community conscience or public sentiment, treats the participants with respect in that it subjects them only to the standards that they had the opportunity to participate in enacting and that apply to others in society.

The second difficulty that arises for the interpretation of the necessity defense as appealing to the informal community conscience involves the legal formulation of this defense. It remains mysterious in what sense this defense could constitute a legal defense insofar as neither the court nor anyone else can determine the parameters of the defense for any particular defendant or circumstances until after a jury makes an idiosyncratic decision that applies only to this case. That is, the interpretation of the necessity defense as appealing to the informal community conscience seems incompatible with the structure of legal defenses generally and of justification defenses specifically.[69]

6.3.4 Nullification as Necessity: Intrasystemic Appeals to Justice

If the necessity defense provides a residual justification defense reflecting the principles of justice embodied in the conventional public morality represented by the criminal law, nullification by appeal to the broader principles of justice that serve as the underlying ends and values of the system apparently collapses

---

69 Defenses at §§ 41, 121.

into that necessity defense. Does any logical space remain for nullification independent of necessity? Recall that nullification involves an act of conscience, so accidental deviation and malicious deviation motivated by considerations such as greed, self-interest, or hate do not constitute nullification. Misguided appeals to conscience would constitute nullification, and the possibility remains that the institutional conditions that allow nullification would also provide the opportunity for malicious deviation. The mere possibility of erroneous or malicious misapplication of a doctrine does not differentiate nullification from necessity or other legal doctrines, however, although the relatively unstructured nature of nullification might facilitate such departures.

Jurors might conclude that a conviction required by law would violate the principles of justice embodied in the conventional public morality at either of two levels of specificity. First, they might conclude that circumstances specific to the case render unjust a verdict required by some generally justified rule of the criminal justice system. Second, they might conclude that some general legal rule represents a malignant deviation within the liberal structure. They might conclude, for example, that the specific statute supporting a conviction for this defendant violates the liberal principles underlying the broad system.

Consider first the more specific variation in which nullification appeals to the principles of justice embedded in the law in order to avoid an unjust verdict resulting from circumstances specific to the case. This variation duplicates the corrective function of the necessity defense, and, therefore, nullification and necessity differ only in legal structure. Necessity takes the form of an explicitly recognized and instructed defense with relatively clear parameters, but nullification remains implicit, uninstructed, and relatively vague. Providing nullification instructions would render this option explicit, leaving the relative degree of structure as the only remaining difference. Thus, if one interprets both as intrasystemic corrective devices intended to allow departures from specific provisions when circumstances necessitate doing so in order to comply with the underlying principles of the conventional public morality, the advisability of nullification instructions seems to rest on an empirical question. That is, would providing these instructions increase or decrease the degree to which jury decisions would converge with the purposes and principles underlying the system? Furthermore, if both doctrines are to serve as corrective devices with explicit instructions, how would the nullification instructions differ from the necessity instructions, and what would justify that difference?[70]

Insofar as nullification appeals to case-specific circumstances in light of the

---

70 Instructions that have been recommended differ from those for the necessity defense, of course, but insofar as nullification serves as an intrasystemic corrective device, it is difficult to justify the difference.

principles of justice in the conventional public morality represented by the law, it collapses into the necessity defense, and jury instructions regarding this process would duplicate those for the necessity defense. Furthermore, the process by which the court would determine whether such instructions were appropriate would duplicate the process of legal analysis appropriate to the necessity defense. Thus, jury instructions for this variation of intrasystemic nullification appealing to principles of justice either would duplicate necessity instructions, possibly confusing the jury, or would reflect error in the legal analysis regarding at least one of the two sets of instructions.

Alternately, suppose the jury concludes that the statute supporting conviction of the defendant constitutes a malignant deviation from the liberal principles of political morality represented by the law. Either honest error on the part of legislators or corruption might produce a statute that is inconsistent with the principles embodied in the system. Arguably, instructions authorizing nullification in these circumstances would preserve the underlying principles by protecting the participants from systemically unjustifiable rules. This argument cannot support nullification instructions, however, due to the following dilemma.

Such nullification instructions require that jurors accurately interpret the principles of conventional public morality embodied in the legal system, identify the malignant rules that undermine these principles, and nullify when, but only when, these rules provide necessary conditions for conviction. It seems quite implausible that juries can fulfill these requirements. If one assumes that they cannot, this argument provides no support for nullification instructions. If one assumes for the sake of argument that they can, this line of reasoning still fails to support nullification instructions. Rather, it supports vesting juries with the authority to categorically invalidate the malignant rules. Given the unrealistic assumption that juries can perform and apply this complex analysis of specific rules, the legal system, and the underlying principles, nothing justifies a process that exempts these particular participants from the malignant rule but leaves it in place as a defect in the system to which other citizens are subject. That is, the argument supports either the current instructions or jury authority to overturn legislation, but it does not support the authority to nullify.

These arguments suggest that no logical space remains for intrasystemic nullification appealing to the principles of justice embodied in the legal system. The possibility remains, however, that jurors who receive nullification instructions roughly similar to those endorsed by some commentators might engage in at least two types of nullification based on appeal to conscience that would extend beyond the scope of necessity. First, they might appeal to principles other than justice embodied in the legal system. This type of nullification would resemble necessity insofar as it remains intrasystemic, but it would not entail the judgment that the defendant's conduct was justified. Second, they might depart from the legal rules in order to conform to their own consciences independent of the ends and values of the system.[71]

6.3.5   Nullification beyond Necessity: Intrasystemic Appeals to Mercy

Nullification of the first type might occur, for example, if the jurors were to acquit a legally guilty defendant out of mercy. Advocates of nullification instructions sometimes discuss nullification and nullification instructions in a manner suggesting that "merciful juries" nullify when strict adherence to the law would violate community notions of justice.[72] Justice and mercy, however, are ordinarily understood as two distinct virtues. Virtuous persons might determine that they ought to temper justice with mercy or that they ought to exercise mercy rather than justice in some circumstances, but such a decision reflects an effort to resolve a conflict between justice and mercy rather than an exercise of mercy in order to do justice or avoid injustice. Justice requires that each person receive the treatment he or she deserves or merits under the applicable criteria. An individual has a claim in justice when he or she has not received the treatment due under those criteria, and a decision maker does justice by distributing punishment, reward, benefit, or burden according to merit as defined by the relevant criteria. Retributive justice requires that officials administer criminal punishment according to desert as measured by culpability for offenses as defined by the criminal law.[73]

Persons engage in acts of mercy when they act from kindness or compassion in treating another better than justice demands. If *X* has a claim in justice

---

71 Some might suggest departure from the legal rules in order to conform to the informal community conscience as a third alternative. Such a criterion might suggest that in this manner the jury could serve as the "conscience of the community" through nullification.

    This interpretation of nullification encounters most of the same difficulties previously discussed regarding the corresponding interpretation of necessity. There is no reason to think that the community will arrive at a consensus regarding the contentious issues often involved in crimes of conscience or that a jury would reflect any community consensus more accurately than would the criminal law. A jury that nullifies on the basis of its perception of an informal community conscience violates liberal principles of political morality by subjecting the participants to unenacted standards that were not in effect when they acted, that were not developed through a political process in which they had an opportunity to vote, and to which others, including these jurors, are not subject.

    Finally, it is not clear in what sense one can say jurors bring a verdict of conscience if they ground their decision on the belief that the community endorses these standards rather than on their own conclusions of conscience. Jurors might believe that a community consensus has developed regarding a particular issue and, further, upon careful reflection, they might concur. In this case, however, they nullify on the basis of an extrasystemic standard that they have adopted as a position of conscience. Thus, they fall into the second category. For all these reasons, I will not address this interpretation as a distinct type of nullification as an appeal to conscience.

72 Scheflin & Van Dyke, *supra* note 3.

73 Joel Feinberg, Rights, Justice, and the Bounds of Liberty 265–306 (Princeton: Princeton Univ. Press, 1980).

against *Y,* for example, *X* might exercise mercy by forgoing that claim against *Y* as an act of compassion. *X* might forgo payment of a debt or decide not to collect compensation owed by *Y* because *Y* has suffered some misfortune that would make it very difficult for *Y* to pay the justly owed debt or compensation. Thus, in order to qualify as an act of mercy, *X*'s act must be motivated by kindness or compassion, and *X* must treat *Y* better than justice requires by forgoing some claim against *Y.*[74]

Nullification of this type would stand in clear contrast to acquittal under the necessity defense because jurors who engaged in this type of nullification would not acknowledge the defendant's conduct as justified by the ends and values of the system or by any over other criteria of justice. Rather, they would decide to forgo justified punishment as a matter of compassion. Suppose, for example, that *X* steals a car, is pursued by the police, and in the course of the chase crashes the car into a tree, rendering himself quadriplegic. Jurors might acquit despite clear evidence of legal guilt because they believed that *X* has already suffered enough and that prison would be intolerable for a quadriplegic person. These jurors might understand their decision as consistent with principles embodied within the system in that they might interpret certain criminal law doctrines such as mitigation or duress as reflecting recognition of mercy or compassion in the conventional morality underlying the system.[75]

This type of nullification would not adequately address crimes of conscience for at least two reasons, the first of which applies more broadly to crimes generally. First, by exercising mercy in the decision to convict or acquit, rather than in sentencing, this type of nullification distorts the expressive function of the criminal law. Although it seems unnecessary, and perhaps even cruel, to subject the quadriplegic thief to imprisonment, these considerations address appropriate disposition. Conviction condemns this illegal conduct as a violation of the conventional public morality and the actor as one who engaged in such conduct under conditions of accountability. Although the subsequent injury may well provide a good reason to exercise leniency in disposition out of compassion, it does nothing to undermine the appropriate institutional condemnation of this type of conduct or the specific condemnation of this act as violating the conventional public morality and of this defendant as one who violated that morality under systemic conditions of accountability and blameworthiness.[76]

Furthermore, and most importantly, the acquittal fails to condemn the defen-

---

74 Kathleen Dean Moore, *Pardons* 188–92 (New York: Oxford Univ. Press, 1989).
75 MPC at §§ 2.09, 7.01(a). Even if these doctrines are not best interpreted in this manner, this would remain an instance of intrasystemic nullification, although a misguided one, as long as the jurors were acting out of conscience by appeal to the ends and values that they understood as embodied in the system.
76 *See supra* §§ 2.3, 5.3.

dant's violation of the victim's sphere of sovereignty. Thus, it undermines the standing of the victim by acquiescing in the perpetrator's imputation of lesser status to the victim. By refusing to condemn this violation of the innocent victim's sovereignty in order to exercise compassion for the perpetrator who violated the victim's standing, the jury indirectly reaffirms the perpetrator's denial of the victim's status, effectively announcing that violation of this victim's property rights does *not* constitute a violation of the conventional public morality.[77] Although the jury may not intend to express this denigration of the victim's standing, by virtue of their decision to withhold condemnation of this violation by applying a standard that does not apply similarly to violations against themselves or others, the jurors treat this victim as one whose interests merit less protection than those of other citizens, including themselves.

Second, nullification as an exercise of mercy distorts the symbolic significance of the conduct engaged in by those who commit crimes of conscience, and it does so in a manner that demeans these defendants and denies the significance of their actions. Those who violate a criminal statute out of the conviction that conscience demands such conduct do not contend that they should be excused out of mercy, compassion, or pity. They do not ask to avoid responsibility for admittedly faulty behavior. Rather, they violate criminal prohibitions after careful reflection in order to fulfill their moral obligation as they understand it, and often for the purpose of confronting officials and the population at large in order to elicit public review of the law or policy to which they object. Those who sincerely engage in crimes of conscience demand and deserve that officials and the public directly confront their claims of justification.

Nullification based on mercy denies them this explicit consideration of their claims of justification. It redirects attention away from the putative justification for their conduct and for the law or policy at issue and toward considerations of mercy and compassion. Under the guise of special consideration, such a response denies these defendants respect. Perhaps most importantly, by framing the issue as one of mercy rather than of justification, officials and the general population evade their responsibility to reflect upon the law as the official representation of the conventional public morality and to decide whether it is one that a conscientious person can support and apply. Thus, if crimes of conscience merit an intrasystemic response beyond an ordinary application of the law to the evidence, that response must confront the claim that the conduct in question was justified rather than appealing to mercy for the defendant.

For all these reasons, intrasystemic nullification appealing to principles of mercy in the conventional public morality provides an unsatisfactory response to crimes of conscience. In addition, instructions suggesting such a possibility

---

77 *See supra* § 3.3.2.

to the jury as falling within their authority in the conventional public morality, would distort the expressive significance of conviction and acquittal, misrepresenting the conventional public morality embodied in the legal system because the current system exercises mercy through mitigation in sentencing rather than through acquittal. Thus, nullification instructions of this type, rather than the current lack of such instructions, would violate the principles appealed to in the argument from deception and the integrity of the system.

6.3.6   Nullification beyond Necessity: Extrasystemic Nullification

The second type of nullification that does not collapse into necessity occurs when jurors depart from legal rules because they consider some extrasystemic standards superior. Suppose, for example, that an elderly couple, Mary and Jim, have had lengthy discussions about the types of health care they want to accept or reject should either of them become severely disabled. They each promise the other that they will not allow the other to "live like that – hooked up to machines," but they do not write living wills or otherwise clarify the meaning and scope of this promise. Mary then suffers a severe stroke that renders her comatose and dependent on a respirator. Jim requests that the hospital remove the respirator, but in the absence of a written advanced directive by Mary or other witnesses who can confirm and clarify Mary's intention in the earlier conversations, the hospital officials refuse to remove the respirator without a court order. When it becomes clear to Jim that Mary will remain on the respirator for a relatively lengthy period during the legal process, he concludes that he is failing Mary in his last promise to her. He quietly walks into her hospital room, wedges the door closed, and turns off the respirator. When the nursing staff successfully force open the door, they find Jim holding Mary's hand. He says to them, "You can come in now; she doesn't have to live like that anymore, just as we promised."

Jim explicitly states that he understood that removing Mary's respirator would cause her legal death and that he deliberately did so because he had promised her that he would in these circumstances. He accurately understood that doing so was illegal, and he suffers no disability that might support an excuse. Jim might even agree that he has a moral obligation to obey the law generally or the homicide law specifically. He concluded, however, that his promise to Mary supported a more weighty obligation.

Some jurors might decide to acquit Jim of the homicide charge despite clear legal guilt. They might acknowledge that neither the legal rules nor the ends and values underlying the system justify Jim's conduct.[78] They might also

---

78 Some might cogently argue that the values underlying liberal legal institutions support Jim's decision, but the point here is that some jurors might nullify while denying this.

agree that the law ought not allow such action because a system with provisions that allowed individual decisions in such circumstances would be vulnerable to many unjustified killings by those who would knowingly abuse the rules for their own convenience or by those who would make misguided decisions under severe stress. These jurors might still acquit, however, because they believed that Jim's conduct was justified by his personal moral obligation to Mary and that it would be wrong for them to punish Jim for fulfilling his obligation. That is, they might agree with Jim's conclusion that his relationship with Mary generates obligations in the nonpublic domain that override any obligation he has as a citizen of the public domain to obey the law against homicide. Furthermore, they might conclude that as independent moral agents they have an obligation to refuse to punish Jim or to express any condemnation of Jim or of his conduct and that this obligation overrides their obligation as citizens to apply the public morality.[79] Thus, they might conclude that Jim's killing Mary and their acquittal of Jim were justified by moral standards external to the conventional public morality represented by the legal system.

Jim's conduct would not fit the corrective model because it would not involve deviation from specific provisions in order to promote the broader purposes and principles of the system. Similarly, the acquittal would not reflect the corrective model because it would not constitute a legitimated rule departure by officials in service of the purposes and principles underlying the system. Rather, the acquittal would reflect the jurors' judgments that Jim's personal moral obligation outweighed his obligation to conform to law and that their duty to exercise moral judgment as persons outweighed their duty as officials to apply the rules and broader principles of the law.[80]

Instructions suggesting that resort to extrasystemic nullification falls within the legitimate scope of jury responsibilities would violate the fundamental principles of a liberal society. The conventional public morality of the liberal society provides that society with principles of political morality and with political institutions upon which individuals can converge as establishing a

---

79 It is also possible that other jurors, with other comprehensive doctrines, might conclude that Jim's obligation to Mary outweighed any obligation he had to conform to the public morality but that their obligation to apply the public morality required that they convict.

80 Notice that as Jim and the jurors diverge from the conventional public morality by appealing to extrasystemic principles, they might reach the same conclusions or different conclusions, and if they reach common conclusions, they might do so for different reasons. Jim, for example, might be a substantive liberal who believes that his obligation to Mary and her prior autonomous decision to forgo such treatment override the obligations grounded in the conventional public morality. One juror, who is a Utilitarian, might decide to nullify because he believes that doing so in this instance will maximize utility, while another Utilitarian juror might refuse to nullify because she believes that doing so would encourage such decisions, promoting disutility in the long run. Finally, a third juror, who adopts a particular religious comprehensive doctrine, might refuse to nullify because, in her view, Jim's conduct violated God's will.

common moral foundation for the public jurisdiction despite divergent comprehensive doctrines. This public morality grounds common obligations that provide reasons to act in the public domain. At least in modern complex societies, any plausible institutional structure for the conventional public morality will include a system of law that can represent that conventional morality in a relatively consistent, predictable, and enforceable manner and a process of lawmaking that conforms to liberal principles of political morality, recognizing the equal standing of citizens as participants in the democratic lawmaking process. Thus, obligations of the public morality that provide reasons to support and conform to that public morality also provide reasons to support and conform to legal institutions that instantiate it. The claim here is not that liberal political morality entails a general obligation to obey law, but rather that, at least in the context of modern complex societies, it generates an obligation to support the rule of law as a process for institutionalizing the conventional public morality.

Instructions legitimizing extrasystemic nullification would undermine the conventional public morality as embodied in legal institutions by licensing the jurors to subject the defendant and the victim to judgments reflecting the jurors' nonpublic moral doctrines or their conceptions of the public morality that ought to be established rather than to judgments reflecting the conventional public morality as established by the political process. By authorizing such decisions by jurors, the court would misapply the coercive force of the law in subjecting the participants to unpredictable standards that they had no opportunity to participate in establishing and that the court will not apply to other citizens, including the jurors who apply them. Such instructions would sanction treatment within legal institutions, violating the boundaries of the public and nonpublic jurisdictions and undermining the equal standing of both participants as citizens subject only to the public morality they had the opportunity to participate in establishing, and not to the individual moral standards of other citizens. Thus, instructions authorizing extrasystemic nullification undermine the equal standing of the participants and the distinction between public and nonpublic morality that lies at the core of the liberal principles of political morality and provides the common moral commitment of citizens who endorse different comprehensive doctrines.

6.3.7 Summary

The necessity defense and three different variations of jury nullification fulfill different roles in relation to the normative structure of a liberal society, and they represent markedly different responses to crimes of conscience. Acquittal through the necessity defense expresses the conclusion that the putative crime of conscience was no crime at all. Rather, the conduct was justified by appeal to the purposes and principles embodied in the conventional public morality underlying the law. This justification defense precludes the condemnation inherent in criminal conviction and punishment because the defendant did not violate the fully articulated conventional public morality. This defense provides a corrective device within the general category of justification defenses in that it exculpates defendants who do not qualify for specific justification defenses, although the principles of the public morality justify their conduct. The roles of the judge and of the jury, as well as the instructions regarding this defense, appropriately reflect the justificatory principles embodied in the law as the official representation of the conventional public morality.

Intrasystemic nullification by appeal to the principles of justice embodied in the conventional public morality collapses into the necessity defense in that it represents the judgment that those principles justify the conduct in question, and, thus, that the conduct did not violate the fully articulated conventional public morality. Instructions regarding this variant of nullification would either duplicate necessity instructions or reveal an error in the court's analysis of either necessity or this form of nullification.

Intrasystemic nullification by appeal to principles other than justice that are embedded in the system, mercy for example, distorts the expressive function of the criminal justice process and fails to confront the claim advanced by those who engage in crimes of conscience. Such a verdict vindicates neither the defendant's conduct, the current law, nor the standing of the victim. Thus, it demeans the defendant as well as the victim and abdicates the responsibility of the court and of the public. Nullification instructions of this type, rather than the current lack of instructions, would undermine the integrity of the criminal law.

Extrasystemic nullification appeals to moral principles outside of the conventional public morality. It reflects the jurors' judgment that the defendant acted rightly according to principles that neither establish any specific defense within the conventional public morality represented by the criminal law nor provide the basis for acquittal under the residual necessity defense. Jurors who acquit a defendant on this basis abandon their responsibilities under the conventional public morality and transgress the boundary between the public and nonpublic domains of jurisdiction in a liberal society. Instructions legitimizing such a decision as within the discretion of jurors as participants in the public morality would undermine the distinction between the public and nonpublic domains that lies at the foundation of liberal political morality, and it might render the public morality incoherent.

Thus, neither of the two types of nullification that do not collapse into necessity falls within the boundaries of the general category of justification defenses. They violate the limits of systemic justification defenses because they do not justify by appeal to the principles of justice contained in the fully articulated conventional public morality. Any attempt to extend the general category of justification defenses to include such nullification undermines the role of this category of defenses in the system of criminal law that represents the conventional public morality in a liberal society.

6.4   The Responsibilities of Persons in a Liberal Society

6.4.1   The Zenger Trial and Jurors as Persons

Some might object that those who reject a role for nullification within the criminal justice system of a liberal society must contend that jurors should not have nullified in famous historical cases such as that of Peter Zenger.[81] The liberal has two responses to this objection. First, the case does not apply because the conditions that obtained in colonial America at the time of the Zenger trial did not constitute a liberal society with a legal system institutionalizing a conventional public morality through a democratic political process.[82] Second, and more central to this chapter, from the claim that the law of a liberal society ought not authorize nullification, it does not follow that jurors ought never nullify.

Although the conventional public morality gives rise to obligations that provide reasons for all those who endorse liberal principles of political morality to conform to that morality in the public domain, reasons to engage in a certain action do not invariably constitute decisive reasons. Obligations provide reasons to act, and these reasons sometimes conflict. Just as the common principles of public morality in a liberal society provide good reasons to conform to that public morality, the principles of nonpublic morality contained in the comprehensive doctrines of the individual citizens provide good reasons to act in a manner consistent with those doctrines.[83] Given relatively coherent comprehensive doctrines with shared principles of public morality, it is reasonable to expect that conflicts among reasons arising within the public and nonpublic domains will occur relatively infrequently. Absent implausible assumptions regarding the morally relevant conditions of human life and the theoretical consistency and completeness of comprehensive doctrines, however, it is reasonable to expect that such conflicts will occur.

Recall, for example, the case of John and Mary in which John commits a crime of conscience grounded in personal obligation arising from his relationship with Mary. In these circumstances, John might well recognize the homicide statutes prohibiting his action as legitimate components of the legal representation of the conventional public morality. Given the need for generality in

81 Scheflin & Van Dyke, *supra* note 1, at 89.
82 Scott, *supra* note 9, at 423–4; Simson, *supra* note 3, at 503–5.
83 This is not an argument for ethical relativism. Rather, insofar as conscience consists of sincere beliefs based on careful reflection, each citizen has an obligation of conscience to follow the comprehensive doctrine derived from that process of careful reflection, although that doctrine may be misguided. Structural liberals, as such, remain agnostic as to the obligations of various comprehensive doctrines, although each also endorses a particular comprehensive doctrine as a moral agent. Substantive liberals derive obligations from both the public and private aspects of their liberal morality.

law and the danger of deliberate abuse or unintentional misuse under stress, he might even agree that these statutes should not provide an exception for the circumstances such as those he encountered. John might endorse the conventional public morality prohibiting his conduct, therefore, and agree that he has a strong obligation to conform to the statutes representing that conventional morality. He might conscientiously decide, however, that the extended relationship with Mary that has defined a central aspect of his life gives rise to obligations to keep his promise to her that outweigh any reasons he has to conform to the conventional public morality.

Those who engage in crimes of conscience act on the determination that some source of moral obligation provides reasons to act that outweigh any obligations they have to conform to the law representing the conventional morality. Those who engage in civil disobedience or conscientious resistance contend that some aspect of law or policy represents a misguided component of the conventional public morality, and they commit crimes of conscience with the intent to elicit change in that misguided law or policy, or to ameliorate the effects of it. Others, like John, who engage in crimes of personal obligation violate the public morality in service of more weighty moral obligations grounded in their comprehensive doctrines.

Nullification instructions would trivialize these decisions by authorizing jurors to treat the defendants who acted upon them as if they had engaged in mere variations within the officially established conventional public morality. These instructions would also trivialize verdicts of conscience by treating these decisions by jurors as mere corrective devices for smoothing certain rough edges on the legal system, rather than as profound decisions of conscience that the personal responsibility of the juror as a moral agent overrides any responsibility to conform to and to apply the official representation of the public morality as a member and temporary official of the political system. Thus, jury instructions regarding nullification would reduce the role of citizen and juror from that of an independent moral agent who participates in a legal system as an institution of social cooperation to that of a functionary whose only significance is that of a participant in that system.

By blurring the distinction between the juror's roles as participant in the legal system and as independent moral agent, nullification instructions would undermine the democratic process and the fundamental premise of the liberal structure. The liberal political structure rests on the fundamental premise that independent moral agents can derive common principles of political morality for the cooperative governance of the public jurisdiction while endorsing a variety of comprehensive doctrines through which each orders the nonpublic domain. This distinction between the public and nonpublic jurisdictions provides the institutional mechanism through which the liberal society recognizes the dual roles of the person as a member of a cooperative society and as an independent moral agent.

These roles ordinarily converge in the democratic process that allows the individual to participate in the public jurisdiction by exercising the capacities that render him or her a moral agent. When unusual circumstances generate a conflict between obligations attaching to each role, however, the legal system cannot incorporate the obligations of the nonpublic sphere into the public jurisdiction through nullification instructions. Any attempt to do so would undermine the democratic process by authorizing the application of standards that had not been democratically enacted, and it would violate the standing in the public sphere of the participants in the case. Furthermore, it would minimize the significance of individual conscience by treating it as merely a variation within the conventional public morality. By recognizing the limits of legal justification defenses as excluding nullification, the criminal justice system preserves the distinction between the public and nonpublic domains and respects the dual roles of a person as a citizen of the public jurisdiction and as an independent moral agent.

Political liberals can provide no rule or formula by which jurors can determine when their obligations as moral persons override their obligations that attach as citizens of the conventional public morality. One important consideration involves the standing of individual victims. Acquittal of a responsible defendant who has violated the rights of an identified victim indirectly violates the equal standing of that victim by reaffirming, or at least acquiescing in, the imputation of lesser standing to the victim by the defendant.

Certain crimes of conscience such as demonstrations involving disruptions of traffic or of business in public buildings might inconvenience many people. These offenses do not impute lesser standing to any identified individual, however, because those who engage in them do not single out particular persons, violate their ordinarily protected interests, and ask the courts to ratify these violations of these individuals' interests as justified. Thus, nullification regarding these demonstrations would not impugn the equal status of any identified person by ratifying the violation of that person's protected interests. Some crimes of personal moral obligation might express deep respect for the standing of the other person. Jim's removal of Mary's respirator, for example, reflects his conclusion that Mary's prior expression of her priorities in the context of their relationship gives rise to an obligation that outweighs any supported by the conventional public morality.

Other crimes of conscience, such as those involving trespass to private property or interference with the exercise of individual rights, directly violate the standing of identified individuals. When the offense charged constitutes a violation of the rights of an identified victim, nullification denigrates the standing of that victim by withholding condemnation of that violation and by acquiescing in the defendant's imputation of lesser standing to that person. A jury that nullifies in such a case distorts the expressive function of criminal conviction and punishment in a manner that misrepresents the central liberal principle of equal standing in the public jurisdiction and abdicates the responsibility of the public institutions to respect and protect the equal standing of citizens. These imputations of lesser standing to identified victims provide very strong reasons why jurors ought not nullify regarding these crimes. They do not, however, support an invariable rule that jurors ought never nullify in such cases because persons must weigh any good reasons to act or to refrain from acting against any countervailing good reasons that may apply.

The expressive significance of nullification as ratification of the imputation of lesser standing to an identified victim provides a strong reason for any structural liberal to refuse to nullify in cases with identified individual victims, but it can carry particular significance for the substantive liberal. An imputation of lesser standing violates a central principle of structural liberalism, but the relative significance can vary substantially at the level of the comprehensive doctrine. The structural liberal who endorses a utilitarian comprehensive doctrine, for example, would vest only instrumental value in this aspect of structural liberalism and might expect a particular instance of nullification to promote overriding utility, which would be of intrinsic value to the utilitarian.

The substantive liberal, in contrast, recognizes individual autonomy, including personal sovereignty in the nonpublic sphere, as a fundamental value. Civil disobedience that interferes with a competent woman's opportunity to exercise her legal right to make reproductive decisions, for example, imputes lesser standing to her in the public sphere, and it seriously interferes with her sovereignty in the nonpublic domain as well as with her ability to define a central aspect of her life in that nonpublic domain. Thus, the substantive liberal would interpret such a crime of conscience as a transgression against the conventional public morality, an imputation of lesser standing in the political domain to the victim, and as an intrusion into the victim's domain of sovereignty. These considerations provide the substantive liberal juror with very strong reasons not to nullify regarding crimes of conscience with identified individual victims. They do not, however, establish an invariable rule that substantive liberals should never nullify regarding such crimes of conscience. Rather, they provide very strong reasons that jurors must weigh against all other morally relevant reasons.[84]

---

84 Given the juror's need to carefully weigh such a complex set of reasons, it may seem reasonable to ask whether the legal system ought to provide some vehicle by which all relevant information comes before the jury. On the theory advanced here, the criminal justice system should provide only the information relevant to the conventional public morality. The juror, as an independent moral agent, must consider all morally relevant reasons to act, but reasons that carry normative force only in the juror's comprehensive doctrine are not relevant to the conventional public morality. If the criminal justice system provided such information, it would violate the conventional public morality of which it is an institutional representation and undermine the principles of liberal morality that justify its function. That is, from the perspective of the conventional public morality, the legally relevant information is the only relevant information.

In order to constitute verdicts of conscience or crimes of conscience, the actions of jurors or defendants must be deliberate rather than accidental and conscientious rather than malicious.[85] Does deliberate action motivated by sincere belief that principle requires that action suffice, however, to qualify an act as an act of conscience? Consider, for example, the racial separatist who burns crosses on the lawns of interracial couples because he sincerely believes that the Bible condemns miscegenation and requires that all Christians publicly repudiate the practice. Does this individual's sincere belief qualify these offenses as acts of conscience, and would acquittal through nullification by jurors who share these beliefs constitute verdicts of conscience?

Acting from the sincere belief that morally relevant considerations support one's action is necessary but not sufficient to qualify behavior as an act of conscience. Such belief is analytically necessary because it is inherent in the concept of acting from conscience.[86] Sincere belief is not sufficient, however, because acts of conscience require not only that one act *from* conscience but also that one reason responsibly *to* conscience. That is, conscientious action requires not only that one deliberately acts in a manner that one sincerely believes one morally ought to act, but also that one engages in a careful, responsible process of deliberation in making that determination.[87] Thus, acts of conscience must represent a sincere belief in the moral correctness of the act and a conscientious process of deriving and maintaining that belief. Crimes or verdicts of conscience in a generally justifiable social structure involve choice among morally relevant reasons to act. In confronting this choice, the individual encounters explicit notice that there are at least some morally relevant reasons to refrain from acting in the manner contemplated. This notice provides good reason to question the principles and circumstances the individual understands as supporting the conscientious action.

Thus, the conscientious moral agent can never take it as obvious that a crime or verdict of conscience is justified. Rather, in order to qualify as an authentic act of conscience, a conscientious decision to perform criminal conduct or to bring a verdict contrary to law in a generally just social structure requires that the actor engage in careful deliberation on the proposed action and on the principles thought to support that action. One who purports to act conscientiously but refuses to carefully examine the basis for that conduct does not responsibly

---

85 *See supra* § 6.2.2.

86 II Oxford English Dictionary at 522. Conscience is "[t]he internal acknowledgment or recognition of the moral quality of one's motives and actions; the sense of right and wrong as regards things for which one is responsible." Benjamin, *supra* note 35, at 469. "Conscience" refers most generally to conscious awareness of the moral quality of one's action.

87 II Oxford English Dictionary at 522. One is conscientious if one is "[o]bedient or loyal to conscience; habitually governed by a sense of duty; scrupulous." To be scrupulous is to be "cautious or meticulous in acting, deciding, etc. . . . characterized by a strict and minute regard for what is right." II Oxford English Dictionary at 2686; Benjamin, *supra* note 35, at 470.

reason to conscience and, therefore, does not engage in an act of conscience.[88] Careful deliberation does not guarantee accurate conclusions, however, and one who fulfills this requirement of careful deliberation may engage in unjustified conduct. Acts of conscience do not necessarily constitute justified action.

The expressive significance of nullification for the equal standing of innocent victims must weigh heavily in the process of deliberation to conscience that is required in order to qualify nullification as an authentic verdict of conscience. That a crime or verdict of conscience imputes lesser standing to an innocent victim provides good reason to refrain from engaging in that offense or from bringing that verdict, and it provides good reason to doubt that such conduct is right. These reasons arise from the normative significance of conscience and from the principles of liberal political morality.

The normative significance of conscience reflects its relationship to the integrity of the person. Deliberation of conscience involves conscientious reflection on the convictions and principles that provide the foundation of one's identity as a person and define one's life as an extended project. Thus, respect for acts of conscience reflects respect for persons in that an authentic act of conscience reveals careful reflection on the underlying convictions that define the unique identity of the actor.[89] Putative acts of conscience that impute lesser standing to innocent victims directly conflict with this foundation in respect for persons in that they express disrespect for those innocent victims. This conflict does not categorically preclude such acts, however, because upon careful reflection, one might conclude that overriding reasons require an act despite this very strong reason to refrain from engaging in it.

Conduct that undermines an individual's equal standing violates a basic principle of the liberal political morality. Thus, the mere fact that contemplated acts of conscience will have this effect provides liberals with good reason to doubt and carefully review the process by which they derived their positions of conscience as well as their conclusions that they ought to engage in such conduct. Overriding reasons grounded in the public or nonpublic domain might persuade them that they ought to engage in the conduct or bring the verdict despite this good reason not to do so. If they then act on that conclusion, they ought to do so reluctantly and regretfully, recognizing that they can justify that decision as at best a lesser evil.

Nullification instructions authorizing jurors to exercise their consciences in

---

88 Two clarifications are relevant here. First, the requirement of deliberation does not necessarily require the type of analytic reflection one might expect from someone who is analytically trained. Rather, it requires careful, sincere reflection upon and attempts to ascertain the adequacy of one's reasons for action. Second, the duration of deliberation cannot be evaluated without allowing for circumstances that might require a rapid decision and for prior reflection on related matters.
89 Benjamin, *supra* note 35, at 470–2.

their decisions of legal guilt and innocence attempt to incorporate all obligation and responsibility into legal obligation and responsibility. Such instructions incorporate nullification into the legal structure of the public morality, blurring the central liberal distinction between the public and nonpublic domains. This blending of public and nonpublic morality discourages jurors, officials, and the population in general from fully appreciating and confronting the depth with which crimes and verdicts of conscience challenge the officially established conventional morality. This loss of clarity obfuscates the need for conscientious reflection on the public morality and on the tension that can arise between the obligations of political justice in the liberal society and the obligations that each person assumes through the comprehensive doctrine by which he or she orders a life.

This tension arises from the obligations to support a system of law instantiating the conventional public morality and to retain authority and responsibility for one's own decisions and actions as a moral person. This second obligation is inherent in the notion of a moral agent who is capable of fulfilling the role of a responsible citizen in the public domain and of developing a life in accord with some comprehensive doctrine in the protected domain of nonpublic morality. In short, nullification instructions would trivialize the challenges to the public morality embodied in crimes of conscience and verdicts of conscience, and they would obscure the fundamental questions regarding the responsibilities of persons as subjects of the law representing the public morality and as independent moral agents.

6.4.2   Judicial Nullification

As previously discussed, the necessity defense provides an intrasystemic corrective device through which courts acquit defendants who have performed conduct violating an offense definition in circumstances in which no specific defense applied and in which that conduct was necessary in order to avoid a greater evil according to the conventional public morality represented by the law. The judge must determine whether the defendant has met the burden of production regarding the elements of the defense in order to decide whether to allow evidence and instruct the jury regarding the defense. In making this determination, the judge should appeal to the principles of the conventional morality represented by the legal system, rather than to the principles of his or her comprehensive doctrine because the defense serves as an intrasystemic corrective device.[90]

Suppose that Jim is brought to trial for murdering Mary by removing her respirator. Jim admits that he purposely caused Mary's death; he acted in order

---

90 *See supra* § 6.3.3.

to fulfill their mutual promise not to allow the other to "*live* like that – hooked up to machines." The investigation clearly establishes that Jim premeditated in that the night before he removed Mary's respirator he prepared to carry out his decision by carving the wooden wedge he used to prevent the hospital staff from opening the door and intervening. Psychological evaluation of Jim reveals that at the time he acted, he was distressed about Mary's illness and about his failure to keep his promise to her but that he clearly understood the medical and legal circumstances and that he suffered no disability that might support any type of excuse or claim of diminished capacity.

Jim's defense attorney seeks to admit evidence and elicit jury instructions regarding the necessity defense. The attorney intends to argue that Jim's conduct was necessary in order to avoid a greater evil because Mary's decision in her discussions with Jim demonstrates that continued existence in a state of dependence on the respirator would constitute greater harm to her previously expressed interests than would her death due to the removal of the respirator in compliance with her expressed preference.

The state supreme court has directly rejected this argument in a similar case of euthanasia approximately two years ago. At that time, the trial court refused to allow evidence and instructions regarding the necessity defense. The defendant was convicted of murder, appealed, and the state supreme court affirmed the conviction, expressly ruling that the necessity defense did not apply to cases involving euthanasia. Shortly after the supreme court decided that case, a legislator introduced a bill in the state legislature that would have allowed a spouse to demand the removal of respirators or other life-sustaining equipment in circumstances such as those involved in the case of Jim and Mary and in the earlier case. The bill was defeated by a large majority in the legislature, partially in response to several statewide surveys that demonstrated broad popular opposition to any legalization of euthanasia.

It seems clear in these circumstances that the conventional public morality represented by the law does not authorize the judge to allow evidence, argument, or instructions regarding the necessity defense. The conventional public morality subordinates the judge's authority to interpret that morality to both the legislature and the supreme court, both of which have expressly determined that the public morality does not accommodate the judgment of relative evils the defense attorney wants to argue. Upon review of the defense attorney's argument, the relevant case law, and the legislative history, the trial judge concludes that the conventional public morality does not allow her to instruct or admit evidence regarding the necessity defense in these circumstances.

Suppose, however, that the trial judge is a substantive liberal who firmly believes that if the evidence supports Jim's story, Jim's conduct was morally required both because the ongoing maintenance on the respirator constituted a severe intrusion into Mary's domain of sovereignty and by virtue of Jim's obligation to Mary in the nonpublic sphere arising from their mutual promises in the context of their extended intimate relationship. The judge understands her responsibilities arising from her official position in the political structure as supporting a strong obligation to discharge her official function by applying the public morality represented by the law rather than her comprehensive doctrine when the two conflict. She, like those who serve on juries, however, does not escape her responsibilities as an independent moral agent when she accepts an official role. Her obligations arising from her official responsibilities provide strong reasons to conform to the conventional public morality represented by the law, but strong reasons do not necessarily constitute decisive reasons.

If, for example, the judge firmly believes after careful deliberation that Jim had a strong obligation to Mary to remove the respirator, that it would be wrong to punish Jim for fulfilling that obligation, and that it would be wrong for her to participate in that process, it remains an open possibility that her obligations arising from her comprehensive doctrine and her status as an independent moral agent might override her obligations to apply the conventional public morality. Should this judge decide to allow evidence, argument, and instructions regarding the necessity defense, however, this apparent application of the intrasystemic necessity defense would actually constitute an exercise of extrasystemic judicial nullification as an act of conscience.[91]

The claim here is not that she ought to conclude that her comprehensive doctrine supports stronger reasons than those arising from the conventional public morality and, therefore, that she ought to allow the defense. Rather, the example illustrates two points. First, both the public morality and her comprehensive doctrine support obligations that provide morally relevant reasons, and, thus, the reasons and responsibilities arising from her official role in institutions of the public morality do not take categorical priority such that one can conclude that judges ought never give priority to morally relevant reasons grounded in the comprehensive doctrine over those grounded in the public morality. Second, if she allows evidence, argument, and instructions regarding the necessity defense because she concludes that reasons grounded in her comprehensive doctrine override those grounded in the public morality, she engages in judicial nullification. In short, judges, like jurors, remain persons who may encounter circumstances in which obligations conflict and no algorithm provides a clear decision rule.

By virtue of their official roles, judges arguably take stronger obligations to apply the official public morality than do jurors. Judicial decisions ordinarily carry more profound institutional impact. Judges make decisions that carry

---

91 Notice that Jim differs significantly from the candidates for systemically complete mitigation discussed in § 5.2. They act contrary to law in circumstances in which compliance would require extreme fortitude or discipline. Jim, in contrast, may exercise extreme fortitude or discipline in resisting systemic pressure to conform to law in order to fulfill obligations in the non-public sphere.

precedential force, influencing unpredictable numbers of cases and participants in the future. If citizens conclude that judges frequently depart from the public morality in order to conform to their own nonpublic standards, this belief might well erode public confidence in public institutions and undermine voluntary cooperation with those institutions. Alternately, if citizens interpret these judicial decisions as reflecting the public morality, this perception will distort the expressive function of judicial process by misrepresenting an exercise of the judge's nonpublic comprehensive doctrine as an expression of the public morality.

These arguments support the conclusion that by virtue of their institutional role, judges take a very strong obligation to conform to the public morality rather than to their comprehensive doctrines when the two conflict. Very strong obligations provide very strong reasons, however, rather than necessarily decisive reasons. Nothing in these arguments rules out the possibility that in extraordinary circumstances reasons arising from the nonpublic comprehensive doctrine might prevail. A critic might contend that judges should never consider reasons arising from their nonpublic comprehensive doctrines because they take an oath to apply the law. The oath provides a very good reason for conforming to law, but absent an argument explaining why oaths uniquely provide a special type of reason that can never be overridden by other morally relevant reasons, it does not establish a categorical priority for obligations arising from the public morality.

This potential conflict among obligations grounded in the public and nonpublic domains of morality can arise for any structural liberal. A utilitarian judge, for example, might support structural liberalism as the form of political organization most likely to maximize utility in the long run. Yet, that judge might encounter unusual circumstances in which it appears that departing from obligations arising from the judicial role in the conventional public morality would result in a clear balance of utility over disutility without significantly undermining the utilitarian benefits of the institutional structure.

This conflict can take a particularly cogent form for the substantive liberal. Although any independent moral agent retains a responsibility to evaluate and act upon all morally relevant reasons, the substantive liberal vests fundamental value in individual autonomy, including the exercise of the autonomous capacities such as reflection and deliberation in the pursuit of the autonomous virtues such as self-direction and in the process of defining a human life of one's own. Thus, the substantive liberal grants substantial weight to the importance of retaining the authority and responsibility to consider all relevant factors in any decision that significantly affects the moral quality of one's life. By devoting a significant portion of one's life to the role of a judge in the institutions of public morality, however, the substantive liberal also vests substantial value in discharging that responsibility as a major component of the life he defines. In short, the substantive liberal judge's comprehensive doctrine emphasizes both the responsibility to discharge the institutional obligations associated with the role that constitutes a major commitment in that judge's life and the responsibility to deliberate carefully on all reasons relevant to significant life decisions, including reasons that conflict with those arising from institutional obligations.

This tension among reasons to act encountered by the substantive liberal judge represents a special case of a tension encountered more broadly by substantive liberals. Those who endorse the substantive liberal comprehensive moral doctrine vest fundamental value in a principle of autonomy including the exercise of personal sovereignty in developing a life of one's own and in cultivating the autonomous virtues. Retaining the authority and responsibility for one's central life decisions is critical to this project. Yet, at least in complex modern societies, public institutions ruled by law probably provide the only plausible social structure that can establish the conditions of fair and predictable social cooperation that will allow each to define and pursue a life as an extended project. Thus, the substantive liberal comprehensive doctrine provides good reasons to endorse and protect the rule of law as well as to retain the authority and responsibility to depart from that law when overriding reasons obtain.

6.4.3   Conflicting Obligations: Tension Rather than Contradiction

Some critics might contend that these conflicting obligations arising from the public and nonpublic domains reveal a fatal contradiction in liberalism. A central contradiction in the theory would eviscerate the integrity of the theory in that one can infer any proposition from a contradiction.[92] This unavoidable tension does not, however, constitute a contradiction in liberal political morality. Two statements are contradictory only if they are inconsistent, that is, only if they cannot both be true under any circumstances. Consistent statements can both be true under some state of affairs.[93] Analogously, the obligations to support a system of law representing the conventional public morality and to retain moral authority and responsibility regarding one's actions are consistent in that the individual can fulfill both under some circumstances, and, moreover, these obligations usually converge in a generally just society. Ordinarily, for example, jurors can fulfill both by conscientiously applying the law. That liberal political morality occasionally encounters this tension demonstrates the complex set of principles, concerns, and circumstances that people must consider in their moral decisions as citizens of a society, participants in relationships, and sovereign moral agents. In short, it is a virtue rather than a defect of liberal political morality that it occasionally encounters this tension because in doing so it reflects the complexity of moral life.

92 Pascal Engel, The Norm of Truth 372, 222 (Toronto: Univ. of Toronto Press, 1991).
93 Simon Blackburn, The Oxford Dictionary of Philosophy 78, 81 (Oxford: Oxford Univ. Press, 1994); Engel, *id.* at 372.

6.5   Conclusion

Although some might raise historical or analytic questions about verdicts of conscience and crimes of conscience, those who want to determine whether courts *ought* to instruct jurors regarding necessity or nullification as falling within the scope of their authority as jurors need a normative theory justifying a particular role for jurors within a more broadly justified institution of criminal justice. Liberal principles of political morality support a criminal justice system in which the necessity defense serves as a residual intrasystemic corrective device. It appropriately applies to putative crimes of conscience only when the conduct constituting the offense qualifies as a lesser evil than the evil avoided according to the principles of the conventional public morality represented by the law. In such cases, the putative crimes of conscience do not actually constitute crimes at all because they do not violate the fully articulated conventional public morality.

Intrasystemic nullification by appeal to the principles of justice embodied in the criminal law collapses into necessity. Intrasystemic nullification by appeal to principles other than justice, for example, mercy, embodied in the criminal law distorts the expressive function of the criminal process and fails to confront the significance of crimes of conscience. Under the guise of concern for those who commit crimes of conscience, such a verdict denies them respect. Extrasystemic nullification and jury instructions regarding this alternative have no legitimate role within the criminal process as an institution of the conventional public morality because extrasystemic nullification involves the decision by jurors that some obligations arising in the nonpublic domain override any obligation they have as participants in the criminal justice process of the public morality. Either jurors or judges may encounter circumstances in which they determine that they ought to act contrary to the public morality, but judicial instructions cannot incorporate these determinations into the public morality. Any attempt to do so would trivialize verdicts of conscience and crimes of conscience. By maintaining a clear distinction between legal justification defenses and extrasystemic jury nullification, the criminal law preserves the public and nonpublic domains and respects the dual roles of a person as citizen of the public jurisdiction and as independent moral agent.

At least in the context of modern complex societies, persons need legal institutions that provide the social structure that allows them to order social interaction in a manner that maintains a relatively predictable public domain and protects a nonpublic domain within which they can define their lives as individuals and as participants in relationships. We should not, however, expect too much of law. It cannot order the nonpublic domain, and it cannot provide an alternative to individual deliberation by persons when obligations arising in the public and nonpublic domains conflict.

7

Conclusions

The criminal law embodies an important component of the official representation of the conventional public morality. As such, it provides a set of behavioral directives and incentives designed to maintain a system of cooperative social interaction, but it also serves important expressive functions. Criminal offense definitions and justification defenses instantiate the more abstract substantive principles of the conventional public morality in a form that facilitates interpretation and application by officials and citizens. These provisions also contribute to the definitions of the parameters of the public and nonpublic jurisdictions. Certain offense elements, excuses, and mitigating factors represent systemic criteria of accountability and blameworthiness.

Justification defenses preclude conviction and punishment of individuals who violate offense definitions in circumstances that preclude the condemnation inherent in conviction and punishment because they support exceptions to the underlying prohibitory norms of the fully articulated conventional public morality. In order to understand the significance and parameters of the general category of justification defenses and of each particular justification defense, one must interpret them in light of the condemnation expressed by conviction and punishment in a system of criminal law that embodies substantive principles of political morality.

Legal conviction and punishment ordinarily expresses condemnation of five types at two levels of analysis, but only the first type of condemnation, expressed at the institutional level by the proscription of certain act-types as criminal offenses, inheres in every institution of legal punishment. Convictions in a retributive system also express condemnation of the actors as having violated the fully articulated conventional public morality as accountable agents by systemic standards, and punishment in a retributive system expresses condemnation of the actor as blameworthy by systemic standards in proportion to the severity of the punishment.

Justification defenses exempt certain defendants who do not merit the condemnation inherent in conviction and punishment because their actions do not violate the fully articulated conventional public morality. Excuses, in contrast, exculpate those who violate the public morality but not in the capacity of accountable agents. Some excused defendants lack the capacities required to qualify as accountable agents, while others lack the knowledge that would provide the opportunity to apply these capacities to the decision to perform the proscribed conduct. This latter group's action-plan selection is internally justified by the reasons they are aware of, although their conduct is not externally justified by all the relevant reasons that apply.

A satisfactory account of the role and parameters of any particular justification defense, as well as of the general category of justification defenses, in a specific legal system must appeal to the substantive principles of political morality supporting that system of criminal law. The law of self-defense in a western liberal democracy, for example, must reflect the underlying liberal principles of political morality that vest fundamental value in the individual's right to self-determination and recognize each sovereign person's equal standing. The criminal law of such a society condemns culpable criminal conduct that infringes on the victim's concrete interests and violates her sphere of sovereignty. The aggressor imputes inequality of standing by culpably violating the victim's protected domain, and in a liberal society any violation of sovereignty constitutes an injury to a fundamental interest. The victim may exercise any force necessary, therefore, to protect her sphere of self-determination against an aggressor whose culpable conduct extends beyond his own protected domain. She has no obligation to observe rules of proportion or retreat against an aggressor, but she must consider the interests of innocent aggressors or shields and must not violate the sovereignty of an innocent party.

Certain common legal provisions requiring retreat or rough proportionality may be justifiable as qualifications of the basic moral principles in light of the formal properties of law, defensible error preferences, and reasonable hypotheses regarding human propensity to err. These provisions should remain open to revision, however, if evidence either undermines the empirical hypotheses that support them or demonstrates that procedural devices can adequately address these considerations. The technical requirements of substantive and procedural law can be significant not only for their effects on the outcome of any specific case, but also for the manner in which they promote or undermine the expressive function of the criminal law.

The perplexing series of cases involving battered women who kill their batterers in the absence of occurrent attacks or threats demonstrates the practical and expressive significance of precise legal formulation. Satisfactory analysis and adjudication of these cases require empirical rigor, careful attention to the jurisprudential foundations of legal doctrine, and the integration of the two. Although expert testimony regarding the battered woman syndrome has been widely endorsed by courts, commentators, and statutes, this syndrome lacks empirical support as a clinical syndrome. Furthermore, it bears almost no relevance to rigorously formulated and interpreted self-defense doctrine, either in its current form or as developed in Chapters 2 through 4 in order to more accurately represent liberal principles of political morality. If future research were to provide adequate empirical support for such a syndrome, it could have limited relevance for the purposes of supporting the defendant's credibility or advancing an excuse for nonculpable mistake regarding justification.

When justification and excuse are distinguished, other central concepts of self-defense doctrine are clarified in a manner that renders them consistent with the underlying principles of liberal political morality, and expert testimony regarding the syndrome is differentiated from ordinary factual evidence and expert testimony regarding the pattern of battering, many of the problematic issues and cases can be addressed more satisfactorily. A statutory scheme reflecting the structure of justification defenses and related excuses as analyzed in Chapter 2 and the moral foundations of self-defense advanced in Chapter 3 would accommodate many of the most troubling circumstances in which battered women kill their batterers in nonconfrontational situations. Some of these defendants would qualify for a justification defense based on necessity, while others would be excused due to nonculpable mistakes regarding justification. Finally, some would fail to qualify for either type of defense. Thus, this approach has the additional virtue of avoiding a new stereotype by treating each defendant in the manner appropriate to the circumstances in which she acted.

Duress and jury nullification raise important questions regarding the boundaries of justification defenses in the criminal law. Duress has traditionally been very difficult to classify as either a justification or an excuse, and so it should remain because it is neither. Duress represents a subset of a broader set of cases that should be subject to systemically complete mitigation resulting in purely vindicating convictions. In a retributive system that punishes in proportion to systemic criteria of blameworthiness, this approach would accommodate defendants who do not merit blame by systemic standards and thus do not merit the fifth type of condemnation, which is inherent in punishment by these retributive systems. Although conviction in a retributive system entails only the first and fourth types of condemnation, punishment also entails condemnation as blameworthy by systemic standards in proportion to the severity of the punishment. Thus, accountable agents who commit unjustified offenses under extraordinarily coercive circumstances merit the condemnation inherent in conviction but not the condemnation inherent in punishment.

Classifying duress as systemically complete mitigation leading to purely vindicating conviction might produce conceptual and practical advantages over the current ambiguous interpretation of the defense. It would retain the explicit condemnation of this type of conduct at the systemic level, possibly enhancing the ability of many people, especially innocent victims, to accept the outcome. The vindicating conviction also affirms the broader structure by explicitly confirming the defendant's status as an accountable agent by systemic standards.

Finally, the vindicating conviction recognizes the separate expressive functions of conviction and punishment in retributive institutions. That is, conviction condemns this person's performing a particular type of conduct as an accountable agent, and punishment expresses the degree of blameworthiness attributable to that agent.

This classification of duress and similar cases within the broader framework of the criminal law might also enable us to avoid certain costly expressive errors. The currently dominant classification of duress as an excuse denigrates the identified defendants by misrepresenting them as lacking the capacities of accountable agents. Perhaps most importantly from the perspective of the expressive function of the criminal law, excusing these actors encourages the rest of us to engage in an insidious form of self-deception in which we direct our attention toward the putative defects suffered by these particular individuals rather than confronting the uncomfortable likelihood that they acted as they did not because they differ from us but rather because they are very much like us.

Careful reflection on necessity, nullification, and the relationship between the two clarifies the limits of justification defenses in a system of criminal law representing the conventional public morality of a liberal society, and it advances the analysis of the responsibilities of persons as citizens of the public jurisdiction and as sovereign moral agents. Liberal principles of political morality support a criminal justice system in which the necessity defense serves as a residual intrasystemic corrective device. It appropriately applies only when the conduct that violates an offense definition qualifies as a lesser evil than the evil avoided according to the principles of the conventional public morality represented by the law. In such cases, the putative crimes do not actually constitute crimes at all because they do not violate the fully articulated conventional public morality.

Intrasystemic nullification by appeal to the principles of justice embodied in the criminal law collapses into necessity. Intrasystemic nullification by appeal to principles other than justice, for example, mercy, embodied in the criminal law distorts the expressive function of the criminal process. Furthermore, when applied to crimes of conscience, it fails to confront the significance of this conduct. Under the guise of concern for those who commit crimes of conscience, such a verdict denies them respect. Extrasystemic nullification and jury instructions regarding this alternative have no legitimate role within the criminal process as an institution of the conventional public morality because extrasystemic nullification involves decisions by jurors that some obligations arising in the nonpublic domain override any obligation they have as participants in the criminal justice process of the public morality.

Either jurors or judges may encounter circumstances in which they determine that they ought to act contrary to the public morality, but judicial instructions cannot incorporate these determinations into the public morality. Any attempt to do so would trivialize verdicts of conscience and crimes of conscience. By maintaining a clear distinction between legal justification defenses and extrasystemic jury nullification, the criminal law preserves the public and nonpublic domains and respects the dual roles of a person as citizen of the public jurisdiction and as independent moral agent.

At least in the context of modern complex societies, persons need legal institutions that provide the social structure that allows them to order social interaction in a manner that maintains a relatively predictable public jurisdiction and protects a nonpublic domain within which they can define their lives as individuals and as participants in relationships. Obligations arising in the public jurisdiction from the conventional public morality can provide strong reasons to conform to particular laws and to support the rule of law as the social institution reasonably expected to maintain a viable system of social cooperation. Strong reasons are not necessarily decisive reasons, however, and in certain circumstances any structural liberal might conclude that morally relevant reasons arising in the nonpublic domain outweigh those arising in the public jurisdiction. Conflicts among reasons arising in the public and nonpublic jurisdictions may become particularly salient for substantive liberals. We cannot eliminate or escape these conflicts by attempting to incorporate all of morality into the conventional public morality represented by the law. Although law fulfills an essential role in the lives of persons, it cannot relieve us of the responsibilities inherent in the status of competent moral agents.

Index

accomplice liability, 47, 53
accountability, 3, 13, 35, 145; criteria of, 26, 199; systemic criteria of, 150; by systemic standards, 26, 36, 72
accountable agent(s), 34, 36, 41, 43, 140, 141; condemnation type and, 24, 26, 27, 29; disabilities undermining status of, 148; duress and, 201, 202; and excuses, 143, 200; and justification defenses, 199; vindicating convictions and, 147
accountable agent by systemic standards, 39, 40, 53, 149, 151
acquittal, 150, 153, 160, 170, 189; despite legal guilt, 156, 157, 164, 180, 181–2, 183–4; expressive significance of, 183; in extrasystemic nullification, 186; through necessity defense, 185–6
act-type(s), 27n25, 43, 53, 199; condemnation of, 149; proscribed, 35
action-plans, 32–4, 35, 36, 37, 39, 40, 41, 43, 53, 141, 200
action-theory, 37
aggressor culpability: harms and, 60–2
arrest, 45
assault, 25, 27, 28, 29, 43, 110; offense definitions, 74; offense elements for, 1, 2; unprovoked, 52
assault statutes, 30, 56, 64
assisting justified acts, 40–2, 46–7
asymmetrical justification, 49, 53, 54
athletic contests, 51
attempt liability, 36, 38, 41, 42, 127
autonomy, 68; fundamental value for, 67–8, 68n34, 70, 190, 196, 197; protection of, in self-defense law, 56–7, 59, 101–2, see also sovereignty, personal
awareness of justificatory circumstances, 3, 5–6, 10, 21, 31, 36, 38

battered woman syndrome, 2, 13, 39, 90, 92, 111–14, 129–30, 131, 133–5, 200–1;
and conventional self-defense law, 98–114; excuse rather than justification, 120, 134; and mental illness, 116–20; or pattern of battering, 104–6; putative relevance of, to self-defense, 93–4; research on, 94–8; and self-defense, 92–4
battered women, 136, 137, 140; culpability and, as justified or excused, 126–34; reasonable belief in necessity of deadly force, 106–8; and self-defense, 12–13, 15, 89–135; self-defense as justification and excuse, 114–34
battered women cases, 200–1
battering relationship, 90, 92, 94, 95, 96–7, 104, 109, 130, 135; failure to leave previously, 111–14; inability to leave, 94, 95; necessary force, 104–6; and necessity of deadly force, 106–7; patterns of legal intervention in, 127; as support for reasonable belief, 111
behavior: exempted by justification defenses, 30, 31, 32
behavioral directives, 73, 74
beliefs, 22; in self-defense, 91; see also reasonable belief
bias, 160, 161
Blackman, Justice, 173n65
Black's Law Dictionary, 99
boxing matches, 21, 51
burden of persuasion, 87, 171
burden of production, 170–1, 193
burden of proof, 132n124
business practices, 21

capacity-responsibility, 148
choice-of-evils defense, 2, 44, 63
circumstances, 32, 37; and justification, 3, 136–7, 143; see also extraordinary circumstances
civil disobedience, 25, 154–5, 156, 173–4, 188, 190
civil protective orders, 110

coercion/coercive force, 138, 139, 141–2
coercive circumstances, 143–4, 146, 201
community conscience, 174–7; jury as, 174–6, 177, 180n71
community consensus, 171
compensation, 63, 80, 81
competition, mutually privileged, 21
comprehensive doctrines: of citizens, 187, 188; of judges, 193, 195, 196
concrete interests, 200; of aggressor, 76, 77, 78, 87, 133; defined, 63n21; injury to, 72; of innocent aggressors, 80; protection of, in self-defense, 75, 79, 82, 83, 88, 102; threat to, 63, 64
conduct, 32, 37; justification directed toward, 13
conflict: between putatively justified actors, 21, 40; mutually justified, 4, 16, 21
confrontation cases (battered women), 13, 107, 108, 109
conscience, 189; acts of, 162, 192–2, 195; defined, 191n86; normative significance of, 192; verdicts of, 188, 191, 193, 198, 203; *see also* crimes of conscience
conscientious resistance, 155, 156, 173–4, 188
consequentialism, 61, 85, 157n16; jury nullification in, 158–9, 161, 167
Constitution, 172
conventional public morality: action according to standards of, 143–4; criminal law as official representation of, 2, 23, 25–6, 31, 43, 52, 56, 71–2, 73, 74–5, 80, 84, 87, 143, 145, 147, 163, 167, 175–6, 199, 202, 203; fully articulated, 19, 28, 29, 30, 31, 34, 37, 38, 39, 49, 53, 64, 89, 140, 151; and judicial nullification, 193–4, 195, 196; jurors' responsibilities in, 154; justification defenses and, 16–54; necessity in, 167, 168, 170–7, 185–6; nullification in, 167, 168, 178, 179, 182–3, 184–6; obligations from, 187, 188, 197; properties of, 30; self-defense theory as component of, 56, 64; social matrix as component of, 48; violations of, 149, 199
conventional social morality, 30–1, 38
conviction, 2, 23, 24, 26, 72, 73, 74, 149–50, 201; condemnation in, 52, 53, 54, 56, 64, 149, 151, 152, 186, 199, 201; expresive function of, 15, 151, 183, 189–90, 202; without harsh treatment, 145, 147; and status of victim, 73; *see also* purely vindicating convictions
corrective device: necessity and nullification as, 170, 178, 184, 186, 193, 202
courts: appellate, 153, 161; battered woman syndrome in, 92, 93–4, 96, 98, 99, 103, 107, 108, 118, 120, 123, 129, 131, 134; and

necessity defense, 170–1, 172–4; decisions under conditions of uncertainty, 132, 135; and jury nullification, 156; and punishment, 146; and self-defense, 115
credibility argument: battered women, 111–14, 134
crimes of conscience, 13–14, 15, 154–6, 168, 170, 181–2, 185–6, 189–91, 193, 198, 202, 203; grounded in personal obligation, 187–8
criminal code(s), 74
criminal justice system, 22, 25–6, 64–5, 145, 154, 189, 198, 202; and blameworthiness, 150; deception and integrity of, 167–8; information provided by, 190n84; in liberal society, 71–3; political morality underlying, 15, 166, 167; reliance on general verdicts, 156; rule-based, 159; *see also* retributive systems
criminal law, 4–5, 29, 132, 200; attribution of blameworthiness in, 145; character in, 38; as community conscience, 175–6; core rules of, 23, 26; expressive function of, 2, 15, 72, 87, 133–4, 151, 181, 199, 200, 202; as guide to conduct, 17; integrated system of, 52; moral force of, 162, 163–7; offense definitions and justification defenses in, 168–9, 173; and personal sovereignty, 71, 73; prospective/restrospective functions of, 34–7; purposes of, 44–5; regulating degree of discipline and fortitude required, 142, 143, 144; role of justification defenses in, 14; and self-defense, 75; violence-preventing function of, 6, 8
criminal law doctrine: theoretical analysis of, 90
criminal punishment, *see* punishment
criminal prosecution: for battery, 110
critical morality, 43, 143
culpable aggressors, 12, 58–9
culpability, 3, 26, 35, 71, 121, 131, 141, 147; and battered women as justified or excused, 126–34; criterion of, 124–5; in distributive justice, 60–1; in duress, 138; for mistaken beliefs, 125–6, 130; and self-defense, 84, 85, 86
culpability elements, 2, 3, 32, 33–4
cycle theory of violence (battering relationship), 92, 95, 96, 97

deadly force, 62; by battered women, 90, 93, 111, 134; reasonable belief in necessity of: battered women, 106–8; in self-defense, 85, 86, 91, 115
deception: and integrity of a liberal criminal justice system, 167–8; and moral force of criminal law, 163–7

defendant: status as accountable agent, 150, 151

defense-of-others, 1, 11, 27, 28–9, 30, 43, 55

defensive force, 56, 57, 75–7, 78–9, 83, 85–7, 88, 90–1, 102, 136–7; battered women, 89, 93, 94, 99–100, 101, 103, 109, 110–11, 120, 126, 127, 128–34, 135; in criminal law, 74; justificatory foundations for, 75, 81–2; necessary, 2; retreat as legal alternative to: battered women, 108–9; *see also* deadly force

deliberation, requirement of, 192

democratic process: undermined by nullification, 188, 189

democratic self-government: and nullification instructions, 162–3

deontic theories, 157n16

depression, 92, 95, 96–7, 104, 113, 116, 118, 119

desert, 26, 43, 146, 158

desert-based approach, 61

deterrence, 71, 163

difficult cases, 10–11, 14, 16, 21, 136–8, 143–4; battered woman syndrome, 135; duty not to resist, 42; justification defenses, 34; and knowledge requirement, 37–40; moral condemnation, 25–6; and revised matrix of social responsibility, 47–52; self-defense, 55, 58, 88; social matrix/incompatibility thesis, 9–10

diplomatic immunity, 18

disability(ies), 142; exculpation due to, 3; giving rise to excusing condition, 140, 141; grounding excuse, 8, 148; in innocent aggressors, 79; undermining status as accountable agents, 148

disability that differentiates, 137, 141, 142, 148

discipline and fortitude, 143–4, 145–6, 147, 148, 150

distributive justice: self-defense and, 60–2

double jeopardy prohibition, 156

Dressler, Joshua, 4, 9, 10, 47, 50, 139–40

duress, 11, 15, 44n59, 54, 83, 88, 181, 201–2; as claim of mitigation, 142; classification of, 152; as excuse, 10, 138, 139–40, 141–2, 148–9, 151, 152, 202; as problematic classification, 10; and systemically complete mitigation, 136–52; theoretical interpretation, 138–42

duties; in social matrix, 47; *see also* obligations

duty not to interfere: and incompatibility thesis, 42–7

duty not to resist, 42

duty to retreat, 55, 58, 59, 60, 77, 83, 85–6; with innocent aggressors, 80

equal standing of citizens, 63, 66, 67–8, 70, 71, 75, 78, 79, 80, 81–2, 83, 162, 177, 185; impairment and, 82–3; legal system and, 72, 73; in self-defense, 102; violated by deception, 167; violated by necessity defense, 177; violated by nullification, 185

equal standing of victims, 182; nullification and, 189–90, 192

error preference, 74, 76, 84–5, 87, 88, 91, 132n124, 200

euthanasia, 194

evidence: and jury deviation, 161; self-defense: battered women, 105–6, 107, 108, 111, 112, 113–14, 129, 133

excuse(s), 1, 3, 7–8, 16, 18, 24, 32, 34, 39, 40, 41, 50, 53, 91, 141, 143–4, 145, 199; action-plan and, 35; battered women, 126–34; and condemnation, 37; duress as, 10, 138, 139–40, 141–2, 148–9, 151, 152, 202; exculpation by, 150, 151–2, 200; exempting from condemnation and punishment, 29; innocent aggressors, 79–80; justifications and, 22; mistaken beliefs and, 7, 58; in prison escape cases, 44; and purely vindicating conviction, 147, 148; reasonable belief in, 120–6; self-defense, 59, 61; self-defense by battered women as, 114–34; structure of, 201; *see also* justification/excuse distinction

excusing condition(s), 137, 140, 141, 142

execution, 23, 26

expert testimony, 126; battered woman syndrome, 89, 90, 92, 93–4, 96, 97, 103, 104, 105, 106, 107, 111, 112, 114, 116, 134, 200, 201

extraordinary circumstances, 140, 144–5, 146, 147, 148, 149, 152

failure-of-proof defenses, 3, 19, 20, 34, 150; action-plan and, 35; and condemnation, 37

Feinberg, Joel, 22, 67, 69

Fingarette, Herbert, 138–9

Fletcher, George, 4, 5, 8, 10; justified conduct as right, 16–18, 18, 20; prohibitory norms, 31, 32, 40; putative justification, 6–7, 21; self-defense law, 56–9, 60, 83n58, 85; unknowingly justified defendants, 29–30

force: justified/excusable, 43, 44; justified use of, 46, 48; in law enforcement, 45, 46; in self-defense, 51; *see also* deadly force; defensive force; necessary force

forfeiture theory, 77–8

fundamental value, 67; for autonomy, 68n34, 70; sovereignty as, 68–9

Furman v. Georgia, 174n65

general defenses, 3
general self-defense, 11–12
good (the), 66, 68; and the right, 157n16
government: individuals and, 70, 71, 73
Greenawalt, Kent, 4, 6, 7, 9–10, 21–2, 39, 42

harm(s), 84n60, 133; and aggressor culpability, 60–2; balancing of, 82, 87; consequentialist weighing of, 59; minimizing, 63; in necessity requirement, 101, 102; in self-defense, 76; undeserved, 138
harm distribution (HD) principle, 60
Hart, H. L. A., 148
home: self-defense in, 86–7, 91, 126
homicide, 31; negligent/reckless, 132; offense definitions, 74; self-defense exception, 36
homicide statutes, 28, 30, 56, 64, 129

immediacy; battered woman syndrome, 98–9
immediate (defined), 99
immediately necessary: imminent or, 99–102, 103
imminence, 74, 75, 87n68; battered woman syndrome, 98–9; in self-defense doctrine, 102
imminence requirement, 55, 91
imminent: defined, 99; or immediately necessary, 99–102, 103
impaired capacity: and culpability, 131; and unreasonable beliefs, 122–3, 125
imprisonment, 23
imputation of lesser standing, 64, 70, 73, 75, 76, 80, 81, 88, 182, 189, 190
incompatibility thesis, 4, 8, 50, 51, 52; duty not to interfere and, 42–7; social matrix and, 3, 7–10, 11, 40–52
individual interests: legal defenses and, 62–4; *see also* concrete interests
information, lack of: and unreasonable beliefs, 121–2, 131–2
injury: in battering relationship, 107; in culpable aggression, 61; directed toward culpable party, 128; in self-defense, 75, 76, 77, 80, 83, 87; undeserved, 49, 54
innocent aggressors (IAs), 5, 12, 200; not culpable, 79–80; and self-defense, 55, 57, 58–9, 61, 79–80, 83, 84, 88
innocent bystanders (IBs), 55, 83
innocent parties, 49
innocent shields (ISs), 200; and self-defense, 55, 58–9, 80–1, 82, 83, 88
innocent victims, 48, 49, 58; standing of, 145
insanity defense, 24, 34, 45n60, 119–20, 124, 137
institutional legal alternatives to defensive force, 109–11

interests: in claims of self-defense, 56; of victims, 57, 59; see also concrete interests
interference, 20–1, 46n63, 53; with justified conduct, 40, 41, 51; *see also* duty not to interfere

judges, 161, 198; instructions to juries regarding power to nullify, 157, 158, 164–6; role of, 186
judicial nullification, 193–7, 202–3
juries/jurors, 24, 25, 171; authority to nullify, 157–63; battered woman syndrome, 93–4, 130, 132, 134; as community conscience, 174–6, 177, 180n71; and nullification, 178, 179–85, 202–3; as persons, 187–93; power to decide facts and law, 156–7, 158, 162, 179, 164; and punishment, 146; responsibilities of, 154; role of, 186, 198; standard instructions to, 164–5, 166–8, 202–3
jury derivation, 160, 162, 169; accidental/malicious, 178; malignant, 160–1
jury nullification, 14, 15, 153–4, 156–7, 201, 202–3; consequentialist argument, 157, 158–9, 161, 167; deontic argument, 157, 162–3, 167; historical argument, 157–8
just outcomes: nullification instructions and, 161, 162
justice, 158; in acquittal, 157; criteria of, 167; different from mercy, 180–1; formal principle of, 60; intrasystemic appeals to, 170, 177–80
justification, 147; battered women, 126–34; duress as, 10, 11, 138, 141; internal/external, 35–6, 37, 38, 39, 40, 41–2, 43, 45, 48, 53, 131, 139, 200; knowledge and, 21–2, 29–40; limits of, 153–98; reasonable belief in, 120–6; self-defense by battered women as, 114–34; wide/narrow senses of, 51–2, 53
justification defenses, 3, 73–5, 126, 151, 168, 199; and conventional public morality, 16–54; exculpation in, 127–8; exemptions by, 199–200; general category of, 14, 15, 56, 89, 136, 199, 200; boundaries of, 154, 156, 170; self-defense by battered women and, 114–34; nullification not in, 186; theoretical debate about, 2–11, 90; theoretical framework for analysis of, 16, 52–4; grounded in justificatory circumstances, 128–9, 130; and condemnation, 37; distinct from excuse and mitigation 16; exculpation by, 150; objective and subjective elements of, 31; preclude conviction and punishment, 149; prospective/retrospective functions of, 52; integrated theory of, 2, 14–15; issues, 1–15;

moral condemnation and, 26–9; preclude condemnation inherent in conviction and punishment, 185–6, 199; self-defense as, 89; structure of, 201; with subjective elements, 31–7
justification/excuse distinction, 6, 14, 88, 90, 130–1, 133, 134, 139; mental states in, 13, 89, 120–6
justificatory circumstances, 3; awareness of, 3, 5–6, 10, 21, 31, 36, 38; justification defenses grounded in, 128–9, 130
justified acts, 51; conflict of, 43, 48
justified conduct, 21; as right/as permissible, 3, 4–5, 7–8, 10, 16–21
justified liability, 121

Kadish, Mortimer, 169, 170
Kadish, Sanford, 169, 170
knowledge: and justification, 21–2, 29–40
knowledge requirement, 5–6, 8–9, 10, 21–2, 31, 34, 35, 36–7; difficult cases and, 37–40; and social matrix, 41

law: in liberal society, 71; role of, 84–5; see also criminal law; rule of law
law of self-defense, 55–6
learned helplessness, 92, 93–4, 95–6, 97, 106, 111–12, 114, 116, 118, 123–4, 129, 130; as disordered thought and special capacity, 102–4
legal alternatives to defensive force, 129, 130–3, 134; availability/lack of, 126–7, 143; institutional, 109–11; retreat, 108–9
legal defenses: and individual interests, 62–4
legal institutions, need for, 198, 203
legal liability: and common moral intuitions, 38
legal powers: and legal rights, 166, 167
legislative preemption, 171–2, 178, 174
lesser-evils defense, 2, 47–8, 49, 62, 139
lesser-evils model: self-defense law, 56
lesser-evils rationale, 12
lesser-harms theory, 61, 77, 81, 85
liability, 36
liberal democracy: deception in, 163–4; justification defenses in, 2
liberal political morality, 2, 185; principles of, 108–9; self-defense, 64–5
liberal political philosophy, 65–71; self-defense theory in, 55, 56, 62, 75, 83
liberal political structure, 188
liberal society: analysis of justification defenses in, 65; criminal justice system in, 71–3; general principles in, 73; law in, 71; law of self-defense in, 56; necessity and

nullification in, 167–86; responsibilities of persons in, 187–97; self-defense as justified conduct in, 74, 75–83
liberties, basic set of, 69
locus of control: battered women, 95–6, 97

McDonald v. United States, 117–18
malicious motives, 38, 41, 127–8, 161
mental illness: battered woman syndrome and, 116–20
mental states, 89, 120–6; and distinction between justification and excuse, 13; and justification, 7
mercy: in acquittal, 157; intrasystemic appeals to, 180–3, 198, 202
mistake: nonculpable, 43, 45, 124, 126, 127, 130, 131, 132, 133, 134, 141, 201; reckless or negligent, 39n49
mistaken beliefs: and excuses, 58
mitigating factors, 199
mitigation, 16, 50, 145, 147, 181; in sentencing, 142, 183; *see also* systemically complete mitigation
Model Penal Code (MPC), 1, 2, 3, 5, 10, 32, 83n58, 100; assault provision, 18; defensive force, 85, 86, 87; duress provision, 141; self-defense in, 62, 91, 121, 122
moral agent(s), 191–2, 193, 197; citizens as, 154; juror as, 188; persons as, 203; responsibility of, 202
moral blameworthiness, 24, 26, 35, 36, 38, 39, 40, 72, 202; assisting justified acts, 41, 42; criteria of, 149, 150, 152, 199; mitigation of, 143, 144; punishment in proportion to, 201; standard of, 145–6, 147
moral condemnation, 2, 29–31, 74; and criminal punishment, 22–9, 37; hard cases for, 25–6; and justification defenses, 26–9; and punishment, 16, 33; first type, 149–50, 152, 201; five types of, in criminal punishment, 22–4, 25–7, 29, 30, 53, 72, 151, 199; fourth type, 32, 34, 38, 39, 40, 42, 43, 49, 140, 141, 147, 149–50, 152, 201; fifth type, 36, 38, 39, 40, 147, 149, 152, 201; institutional, 26; institutional level/level of application, 72, 199; in punishment, 38, 52, 53, 54, 56, 64, 140, 144, 145, 149, 152, 163, 186, 199, 201
moral doctrines, 66–7
moral evaluation, 6, 22, 36
moral force of criminal law: deception and, 163–7
moral principles, 28, 70, 73
moral standards, 23, 30
moral theory, 9, 10, 56, 65
morally justifiable law: self-defense as, 83–7
MPC, *see* Model Penal Code (MPC)

natural events, 63, 78, 80
necessary force: battered woman syndrome/battering relationship, 104–6
necessity, 22, 45, 201; and conventional public morality, 167, 168, 170–7, 185–6; defense, 2, 13–14, 15, 63, 64, 74, 153–98; judgments of, 85, 86; justification, 62; justifying self-defense, 77, 91, 120–1, 126, 127, 133, 134, 137; and nullification, 168–70, 202; and nullification, in liberal society, 167–86; nullification as, 177–80; nullification beyond: extrasystemic nullification, 183–5; nullification beyond: intrasystemic appeals to mercy, 180–3; as residual justification defense, 13, 154, 168–9, 170, 171–2, 177, 186, 193–5, 198, 202
necessity requirement, 102; in self-defense, 91, 94, 101
negligence, 39n49
nonconfrontation cases (battered women), 13, 98, 103, 106–8, 114, 126, 130, 134
nonexculpatory policy defenses, 18
nonpublic domain, 66, 67, 28, 71, 73; sovereignty in, 69–70; *see also* public/nonpublic domains/jurisdictions
nullification, 13–14, 153–98; beyond necessity: extrasystemic nullification, 183–5, 186, 198, 203; beyond necessity: intrasystemic appeals to mercy, 180–3, 186, 198, 202; expressive significance of, 190, 192; indirect or subconscious, 160, 161; and jurors as persons, 187–97; as necessity, 177–80; necessity and, 168–70; necessity and, in liberal society, 167–86
nullification instructions, 157, 158–60, 161, 162–3, 164–6, 169, 178, 185, 186, 188, 189, 192–3, 198, 202

obligation of conscience, 187n83
obligations, 187–8, 189, 193; conflict among, 196–7, 198; of judges, 195–6, 197; positive, 28; and reasons to act, 196; in social morality, 30–1; *see also* personal moral obligation
offense definitions, 19, 53, 64, 72, 89, 168, 199; articulation of, 149; criminal assault, 43; defined, 19; in Fletcher, 4; justified violations of, 49; legal, 74–5; objective elements of, 27, 28, 29; permission to violate, 20; prospective/retrospective functions of, 32–3, 34, 36; as representation of conventional public morality, 73; violation of, 150
offense elements, 1, 2–3, 141, 145, 147, 199; crimes of conscience, 156

Otey v. Stenberg, 174n65
pathognomonic syndrome, 112–13
penal code(s), 22, 23, 28, 35, 127, 145; and conventional morality, 25, 26; justification/excuse distinction in, 131, 133
penal statutes, 84
People v. Young, 9
perception of imminent violence: battered women, 93, 103–4
perjury, 71n43
permissible, justified conduct as, 3, 4–5, 10, 16–21
"person of reasonable firmness," 141, 142
personal moral obligation: crimes of, 155–6, 187–8, 189
persons: as citizens/as moral agents, 188–9, 203; jurors as, 187–93; responsibilities of, in liberal society, 187–97
police intervention: for battered women, 109, 137
political institutions, liberal, 65–6, 67, 68, 70–1
political liberalism, 65–71
political morality, 38, 66–7, 163; underlying criminal justice system, 15, 166, 167; and legal system, 64–5; liberal principles of, 62, 74–5, 83, 102, 202; principles of, 55–6, 65–6, 70, 89, 154, 184–5, 199, 200; self-defense in, 64; theory of, 54
political process, participation in, 66, 69, 164
political protest, 171, 172
"preemptive strike," 12, 101
prison escape cases, 9–10, 43–4, 45, 51, 136, 140
privileges, 19; conflicting, 20; justification defenses as, 20–1; in social matrix, 47
probation, 146
prohibitory norms, 4, 29–31, 35, 73, 74, 168; defined, 19; exceptions to, 5, 18–29, 20, 21, 28, 29, 31, 32, 38, 41, 45, 64, 89, 149; modified by justifications, 40; violation of, 53
propensity to err, 87, 88, 200
proportionality, 12, 74; rough rule of, 85, 87, 88, 200
proportionality principle: in harm distribution principle (HD), 60
proportion(ality) requirement, 55, 57, 59, 61, 75, 76, 83, 85–6, 87, 88, 91, 200
psychological disorders, 137; battered woman syndrome, 116–20, 123–4, 129
psychological responses to battering, 92, 95–6, 104, 106, 111, 116
psychological syndrome(s), 2
psychopathology, 119, 120, 140

public morality, 54; minimal standards of, 26; principles underlying 87–8; shared principles of, 187, 188; *see also* conventional public morality

public/nonpublic domains/jurisdictions, 66, 67, 68, 70, 71, 198, 199, 203; boundaries of, 145, 185; conflict among obligations grounded in, 196–7; conflicts among reasons to act in, 187, 189; distinction between, 188, 189, 193; nullification instructions undermine boundary between, 186

punishment, 2, 71, 75, 146, 201; and blameworthiness, 150; complexity of institution of, 147; condemnation in, 38, 52, 53, 54, 56, 64, 140, 144, 145, 149, 152, 163, 186, 199, 201; for crimes of conscience, 14, 156; expressive function of, 15, 151, 189–90, 202; five types of condemnation in, 22–4, 25–7, 29, 30, 53, 72; harsh treatment in, 144, 145; institution of/application of, 22–3, 24, 26; justification of, 148; mitigation of, 142, 143; moral condemnation and, 16, 22–9, 37; paradigmatic methods of, 26; and status of victim, 73

purely vindicating convictions, 145, 146, 150–1, 152, 201–2; objections to, 146–51

putative justification, 6–7, 8, 11, 21–2, 37, 39, 43, 44, 45, 53, 141

putative self-defense, 58, 91

rational agency, 140, 141, 143

"reasonable battered woman" standard, 123, 130

reasonable belief, 13, 22, 89; arrest on basis of, 45; battered woman syndrome, 129–30, 133–4; justification and excuse, 120–6; that legal alternatives not available, 109–10; in necessity of deadly force: battered women, 106–8; pattern of battering as basis for, 111; in self-defense, 112; in self-defense of battered women, 98, 104–6, 114–16

reasonable but mistaken belief, 3, 6–7, 39

"reasonable person with impaired reasoning," 123

reasonableness, 125–6, 127; and psychological disorder, 123–4

reasonableness requirement: in self-defense, 91

reasonableness standard, 116, 130–1; subjective/objective, 115

recklessness, 39n49

religion, 67

residual justification defense, 2; duress as, 15; necessity as, 13, 154, 168–9, 170, 171–2, 177, 186, 193–5, 198, 202

resistance, 46, 53

respect, 66, 69; denied in nullification, 182, 202

responsibility(ies), 26, 148; of persons as citizens, 202; of persons in liberal society, 187–97

responsibility, principle of, 61

restraining orders, 109

retreat, 5, 12, 74, 75; as legal alternative to defensive force: battered women, 108–9

retreat requirement: dwelling-place exception, 86–7, 91, 109; in self-defense, 88, 91, 109, 126, 200; *see also* duty to retreat

retributive justice, 180

retributive systems, 26, 53, 149, 201, 202; conviction in, 149–50, 151, 199; punishing in proportion to blameworthiness, 144, 152

revenge, 127

right: justified conduct as, 3, 4–5, 7–8, 10, 16–21, 58; yielding to wrong, 102

Right (Recht), 57, 29; should never yield to wrong, 57, 85,

right action, 16–18, 157n16

rights: and harms, 173–4

rights of victims, 59

risk, 133; in self-defense, 76–7, 84n60

Robinson, Paul, 5, 10, 101n42, 140, 141–2

rule of law, 71, 203; and conventional political morality, 185

sacrificing one's life, 50, 144; requirement of, 48, 54

se defendendo, 58, 61, 88, 137

self-defense, 1, 36, 48, 54, 55–88; battered woman syndrome and, 92–4; and battered women, 12–13, 88, 89–135; by battered women: as justification and excuse, 114–34; and distributive justice, 60–2; integrated theory of, 61–2; justification rather than excuse, 120–1, 134; as justified conduct in liberal society, 74, 75–83, 136; law of, 200; moral foundations of, 201; moral justification of, 87–8; as morally justifiable law, 83–7; mutually justified, 52; normative structure, 56, 64–75; as problematic specific justification defense, 11–13; and social order, 56–9; theory of, 11–12, 15, 55, 56–62; use of force in, 2, 5, 12, 51

self-defense doctrine, 91–1, 101–2, 108, 109, 112, 135, 136–7; deadly force in, 106; self-defense by battered women in, 114–34, 201

self-defense law: battered woman syndrome and, 98–114

self-defense provision (MPC), 18

self-determination, 66, 164; right to, 67–8, 69, 70, 71, 75n6, 77, 80, 83, 86, 87–8, 200
self-esteem, decreased, 92, 94, 95–6, 104, 116
self-respect, 66, 69, 70, 79, 80
sentencing, 23, 149, 150
social cooperation, 65, 70, 163–4, 197, 199, 203; mitigation in, 143, 144, 145
social institutions: demands on individuals, 54
social matrix, 50; and incompatibility thesis, 3, 7–10, 11, 40–52; negative aspect of, 41, 51; privileges and duties in, 47; revised, 47–52, 53
social morality, standards of, 4–5
social order, self-defense and, 56–9
sovereignty, personal, 66, 68–71, 190, 197; categorical, underivative, noncompensable, 68–9, 70, 76; impairment and, 82–3; self-defense as protection of, 75–9, 80, 81–2, 85–6, 87–8, 102; threat to, 63, 64; violation of, 72–3, 133, 182, 200
specific justification defenses: self-defense, 11–13
state: intrusion to protect interests, 82–3; *see also* government
structural liberalism, 65–7, 69–70; and nullification, 190, 196; and obligations, 187n83
subjective elements: justification defenses with, 31–7
substantive liberalism, 65, 67–9, 70–1, 203; and nullification, 190, 194–5, 196–7; and obligations, 187n83
suspended sentences, 146
symmetrical justification, 48, 49, 53

symptom, defined, 116–17
syndrome, defined, 116–17
systemic condemnation, 26, 27, 29
systemically complete mitigation, 142–6, 195n91, 201–2; duress and, 136–52

testimony: self-defense: battered women, 105, 106, 113–14
third parties, 57, 133; assisting justified acts, 40, 41, 42; legal rights and duties, 8, 11
Thoreau, Henry David, 155n6
trial by jury, right to, 158

understandability, 125–6, 127, 129
unknowingly justified defendants, 5–6, 21, 22, 29–31, 34–5, 36, 37–8, 121, 127
unreasonable beliefs, 121–2, 125
Urbom, Judge, 174n65
utilitarians, 67, 191, 196
utility (principle), 70

vicious motives, 6, 21–2, 30
victimization, duress as, 138–9
violence, mutually justified, 44, 45, 46, 50, 51–2, 53, 136
voluntary act(s), 3
voluntary act requirement: in duress, 138

Walker, Lenore, 92, 94–7, 113
Wisconsin: civil commitment statute, 117, 118

Zenger, Peter, 187
Zenger trial, 187–93